VOLTAIRE AND THE ENGLISH DEISTS

VOLTAIRE

AND THE ENGLISH DEISTS

BY

NORMAN L. TORREY

ARCHON BOOKS

1967

TO MY FATHER
REV. DAVID C. TORREY
WHO HAS EVER FEARLESSLY ENCOURAGED ME
TO THINK FREELY

PREFACE

IN the preparation of this monograph, research in the National Library at Paris during the winter of 1923–24 was made possible through a Rogers Fellowship from Harvard University. Thanks to a Sterling Fellowship from Yale University I was given the rare opportunity of working during the summer months of 1927 in Voltaire's private library, now a part of the Public Library in Leningrad.

Special thanks are due and gratefully rendered to Profs. Irving Babbitt and André Morize for initial encouragement while I was a candidate for the Ph.D. degree at Harvard University, and to Prof. Albert Feuillerat of Yale University for helpful suggestions and criticisms during the composition of the present study; also to the staff of the Public Library of Leningrad who greatly facilitated for me the handling of Voltaire's books.

N. L. T.

New Haven, Connecticut
July, 1929

CONTENTS

VOLTAIRE AND THE ENGLISH DEISTS

CHAPTER I

INTRODUCTION

THE original inspiration for this study of the influence exerted upon Voltaire by English deists of the first half of the eighteenth century came from Joseph Texte, who wrote, in suggesting important influences still to be studied, that among the many critics who had expressed such contradictory opinions on this question, very few had taken the trouble to read carefully the works of Toland, Collins, or Tindal.[1] Some steps have been taken since that writing, but no comprehensive study based on the examination of the actual texts has appeared. It was discovered, moreover, as the work progressed, that due to Voltaire's transforming genius the evidence thus obtained needed in many cases the corroboration of the books and notes in his own library.

Contrary opinions have often been expressed on this influence, partly because critics have been speaking of different aspects of deism, and partly because they were early put on the wrong track by Voltaire himself. It is convenient to keep to the rather arbitrary distinction made by Leslie Stephen in *English Thought in the Eighteenth Century* between constructive and critical deism. In so far as deism means the adoption of a natural religion based on common ideas of morality and including the worship of a rather indefinite Supreme Being whose laws are plain and engraved in the hearts of all men, as opposed to Christianity with its supernatural doctrines and positive religious duties, Voltaire was a deist, one might say, from birth.[2] This attitude is commonly referred to as *constructive* deism, and it was as a constructive deist that Voltaire wrote *Le Pour et le contre*, in 1722. This natural religion was considered as old as creation and embraced the favorite heroes of the deists, Confucius, Socrates, and Cicero. Con-

---

[1] Betz, *La Littérature comparée* (Strasbourg, 1900), p. xxiii.
[2] Cf. Edouard Sonet, *Voltaire et l'influence anglaise* (Rennes, 1926), p. 158.

structive deism began as a movement in England with Lord
Herbert of Cherbury and Blount, under the direct influence of
humanism, and especially of the great humanists Erasmus and
Jordano Bruno.[3] It had a similar and earlier development in
France with Rabelais, Montaigne, and the *libertins* Gassendi,[4]
Vanini, La Mothe le Vayer, and their successors.[5] Voltaire's con-
structive deism was undoubtedly French in origin, but was
strengthened by his acquaintance with the works of Dryden,
Shaftesbury, Tindal, Trenchard, Gordon, Pope, Bolingbroke,
and others.

The influence of critical deism on Voltaire presents an entirely
different problem. The critical deists were not content with the
acceptance of this natural religion, but considered Christianity, in
so far as it diverged therefrom, an obstacle to the natural morality
and goodness of man and hence an object of attack. With varying
degrees of antipathy, but usually with bitter hatred for the Christian clergy which was admittedly corrupt and self-seeking, they
set about to undermine the foundations of the established religion.
Although critical deism is essentially a part of the larger rational-
ist movement, the critical deists may be distinguished from the
later rationalists because of their unbounded faith in the light
of nature for the solution of religious and metaphysical problems, thus avoiding the universal skepticism of Hume and later
thinkers.

It is unfortunate that the point of departure for the study of the
influence of the English deists on Voltaire's attacks on the Bible
and Christianity has been the years of his exile in England. Of
the controversies that were embittering English Christendom at
the very time of his visit, he seems then to have known very little.
His English notebook, nevertheless, shows his primary interest in
religious questions and the apparent acceptance of a sort of politi-

[3] Erasmus is continually referred to in the works of the whole deist school, while
Bruno exerted an especial influence upon Toland. See the *Collection of Pieces of John
Toland* (London, 1726), I, 304–349.

[4] "Locke borrowed more from Gassendi than from any other writer." J. M. Robertson, *A Short History of Freethought* (London, 1915), II, 114, and note.

[5] See Lanson, "Origines et premières manifestations de l'esprit philosophique dans la
littérature française," *Revue des Cours et Conférences*, 1908–1910; "le Rôle de l'expérience dans la formation de la philosophie du XVIIIe siècle," *R. Mois*, 1910.

cal, anticlerical deism such as he could have found in the *Independent Whig* and *Cato's Letters* by Trenchard and Gordon, in Tindal's early *Rights of the Christian Church Asserted*, or in Mandeville's *Free Thoughts on Religion, the Church, and National Happiness*. From English poets his extracts concerning religion are surprisingly numerous. Deistic passages from Dryden's poems appeared in many forms in his later works, and verses from *The Medal, a Satyr against Mankind* inspired the central theme of his tragedy *Zaïre*.[6] Voltaire's habit of paraphrasing, whether for his own instruction or for the deliberate purpose of hiding his sources, is already apparent, as well as his dependence on notes jotted down in his notebooks as he read for repeated use in later life. There is no evidence in the notebook, however, that he had ever heard of Toland, Collins, or Woolston, or of the main deistic controversy. The evidence from the *Lettres philosophiques* is likewise mainly negative. Among the bolder deists, Collins and Toland alone are mentioned, and merely named as philosophers.[7] Neither they nor their fellow laborers are ever mentioned as *incrédules* by Voltaire until after 1762. The *Remarques sur les pensées de Pascal* stand out as an early and quickly discouraged attempt at critical deism, and lead us to suspect that Voltaire would have interested himself in the controversy much earlier and much more thoroughly if he had dared. For in commenting on the persecution which followed their publication, he wrote to Maupertuis, in 1734:

Savez-vous que j'ai fait prodigieusement grâce à ce Pascal! De toutes les prophéties qu'il rapporte, il n'y en a pas une qui puisse s'expliquer honnête-ment de Jésus-Christ. Son chapitre sur les miracles est un persiflage. Cependant, je n'en ai rien dit, et l'on crie. Mais laissez-moi faire; quand je serai une fois à Bâle, je ne serai pas si prudent.[8]

Voltaire's sojourn at Bâle was very brief and he did not abandon prudence until many years later. He appears to have begun his

---

[6] "Voltaire's English Notebook," *Mod. Phil.*, XXVI (February, 1929), 308-310.

[7] Lanson, *Lettres philosophiques*, I, 175.

[8] XXXIII, 417. Except where critical editions of separate works are available, references to Voltaire's works will be taken from the *Œuvres complètes* (Moland edition) without further indication.

serious documentation at Berlin,[9] reserving his active publication against Christianity until he felt himself secure at Ferney some ten years later. The threats in his letter to Maupertuis show that he probably knew of Collins' *Grounds and Reasons of the Christian Religion,* as he certainly knew of Woolston's *Discourses on the Miracles of our Saviour,*[10] but the edition of Collins' work that he used was printed only in 1737, and probably came into his hands much later.

"In England," Ballantyne writes, "Voltaire lived almost exclusively with the wits and men and women of fashion."[11] Nevertheless he made intellectual contacts with many of the serious thinkers of the age. Samuel Clarke, the latitudinarian and Arian divine, was radical enough to captivate his admiration, and this was the very man whom some of the deists were hotly attacking. His other interests were Locke and Newton, Dryden, Pope, Swift, and other men of letters. It was the attitude of these men that he adopted in discussing the Quakers, the Anglican Church, and the Dissenters in the *Lettres philosophiques* and in his metaphysical works and philosophical poems of the next ten years. Churton Collins was evidently guessing widely when he said of Voltaire's visit to England: "But what most engaged his attention was the controversy then raging between the opponents and the apologists of Christianity."[12] The English exile is closely connected, too, with the supposedly great influence exerted on Voltaire by Bolingbroke. From Villemain to Aldington and Sonet, one finds the practically unanimous opinion that Voltaire got his impetus to criticize Christianity from that English lord. Voltaire is largely responsible for this error through his numerous gratuitous references to Bolingbroke and through his continued careless use of Bolingbroke's name to cover his borrowings from the most varied sources. This is a matter that can be checked up only by an actual comparison of the texts and a careful weighing of other possible

[9] H. Droysen and R. Koser, *Briefwechsel Friedrichs des Grossen mit Voltaire* (Leipzig, 1908), II, 380, 381, 386, 387. Cf. Voltaire, *Œuvres,* XXXVII, 491, 497.

[10] Lanson, *op. cit.,* II, 264.

[11] A. Ballantyne, *Voltaire's Visit to England* (London, 1893), p. 329.

[12] Churton Collins, *Voltaire, Montesquieu and Rousseau in England* (London, 1908), p. 61.

sources. In our study of the time and the extent of the deistic influence, it will appear that the visit to England and the Bolingbroke influence are equally treacherous starting points and should be treated with the greatest caution.

The mere proof or disproof of the influence of the individual English deists on Voltaire is interesting chiefly in so far as it throws light on the general history and interchange of ideas in the very interesting and cosmopolitan eighteenth century; and in particular as it reveals Voltaire's literary and scholarly methods in handling his sources, and his purpose in attacking the Christian religion of his day. If Voltaire's name has persisted as the greatest French genius of the eighteenth century, it is because he understood so well the necessity of dressing up in literary form the results of his patient and erudite research into the dusty volumes of scholars whose names are now almost forgotten, but who live on, often anonymously, in the works of their brilliant successor. Many of Voltaire's later admirers have attempted to minimize the force and extent of his attack on revealed and established religion.[13] Such exculpatory offerings on the altars of orthodoxy are as contrary to the spirit of Voltaire as to that of his English predecessors.

One of the difficulties of the present study has been the inadequacy of treatment which several of the English deists have received, in comparison with the scholarly study that has been accorded Voltaire. Hostile criticism has succeeded in robbing them of much of their due claim to fame, and has seriously blackened their reputations. Among these writers, Toland, Woolston, and Annet were social outcasts; Toland was forced to gain his livelihood by stockjobbing, and the other two suffered ignominy and imprisonment. Justice, as well as expediency for the subject in hand, demands that they be treated sympathetically and in the Voltairean spirit, rather than as "infidels," "atheists," or "denizens of Grub Street." Antidotes can be found at every hand. The deists have long been buried and their works often burned or suppressed, but their spirit is very much alive today and many of their opinions and arguments are still valid. The often repeated

13 Cf. E. Champion, *Voltaire: études critiques* (Paris, 1893), pp. 178–189.

charge of insincerity has touched only their confessions or concessions to Christianity, but never the purpose and ardor of their attacks on the established religion. Many of them owe much to Voltaire and the French philosophers for the continuation of their spirit and opinions.

The deist controversy has best been treated by Leslie Stephen in his *English Thought in the Eighteenth Century.* Stephen harbored the prejudice that the critical deists were the intellectual inferiors of their orthodox opponents, and this prejudice is apparent in his introductions and summaries. But in the body of his treatment, when he was studying the controversy in detail, and reading the deists as well as their opponents, he tends to prove the opposite, as Robertson has in some measure pointed out in his *Short History of Freethought.*[14]

Stephen's division of treatment by method of attack is especially helpful, for each deist approached the problem from his own peculiar angle. Toland dwelt chiefly on the historical argument. His noteworthy contributions were his attacks on the Christian mysteries, his defense of the necessity and sufficiency of the use of reason in matters of religion, his catalogue of apocryphal works which first appeared in *Amyntor,* and his theories concerning the origins of belief. Although Voltaire had relatively little direct contact with his thought, his important contributions to the general movement of deism and freethought profoundly altered the intellectual temper of the century. The brief study of the two men will show especially the cosmopolitan character of the historical argument against the established religion and the importance of Holland in the development of the philosophic and scientific spirit, as well as Voltaire's methods of mystification. After Toland, the historical argument was continued chiefly by Bolingbroke and Middleton, of whom the latter will be found to have given much material and a great impetus to Voltaire's studies in that connection.

Next in importance to Toland, Anthony Collins will be treated to show the nature and date of the influence of his metaphysical works on Voltaire, especially in regard to the soul and the will.

[14] *Op. cit.,* II, 149–151.

This influence was early exerted, but was not in the field of purely critical deism. Collins' critical attack took the form of the argument from the prophecies. This attack, one of the sorest points of the English controversy, was bodily transplanted in France by d'Holbach, but with many reflections in Voltaire. Mandeville attacked chiefly the ethics of modern Christianity and will not be studied here. His influence on the English ethical philosophers has been very adequately handled in F. B. Kaye's work on *The Fable of the Bees,* a remarkable treatise which Voltaire was translating with Mme. du Châtelet at Cirey, and the influence of which on his *Mondain* and other works of economic theory has been carefully studied in A. Morize's *l'Apologie du Luxe au XVIIIe siècle.* The attack was oblique and did not enter directly into the deist controversy. Mandeville stands out among English deists as owing the most to Bayle.[15]

Woolston followed Collins closely with the argument from the miracles. His six *Discourses on the Miracles of our Saviour,* which brought him a prison sentence, exerted a marked influence on Voltaire, both in material and method. His earlier works will be considered as a preparatory study of method and to show that his argument, like Voltaire's, was double-edged, against both the literal and allegorical interpretation of the Scriptures. Chubb succeeded in arousing a great deal of animosity, but he was long merely a constructive deist, contributing little except volume to the critical movement. It was as a constructive deist only that he was translated and known to Voltaire.

Tindal and Annet are important for their "common sense" criticisms of the morality of the heroes and preachings of the two Testaments, a popular method and popular arguments which Voltaire greatly favored and borrowed chiefly from these two men. Tindal published little, but effectively brought "the light of nature and reason" to bear upon the patriarchs and prophets and upon the moral teachings of Jesus. He wrote with some moderation, a trait which Voltaire did not imitate. But Annet was an

---

[15] Mandeville admits his great indebtedness to Bayle in the preface to his *Free Thoughts on Religion, the Church, and National Happiness* (London, 1720). This work is political and anticlerical rather than directly deistic.

extremist among English deists. He wrote scathing attacks especially upon Moses, Paul, and David, of which the last at least was well known and directly used by Voltaire before it was translated by d'Holbach. Annet, who continued the English controversy beyond its natural lifetime, published his last important works in 1761. As this was approximately the date when Voltaire took up his acid pen and seriously and openly began his attempt to undermine the foundations of Christianity, there is no actual breach in the passing of the movement from England to France.

In delaying his directly critical attacks until 1761, Voltaire was following the movement of the century in France. Many reasons have been suggested for the comparatively sudden and almost simultaneous entry into the field of deistic criticism of Voltaire, Rousseau, and d'Holbach. A change in public opinion and a weakening of authority had taken place which removed fear of persecution and manifested itself in the expulsion of the Jesuits. Voltaire's poem *Sur la loi naturelle* was burned in 1755, and his imitation in verse of *Le Cantique des cantiques,* which was actually milder than the biblical original, met a similar fate in 1759. *Candide,* in 1759, displays great daring. But there is still a very notable gap between these works and the *Sermon du rabbin Akib* in 1761, and the *Sermon des cinquante,* published first in 1762 and noted by Beuchot as Voltaire's first overt assault on Christianity. Moreover, there appears no well-defined trace of English biblical criticism in any of Voltaire's works before 1762. He had studied the metaphysical works of Collins and Chubb, and *The Fable of the Bees,* all of which could be safely translated into French in the early thirties. Certain aspects of English philosophical deism are apparent during the twenty-five years between *Le Mondain* and *Candide.* But it is only after the latter work that Voltaire began in earnest to use the original English texts of the deists; and it is not until 1763 that the names of the English deists appear as authorities for his biblical criticism.

That Voltaire's command of English was entirely adequate for a detailed study of the English movement, the present discussion will make evident. Some corroborative testimony may be suggested.[16] From 1735 to 1753, he was corresponding in English with his friend Faulkener. By 1764, he had thoroughly digested much of Warburton's *Divine Legation of Moses*,[17] of which there was no French translation, and was writing reviews of books for the *Gazette littéraire* which prove a very adequate reading knowledge of the English language.[18] The most conclusive evidence of his ability is found in the large numbers of English volumes in his private library at Leningrad,[19] which he read carefully and in some of which he left marginal notes in English indicating a complete comprehension of the text. In the thirties at the time of his metaphysical borrowings, he seems to have preferred French translations, while in his later period of deistic criticism, he was reading widely the English originals of works which no one until d'Holbach had bothered or dared to translate; and even after these translations had appeared, he seems to have preferred his own free versions in *La Bible enfin expliquée*, published shortly before his death. For the historical argument only, he was more willing to read the many available sources in Latin. Yet even here, Middleton's works were very carefully read and extensively used, and Bolingbroke's, though they were, by Voltaire's own admission, not worth the effort, received painstaking consideration.

The examination of Voltaire's private library in Leningrad and especially of his own copies of the works of the English deists, most of them containing markers, stickers, or marginal notes indicating the passages that most attracted his attention, offers invaluable confirmation of the importance of the deists in the development of his own thought and of the extent to which he borrowed the ideas which he was so capable, through his literary genius, of making so thoroughly his own. These books, hardly disturbed since they were ushered into Russia by Wagnière, Voltaire's secretary, at the bidding of Catherine the Great, present undeniable evidence of Voltaire's painstaking methods, his exten-

---

[16] See also Desnoiresterres, *Voltaire, son retour et sa mort* (Paris, 1876), pp. 115 ff.
[17] XX, 348.
[18] XXV, 152 ff., 159 ff., 163 ff., 167 ff., 169 ff., 176 ff., etc.
[19] See G. R. Havens and N. L. Torrey, "The Private Library of Voltaire at Leningrad," *PMLA*, XLIII (1928), 990–1009; and "Voltaire's Books: A Selected List," *Mod. Phil.*, XXVII (1929), 1–22.

sive and often erudite reading, and the vivacity of his intellectual reactions. We are indebted to Wagnière for the following account of Voltaire's method of reading, his habit of making marginal notes, and his use of markers for future reference:

Il avait la méthode, quand il recevait un ouvrage nouveau, de la parcourir rapidement, en lisant quelques lignes de chaque page. S'il apercevait qu'il y eût quelque chose qui méritât l'attention, il y plaçait une marque; après quoi il relisait tout fort attentivement, et même deux fois quand l'ouvrage lui paraissait intéressant et bien fait, et il faisait des remarques aux marges. Il y en avait de très-curieuses, ainsi qu'une quantité prodigieuse de *sinets,* sur lesquels il y a quelques mots écrits de sa main ou de la mienne.[20]

Wagnière testifies likewise to Voltaire's prodigious memory, which enabled him to find a reference needed for work in hand at a moment's notice. In the volumes of the English deists, there are few marginal comments. Voltaire reserved these principally for works to which he took more or less violent exception. We shall find a few in Middleton's works when Voltaire feels he must rise to the defense of Tindal. On the other hand, the volumes abound in markers, or slips of paper on which Voltaire often wrote a few words or a sentence from a passage which he intended to use. He had also the habit, not mentioned by Wagnière, of wetting a tiny end of paper and sticking it over a passage that especially interested him. Markers accompanied the stickers, and passages thus indicated, with the important exception of those in the Bolingbroke volumes, are almost sure to be found repeated in Voltaire's own works.

In the following study, a chapter on the early deists, with special reference to Toland, will show Voltaire's neglect and misuse of these men. Following Collins, Woolston, Tindal, and Annet were more popular writers whose works were more readily adaptable to Voltaire's direct use. The chapter on Chubb and Bolingbroke explains Voltaire's relative neglect of the arguments of the constructive deists to prove what every "honnête homme" already knew by the light of reason, and also how much he valued his English authorities and how loosely he played with

[20] Longchamp et Wagnière, *Mémoires sur Voltaire* (Paris, 1826), I, 53.

their names; while the study of Middleton reveals the source and the inspiration of many of his attacks on the historical side of the movement to undermine the foundations of the Christian religion.

CHAPTER II

THE INFLUENCE OF THE EARLIER DEISTS:
IGNORANCE AND EXAGGERATION

VOLTAIRE borrowed very little critical material from the earlier English deists. He appears to have had no direct contact with the works of Lord Herbert of Cherbury, whom he frequently mentions and pretends to quote, nor with Blount, whom he utterly ignores. There was no trace of either author in his library at the time of his death. His quotations from Shaftesbury are correct and his judgments remarkably sound when he considers that author as a moral philosopher,[1] but very untrustworthy when he treats him as a critical deist.[2] He was also very scantily supplied with the works of John Toland. Except for the latter's dying words and epitaph, which he could have found in any one of numerous dictionaries of authors, all his quotations are false.

We are therefore confronted with mystification and falsehood at the very beginning of our study, and are forced to admit that Voltaire had no sweeping command of the deistic movement as a whole, as witnessed especially by his relative neglect of Toland. Yet he sought to give the impression that his antibiblical attacks were of English origin. England was to him the land of philosophers and freethinkers, and it was largely due to him, at the cost of some exaggeration, that this opinion became current in France in the latter half of the century. He felt it necessary to cover himself with the tradition of English freethought, hence the frequent lists of imposing authorities too often chosen at random. A charitable interpretation is, as has been suggested,[3] that he lied in order that he might live to lie again another day. One of his most devastating pamphlets was written under the name of Lord Bolingbroke, while many others were published under English

---

[1] IX, 465-466; XVII, 584.   [2] XXVI, 482.
[3] In a speech on Voltaire by Clarence Darrow.

pseudonyms. In his *Dieu et les hommes* (1769), given as a translation of the work of a pseudo-Englishman, Doctor Obern, the chapter on the subject "Si Moïse a existé" begins thus:

> Nous avons parmi nous une secte assez connue, qu'on appelle les *Freethinkers,* les francs-pensants, beaucoup plus étendue que celle des francs-maçons. Nous comptons pour les principaux chefs de cette secte, milord Herbert, les chevaliers Raleigh et Sidney, milord Shaftesbury, le sage Locke, modéré jusqu'à la timidité, le grand Newton, qui nia si hardiment la divinité de Jésus-Christ, les Collins, les Toland, les Tindal, les Trenchard, les Gordon, les Woolston, les Wollaston, et surtout le célèbre milord Bolingbroke. Plusieurs d'entre eux ont poussé l'esprit d'examen et de critique jusqu'à douter de l'existence de Moïse.[4]

The passage is typical of at least one important use to which Voltaire put the English deists; the more "chevaliers" and "milords" he could cite, the more impressive the note of authority. As the years came upon him his mystifications become more apparent. In *La Bible enfin expliquée* (1776), he quotes "les incrédules," and, with rare lapses into truthful citation, gives as authorities any name or list of names that comes into his head. In the *Histoire de l'établissement du christianisme,* published the following year, a long list of doubts are signed by English deists who usually never entertained such doubts and certainly never put them in print. Voltaire's two quotations from Lord Herbert of Cherbury[5] which occur in these last deistic works are false, and his knowledge of that early English deist[6] was extremely superficial.

The study of the influence of Toland on Voltaire's deistic thought reveals a minimum of direct contact, much ignorance, some of it wilful, and frequent falsification. Yet Toland's contribution not only to deism but to the history of thought in England was more important than that of any other member of the group, with the possible exception of Collins. In Toland we find the genesis or at least a selection and early expression of a great number of deistic ideas which were to become the stock in trade of both insular and continental deism. Robertson commends him

---

[4] XXVIII, 177. The table of contents in the Moland edition wisely pays no attention to these pluralized names, but omits many casual individual references.

[5] XXX, 66; XXXI, 62–63. [6] XXVI, 482.

for the originality of his ideas and for the impetus he gave to rationalistic biblical criticism.[7] Deists who followed him, Collins, Bolingbroke, and Annet, borrowed the results of his minute scholarship, usually without acknowledgment. His chief handicaps were his unbounded curiosity and the unorthodoxy of his conclusions. His importance is illustrated by the fact that to him was first applied the word *freethinker*,[8] and to him was due the coinage of the word *pantheist*.[9] But it was chiefly through later English deists, through the learned Fabricius, and through the Encyclopedists, that his contributions received from Voltaire some of the attention that they deserved.

His brief article on Toland, written in 1767, in the *Lettres . . . sur Rabelais, et sur d'autres auteurs, accusés d'avoir mal parlé de la religion chrétienne* shows acquaintance with Desmaizeaux's *Life of Toland,* or with a dictionary abstract of that work. He was struck particularly by the account of Toland's death and of his epitaph. "Toland mourut," he writes, "avec un grand courage en 1721.[10] Ses dernières paroles furent: *Je vais dormir.*"[11] In his dictionary article, "Identité," written in 1771, Voltaire again mentions the epitaph and comments on it irrelevantly:

> Le célèbre Toland, qui fit sa propre épitaphe, la finit par ces mots: *Idem futurus Tolandus numquam;* il ne sera jamais le même Toland. Cependant il est à croire que Dieu l'aurait bien su retrouver s'il avait voulu, mais il est à croire aussi que l'être qui existe nécessairement est nécessairement bon.[12]

Whether justly or not, Toland, along with Spinoza, was branded as an atheist by the eighteenth century. This may explain Voltaire's coolness toward Toland in the later years of his life when

---

[7] J. M. Robertson, *A Short History of Freethought* (London, 1915), II, 127, 197.

[8] *Ibid.*, I, 6.

[9] J. F. Nourrisson, in his *Philosophie de la nature* (Paris, 1887), p. 87, finds that Toland coined this word and used it first in his *Adeisidæmon* (1709). The French equivalent was first used by Élie Benoît in his *Remarques* on Toland's dissertation (Hatzfeld et Darmsteter, *Dict. de la langue française*). Desmaizeaux, however, says that Toland published a pamphlet in 1705 as from a "Pantheist" to a friend (*Collection of Pieces* [London, 1726], I, lvii).

[10] The correct date is March, 1722, Desmaizeaux having written 1721–22.

[11] XXVI, 483.

[12] XIX, 402. Toland, *Collection of Pieces,* I, lxxxix.

he was combating the rising school of atheism. But Toland was only inferentially a deist.[13] In many of his works he defended primitive Jewish Christianity against the Gentile institutionalized Christianity that superseded it, and attempted to rationalize the miracles and the Christian mysteries. In writing an appreciation of his independent spirit, Voltaire greatly exaggerated his hatred of the Christian religion:

> Toland a porté des coups plus violents. C'était une âme fière et indépendante; né dans la pauvreté, il pouvait s'élever à la fortune, s'il avait été plus modéré. La persécution l'irrita; il écrivit contre la religion chrétienne par haine et par vengeance.[14]

It has often been argued that since Voltaire was influenced by the English deists, since Toland was an important deist, and since *Christianity not Mysterious* was his best-known work, therefore Voltaire was influenced by that work. There appears no evidence, however, either in Voltaire's works or in his library, that he ever even read the book. Published in 1696, the year of the publication of the first edition of Bayle's dictionary, when Toland was only twenty-five years old, *Christianity not Mysterious* clearly and emphatically marks the beginning of English eighteenth-century critical deism. When Voltaire entered the field some sixty-five years later, the cause of free lay inquiry in questions of religion had long since been won, nor could he be expected to be interested in Toland's theory that the true Christian mysteries were not mysteries after all, but had been made clear by special revelation.

In his *Life of Milton,* published in 1697, Toland's purpose was to prove that the *Eikon Basilike* was a forgery and a cheat which had been imposed on the people, in part by the Anglican clergy. Toland was right, in spite of many protests, but a significant paragraph on the unreliability of historical evidence, especially when religion was concerned, brought a storm about his ears. His answer was *Amyntor,* published the following year, in which he included a "Catalogue of Books attributed in the primitive times to Jesus Christ, his Apostles and other eminent Persons." This publication marks the first serious criticism by an English layman

13 Robertson, *op. cit.,* II, 129.   14 XXVI, 483.

in the hallowed regions of Scriptural canon. Yet again it may be stated that Voltaire was not at all directly influenced by, and perhaps never read, either the *Life of Milton* or *Amyntor*. Toland's sympathetic treatment of Milton's political and religious beliefs found no echo in Voltaire's heart or works,[15] while the important material that Voltaire used for his *Collection d'anciens évangiles ou Monuments du premier siècle du christianisme*, and in practically every deistic treatise that he wrote, came entirely from the *Codex Apocryphus Novi Testamenti*[16] by the German scholar, Johann-Albertus Fabricius, and from Grabe's *Spicilegium SS. Patrum*,[17] both of which works are found in Voltaire's library abundantly marked for ready reference.

Toland's *Letters to Serena*, written for the Queen of Prussia and published in 1704, were better known in France, chiefly through the translation by d'Holbach in 1768. The first three letters contain a discussion of the origin and force of prejudices, of the history of the soul's immortality among the heathen, and of the origin of idolatry and reasons of heathenism; the last two present a refutation of the basic principles of Spinoza's system of philosophy, especially on the ground that motion is essential to matter. Voltaire makes no mention of this work in his article on Toland[18] in the *Lettres . . . sur Rabelais, etc.*, in 1767, but wrote, the following year, in a letter to d'Alembert:

> Il paraît des Lettres philosophiques où l'on croit démontrer que le mouvement est essentiel à la matière. Tout ce qui est pourrait bien être essentiel, car autrement pourquoi serait-il? Pour moi, je cesserai bientôt d'être, car j'ai soixante-quinze ans, et je ne suis pas de la pâte de Moncrif.[19]

It is to be noticed that Voltaire does not mention Toland by name, says nothing of the first three letters, which should nevertheless have interested him, and dismisses the question of motion essential to matter with a joke, though he himself had written much on the properties of matter. It seems evident that Voltaire was jealous of his English authors, who played such an important

---

[15] See XVIII, 590; also A. Morize's critical edition of *Candide*, p. 192, n. 2.
[16] Voltaire's copy was the second edition, 3 vols. in 8, Hamburgh, 1719.
[17] Oxoniae, 1700, 2 vols. in 8.
[18] XXVI, 483.   [19] XLVI, 137.

part in his efforts at mystification. In the cases of Woolston and Annet, at least, he preferred his own adaptations of the original English text to d'Holbach's translations. The *Lettres philosophiques* were likewise put away in his library unmarked except for a note on the title-page, "livre dangereux." There is no certain evidence, however, that he possessed or knew the original text of Toland's *Letters to Serena*.

Certain striking similarities of thought and expression in Toland and Voltaire prove, however, that the former had succeeded well in establishing his ideas in the cosmopolitan deistic arsenal. "Toland's mind," writes Leslie Stephen, "was employed upon some questions, especially as to the historical origin of beliefs, which have since assumed greater importance."[20] Taking his text from Cicero, Toland presents the following case:

The foundations of prejudice are laid even before we are born, witness the extraordinary marks which we sometimes bear, due to the longings of our mothers. The midwife hands us into the world with superstitious ceremonies and spells and omens, and the priest is not far behind with his charms and symbols. The nurse infuses her errors into us with her milk. Stories of hobgoblins give way to stories of fairies and ghosts when we are turned over to idle and ignorant servants, and at school we hear of nothing but genii, satyrs, fauns, apparitions and transformations. In the Universities, the professors must accommodate all things to the laws and the religion of the country. Then the clergy are hired, not to undeceive, but to retain the rest of the people in their mistakes. When we are let out into the world, we are slaves to custom, and are considered monsters if we depart from the universal mode; "martyrs to a habit, but not to religion or truth, unless by mere accident." "You may reason yourself into what religion you please; but, pray, what religion will permit you to reason yourself out of it?"[21]

A passage very similar, in spite of the distinctly Voltairean twist and use of detail, is found in the article "Préjugés" of the *Dictionnaire philosophique*, written in 1764:

Si votre nourrice vous a dit que Cérès préside aux blés, ou que Vistnou et Xaca se sont faits hommes plusieurs fois, ou que Sammonocodom est venu couper une forêt, ou qu'Odin vous attend dans sa salle vers le Jutland, ou que Mahomet ou quelque autre a fait un voyage dans le ciel; enfin si

20 *English Thought in the Eighteenth Century*, I, 104.
21 *Letters to Serena* (London, 1704), pp. 4–13.

votre précepteur vient ensuite enfoncer dans votre cervelle ce que votre nourrice y a gravé, vous en tenez pour toute votre vie. Votre jugement veut-il s'élever contre ces préjugés, vos voisins et surtout vos voisines crient à l'impie, et vous effrayent; votre derviche, craignant de voir diminuer son revenu, vous accuse auprès du cadi, et ce cadi vous fait empaler s'il le peut, parce qu'il veut commander à des sots, et qu'il croit que les sots obéissent mieux que les autres; et cela durera jusqu'à ce que vos voisins et le derviche, et le cadi, commencent à comprendre que la sottise n'est bonne à rien, et que la persécution est abominable.[22]

A space of sixty years separated the two books, however, and Toland's material had been well worked in France as well as in England. We find at least in d'Holbach's translation a "note de Fréret trouvé sur son exemplaire anglais de ces *Lettres de Toland à Sérène*,"[23] and suspect that Toland's influence on d'Holbach himself is much more important than has yet been shown, though the latter's translation was published four years after Voltaire's dictionary article, and his *Essai sur les préjugés* did not appear until 1770. It should be noted, however, that Voltaire wrote down in his notebook, while in England, Dryden's famous lines:

> The priest continues what the nurse began
> And thus the child imposes on the man

and translated them with other lines in his *Lettres philosophiques*.[24]

Other similarities in the writings of Toland and Voltaire can be readily explained by the use of common sources or through intermediaries. On the question of the immortality of the soul, both writers used Bayle's article "Anaxagoras" to show that Pherecydes, according to Cicero, was the first to commit the immortality of human souls to writing, as a great and daring innovation.[25] Toland was a student for a time at the University of Leyden and knew thoroughly the works of Van Dale and the Dutch scholars. He recommends to Serena, Van Dale's *Origin*

---

[22] XX, 266–267.

[23] *Lettres philosophiques* (London, 1768), p. 81.

[24] Ed. Lanson, II, 83–84. These lines are from Dryden's *The Hind and the Panther*, and were combined with lines from *The Indian Emperor* (V, ii) to form Voltaire's medley. Cf. my note in *Mod. Phil.*, XXVI (February, 1929), p. 310, n. 3.

[25] *Letters to Serena*, pp. 28–29; Voltaire, XVII, 161–162. See A. Morize, *Problems and Methods*, p. 107.

and Progress of Idolatry, and praised the work highly as an attack on priestcraft in a polite letter to the author.[26] And Voltaire was as quick as Toland and Fontenelle to recognize the utility of Van Dale's works.[27] Among the intermediaries, mention should be made of the Encyclopedists and of Warburton. While Voltaire's library contained very few volumes of Toland, d'Holbach's collection was almost complete.[28] Such influences are extremely difficult to trace unless concrete examples can be found. Toland did much original scholarly research on the story of "Hypatia," which he published in 1720 as part of his *Tetradymus,* and started its vogue in the eighteenth century. The story found its way into the article "Eclectisme" of the *Dictionnaire encyclopédique.* Voltaire gives this article as his source and used the story many times and for various purposes.[29] Again, the origin of the idea of immortality was to undergo considerable development in England between Toland and Voltaire, and to lead finally to the admission by Warburton in the *Divine Legation of Moses* that the doctrine was unknown during the first centuries of Jewish history. Voltaire, who studied Warburton carefully, naturally objected to his conclusions that the Jews must have been providentially guided by God, since they did not have this very essential doctrine to maintain their civilization. Warburton took an idea direct from Toland's "Clidophorus"[30] to the effect that the sages of antiquity had a double doctrine, which allowed them to preach in public the immortality of the soul in order to restrain the populace, while they ridiculed the idea in private. Voltaire reports this theory and comments sarcastically on Warburton's incongruities.[31]

A study of the first three letters to Serena shows merely that Voltaire's thought was running parallel to Toland's on questions that were deeply interesting the century. The last two letters, for which Toland got his information from a careful study of Spinoza's works and from conversation with his disciples in Holland,

26 *Collection of Pieces,* II, 331 ff.
27 Voltaire states his preference for Van Dale over Fontenelle in his article "Oracles," XX, 141.
28 See *Catalogue des livres de feu M. Le Baron d'Holbach* (Paris, 1789).
29 XIX, 393; also XXVI, 289; XXVIII, 9, 124–125; XXXI, 110.
30 *Tetradymus* (London, 1720), p. 63 ff.   31 XXVIII, 154–155.

made little impression on the French eighteenth century, which was all too willing to accept Bayle's condemnation as irrevocable.[32] It is noteworthy that Voltaire's library contains none of Spinoza's works.[33] Three years after the publication of d'Holbach's translation of the *Letters to Serena,* Voltaire used arguments against Spinoza which show that Toland's letters had not in the least influenced him;[34] and he continued to consider the belief in motion essential to matter a vital aspect of the theory of atheism, and therefore almost as dangerous as "superstition."[35]

Voltaire knew of Toland's two Latin dissertations, *Adeisidaemon* and *Origines Judaicae,* published in 1709, only through Élie Benoît's *Mélange de remarques critiques, etc., sur les deux dissertations de M. Toland.*[36] The first was written to prove, against Bayle, that Livy was not at all credulous nor superstitious, and to show that superstition was no less harmful to the republic than pure atheism would have been. Voltaire never attempted to distinguish between what Livy wrote and what he believed, and left the academic question of an imaginary society of atheists aside, in order to prove the superiority of theism over the Christian religion. The second dissertation was an attack against Huet, the learned bishop of Avranches, and an attempt to discredit early Jewish history by stressing Strabo's account of the Jews. Voltaire, who was well acquainted with Huet's works, attacked him directly with his masterful weapon of ridicule, and in his attacks on the Pentateuch paid no attention to Strabo's history. His markers in Benoît's refutation of Toland indicate that he used the former's discussion of the plurality of gods among the Hebrews for his article "Genèse."[37] He was little interested, however, in Toland's main arguments.

Toland's *Nazarenus* came into Voltaire's library in the form of a translation published in 1777, too late to exert any influence.

[32] See XXVI, 524–525.
[33] Voltaire quotes (XVIII, 365, n. 3) as Spinoza's the words of Boulainvilliers from *Réfutation des erreurs de Spinoza.*
[34] XVIII, 368, n. 1.   [35] XXVI, 525.
[36] Delft, 1712.
[37] *Op. cit.,* pp. 84–87, 261. Cf. Voltaire, XIX, 234–235.

Moreover, the chief point of interest, the discovery of a Gospel of Barnabas, which proved to be a late fraud, had been quoted in the second edition of the *Codex* of Fabricius,[38] published in 1719. Voltaire read this volume carefully, used it extensively, and translated long passages from it,[39] but took no notice of Toland in this connection nor of the only pages of English in the whole work. He seems ever too ready to use Toland's name, but obstinately refuses to use his material, even when it is put before his very eyes.

Toland's final efforts, the *Pantheisticon* and *Tetradymus*, published in 1720, two years before his death, likewise left no imprint on Voltaire's mind, in spite of the fact that half of his letter on Toland is taken up with the former work. A striking passage on the formation of fossils[40] in this half serious, half satirical parody on the English Church service and clergy would have saved Voltaire much trouble and enhanced his reputation as a scientist; for Toland saw very clearly that the theory of the English geologist Woodward that fossils were the remains of once living creatures was correct, if it could only be separated from the physically impossible biblical flood. It was d'Holbach again who continued Toland's scholarship in France,[41] while Voltaire, rather than admit the flood, continued late in life to combat Woodward[42] with ridiculous explanations of fossils. Yet if Voltaire betrays no familiarity with the contents of the *Pantheisticon,* he nevertheless knew, perhaps through Desmaizeaux's *Life of Toland,* the controversies that it occasioned. We have already seen that he classed it with two earlier works as "autant de combats qu'il livra ouvertement au christianisme," as one of the most audacious of books. This judgment is typical of Voltaire's usual exaggeration concerning the English deists, in the attempt to lay many of his own audacities at their door. He then attacks the problem of the prayer to Bacchus for which Toland was unjustly blamed.[43]

[38] *Codex Apocryphus Novi Testamenti* (Hamburgh, 1719), III, 387–394.

[39] For his "Collection d'anciens évangiles," cf. XXVII, 542 ff. Voltaire's copy contains many notes and markers, with one on the Barnabas gospel, but none on the pages containing Toland's contribution.

[40] *Pantheisticon* (London, 1751), p. 46. Cf. Leslie Stephen, *op. cit.,* I, 104.

[41] *Œuvres* (Paris, 1759), III, 5–22. [42] X, 206; cf. XXIII, 225.

[43] *Collection of Pieces,* I, lxxxvi.

On l'accusa, [he writes,] d'avoir fini son *Pantheisticon* par cette prière blasphématoire, qui se trouve en effet dans quelques éditions: "Omnipotens et sempiterne Bacche, qui hominum corda donis tuis recreas, concede propitius ut qui hesternis poculis aegroti facti sunt, hodiernis curentur, per pocula poculorum. Amen!"

Mais comme cette profanation était une parodie d'une prière de l'Église romaine, les Anglais n'en furent point choqués. Au reste, il est démontré que cette prière profane n'est point de Toland; elle avait été faite deux cents ans auparavant en France par une société de buveurs: on la trouve dans le *Carême* allégorisé, imprimé en 1563. Ce fou de jésuite Garasse en parle dans sa Doctrine curieuse, livre II, page 201.[44]

Voltaire is wrong in thinking that the English were not shocked; but M. Lantoine gives him entire credit for this erudite note.[45]

As for Toland's *Tetradymus,* Voltaire does not appear to have suspected its existence. Two of the four articles, "Clidophorus" and "Hypatia," have already been discussed, while "Mangoneutes," a continuation of the discussion of the Gospel of Barnabas in *Nazarenus,* was ignored as completely as the parent work. In the remaining article, "Hodegus," Toland attempted to explain on rational grounds the so-called miracle of the pillar of cloud and fire that guided the Israelites in the wilderness. The proofs of Toland's interpretation are given in scholarly fashion, and are in line with modern biblical criticism. Toland was making careful research in the Pentateuch and creating in himself a higher veneration for Moses.[46] He explained that the language of the Old Testament, in which, for instance, a profound sleep is called a "sleep from the Lord," and a numerous army, "the army of God," was hyperbolical.[47] The study of the Pentateuch was also the diversion of the latter years of Voltaire's life, but from an entirely different approach.[48] The situation in France rendered necessary, perhaps, the Voltairean ridicule to prepare the way for the more scholarly and more sympathetic treatment of the Scriptures by Renan, of whom Toland was clearly a precursor.

Of the numerous works published in Toland's lifetime, we have

[44] XXVI, 483.
[45] A. Lantoine, *John Toland, un précurseur de la franc-maçonnerie, suivi de la traduction française du Pantheisticon* (Paris, 1927), p. 134.
[46] *Tetradymus,* p. ii.   [47] *Ibid.*
[48] Cf. Voltaire, XXX, 80, n. 1.

found in Voltaire's library only d'Holbach's translation of the *Letters to Serena* (1768), and a very late translation of *Nazarenus* (1777). There is also a third volume consisting of posthumous pieces, published by Desmaizeaux as *The Miscellaneous Works*.[49] The two longest and most important of these are *The History of the Druids,* which left no echo in Voltaire's works, and *The Constitution of the Christian Church*. On one of the two markers that Voltaire left in this work is written "Voyez Minut. Felix."[50] Voltaire did search Minutius Felix for a quotation on temples which he used for the article "Autels"[51] in his *Questions sur l'Encyclopédie* (1770). This work of Toland's might be compared with Voltaire's late treatise on the *Histoire de l'établissement du christianisme,* but Toland, in attempting to prove that there is "no such satire in nature against Priestcraft as the Gospel of Christ,"[52] maintains his scholarly methods, while Voltaire, seeing only "that long chain of fanatical crimes with which Christians have besmirched themselves,"[53] is reminiscing vaguely on all his past works against Christianity and quoting at random.

Toland may be considered to have had a negligible influence on the development of Voltaire's thought and writings. Ignorance of his works and the false use of his name greatly outweigh correct use based on actual knowledge. Voltaire lists Toland among the great philosophers in his *Lettres philosophiques* (1734), and again in an article devoted to a discussion of the soul, in his *Mélanges de littérature et de philosophie* (1751). In his *Lettres . . . sur Rabelais, etc.* (1767), he gives a superficial account of Toland which betrays little knowledge of his works. The following year he comments jokingly on Toland's idea that motion is essential to matter which the latter had so carefully elaborated in his *Letters to Serena*. Articles in the *Questions sur l'Encyclopédie* (1770–71) show that he used one reference from Toland and that he was struck by his dying words and epitaph. Other and later references to Toland must be classified as falsifi-

---

[49] A reprint, published in 1747, of the *Collection of Pieces*. The first volume containing Desmaizeaux's *Life of Toland* is wanting.
[50] *Op. cit.,* II, 144. [51] XVII, 494–495.
[52] *Op. cit.,* II, 138. [53] XXXI, 113.

cations. Speaking of the books of the Pentateuch in *La Bible enfin expliquée* (1776), he comments on Toland's little faith in that work:

> Toland assure qu'il est visible que tous ces livres ne furent écrits que longtemps après par quelque prêtre oisif, comme il y en a tant eu, dit-il, parmi nous aux XIIe, XIIIe, et XIVe siècles; et qu'il ne faut pas ajouter plus de foi au Pentateuch qu'aux livres des sibylles, qui furent regardés comme sacrés pendant des siècles.[54]

Again, in the *Histoire de l'établissement du christianisme* (1777), Toland is said to believe, on account of the absurd genealogy in the Gospel according to Matthew, that the author of that book was either an ignorant man or a clumsy forger.[55] Toland may have held dangerous ideas concerning pantheism and materialism, but of all the deists he was the most reverent and appreciative in dealing with the Pentateuch, and the most circumspect in his treatment of the gospels. His method of attack and Voltaire's were essentially different. Voltaire knew very little of his actual works, knew that little late, and found it very little to his taste. He therefore imagined a false Toland—often "les Toland"— which suited much better his efforts at mystification.

[54] XXX, 84.   [55] XXXI, 57.

CHAPTER III

VOLTAIRE AND ANTHONY COLLINS: METAPHYSICS AND PROPHECIES

ANTHONY COLLINS, who represents the noblest type of English critical deist, was better known to Voltaire than Toland, and more directly influenced his thought. Voltaire, in his *Lettres . . . sur Rabelais, etc.* (1767), calls him one of the most terrible enemies of the Christian religion:

> Un des plus terribles ennemies de la religion chrétienne a été Antoine Collins, grand trésorier de la comté d'Essex, bon métaphysicien, et d'une grande érudition. Il est triste qu'il n'ait fait usage de sa profonde dialectique que contre le christianisme.[1]

The judgment is just; the reflection is plainly ironical. A disciple of Locke, even more than was Toland, Collins worked with Toland to force ratiocination on the church. He, too, applied Locke's principles in ways that that author had not intended, especially in his theory of determinism. Beginning with a defense of the free use of reason in matters pertaining to religion, he showed early antibiblical propensities, and published in his more advanced years a very forceful attack on literal prophecy directed against the accepted foundations of the Christian revelation.

Collins was born in 1676, six years after Toland, and died in 1729.[2] He had all the advantages of social position and wealth that Toland lacked. Coming from a good family near London, he was educated at Eton and at Cambridge, and was for some time a student in the Temple. He married twice, both times the daughters of gentlemen, and held for many years in Essex and in Middlesex the office of justice of the peace and deputy-lieutenant. Although he was bitterly attacked for his writings, no one ever

[1] XXVI, 485.
[2] See *Dictionary of National Biography*, for details of Collins' life. Also D'Israeli's *Curiosities of Literature* (London, 1840), pp. 380–383.

attacked his character,[3] and as a gentleman widely respected, he did much to make deism fashionable in England. While still a young man he was on very intimate terms with Locke during the last years of the latter's life. Locke wrote of him: "Collins has an estate in the country, a library in town, and friends everywhere." And Collins wrote to Locke: "Believe it, my good friend, to love Truth for Truth's sake is the principal part of human perfection in this world, and the seed-plot of all other virtues; and if I mistake not, you have as much of it as I ever met in anybody."[4] Locke made Collins his chosen friend and trustee, but did not live to meet his antibiblical arguments. Locke's influence is evident in Collins' whole trend of thought, but especially in his *Letter to Dodwell* in answer to Clarke's demonstration against Dodwell of the natural immortality of the soul, and in his most enduring work on *Human Liberty,* which in turn had such great influence on Voltaire.

Like Toland, Collins made several trips to Holland, published several of his books there, and knew well the work of the scholars in Holland, especially Bayle, on the English translation of whose dictionary he was long held to have had a hand.[5] In Holland in 1711, he won the friendship of Le Clerc, who had favored Clarke in the controversy over the natural immortality of the soul.[6] A second trip to Holland in 1713 was evidently to avoid the turmoil[7] created by his *Discourse of Free-thinking,* published in that year. Like Toland and Voltaire, he had great admiration for the freedom and tolerance of Holland, and published there his attack on the prophecies in 1726, a year before the London edition appeared.

In 1729, Collins died and was buried in Oxford chapel, leaving his manuscripts to Desmaizeaux, to whom we are again indebted for the details of his life. As in the case of Toland, it is hard to get a fair estimate of his importance in the history of thought. Leslie Stephen has in general greatly underrated him, though at

[3] Voltaire lists him, in the *Traité de métaphysique* (1734), as a philosopher of rigid virtue. XXII, 229.

[4] Robertson, *A Short History of Freethought,* II, 134.

[5] Thorschmids, *Versuch einer vollständigen Engelländischen Freydenker-Bibliothek* (Magdeburg, 1765), I, 2–3.

[6] *Bibl. choisie,* XXVI, 2ᵉ partie.

[7] Article, "Collins," *Biographical Dictionary,* X, 63.

times he is forced to admit his worth. On his deism, a hostile criticism by Bishop Van Mildert reads as follows:

> Collins is one of the most mischievous of his tribe. He rejects as inadmissible every kind of testimony in behalf of Christianity, except that which may be drawn from Prophecy literally accomplished; and this he represents as the sole and exclusive evidence on which our Lord and his Apostles rested the proof of the Christian faith.[8]

"Only because this evidence could easily be demolished," he might have added. Robertson, who defends Collins against Stephen's unfair treatment, considers his discourse on free will as durable as any portion of Locke, unsurpassed even today in its essentials as a statement of the case of determinism.[9] Collins' attack on literal prophecy was admitted by Warburton to be the most plausible work ever published against Christianity. And finally Voltaire says of his works:

> Ses *Recherches philosophiques* sur la liberté de l'homme, sur les fondements de la religion chrétienne, sur les prophécies littérales, sur la liberté de penser, sont malheureusement demeurées des ouvrages victorieux.[10]

Voltaire can scarcely be considered an authority on the English deists, but on Collins he has expressed the judgment of his century.

Less prolific and much less diffuse than Toland, Collins holds a position of equal eminence in English critical deism. He was a thoroughgoing experimentalist in the Baconian tradition, with none of the inhibitions that hindered Locke, Clarke, and Leibnitz. Robertson maintains that "Locke's position as a believing Christian was indeed extremely weak, and could easily have been demolished by a competent deist, such as Collins." Clarke, when driven to the wall by the ingenuity of Collins' argumentation, could resort to the strongest argument of the orthodox and warn Collins against writing anything detrimental to the holy Religion. Leibnitz employed the same tactics against Toland. But Collins was apparently born with no sentiment of religion. In his search

---

[8] See Allibone's *Dict. of Authors.*   [9] *Op. cit.,* II, 151.

[10] Voltaire's library still contains these four works mentioned, of which the *Discourse on the Grounds . . . of the Christian Religion* (London, 1737), and the *Scheme of Literal Prophecy considered* (London, 1727) are annotated in his hand.

for truth he felt no concern whatever for the traditions he was ably helping to wreck and hence no necessity to build up a system as a substitute. His method and purpose may best be considered in a discussion of his *Essay concerning the Use of Reason,* his famous *Discourse of Free-thinking,* his *Discourse concerning Ridicule and Irony in Writing,* and certain minor works. His metaphysical preoccupations, in which Voltaire was particularly and directly interested, throw light on the English influence; these are found in his controversial interchange of letters with Clarke and in his *Philosophical Inquiry concerning Human Liberty.* His criticisms of the Bible and of the Christian religion, although already manifest in 1707 in the *Essay concerning the Use of Reason,* culminated much later in his *Grounds and Reasons of the Christian Religion* and in his *Scheme of Literal Prophecy considered.* Collins' consistency and unity of thought makes such a threefold discussion both possible and practical.

Collins' search for the truth was less partisan than Toland's and more dispassionate than Voltaire's in the face of bitter attacks and opposition. As an English gentleman of means and social standing, he sought no honor and no recompense. Whether from choice or necessity, he published all his works anonymously. His *Essay concerning the use of Reason in Propositions, the Evidence whereof depends on Human Testimony* is not a plea but a demonstration that individual judgment based on the sum total of human perceptions is the final authority on questions civil and religious, and that such judgment was of necessity practiced by the orthodox as well as by the heretical. A discussion of several (among many) instances of contradiction in the Old Testament is "enough to prove the necessity of Reason to distinguish Falsehood from Truth in matters of Revelation, in order to give all possible Authority to that which can with any reason be suppos'd to be a Revelation."[11] Toland felt obliged to admit divine revelation as part of human testimony upon which to base judgment.[12] Collins is the bolder pupil of Locke in denying any evidence except that through sense perception. Like Toland, Collins denies

---

[11] *An Essay concerning the Use of Reason* (London, 1707), p. 23.
[12] *Christianity not Mysterious,* p. 16.

any valid distinction between that which is contrary to reason and that which is "above reason." Miracles which imply contradictions are absurd, and an absurdity or a contradiction in a proposition is a demonstration of its falsehood. The mystery of the Trinity is as unreasonable as that of Transubstantiation, and Collins treats them both with ridicule. He is too tactful to quote Toland, but with delicate irony he quotes English divines, Tillotson, Clarke, and Gastrel, to support his thesis. Tillotson had declared in a sermon that not even a miracle would persuade him of the divinity of a man's mission if it contained anything repugnant to the natural notions which he had of God, and this was the opening wedge used by other deists against the testimony of the miracles. The grave Samuel Clarke had maintained that man differed essentially from the brutes in that he alone had notions of religion. Collins answers that the brutes are then better off, for they trust their natural faculties. "I would fain know," says he, "in what good sense Religion can be said to be natural to Man, when it is suppos'd to be contradictory to the perceptions of our Faculties."[13]

Collins' use of irony is well illustrated in his epistolary controversy with Clarke in 1707 over Dodwell's position that the soul is mortal unless upheld by the extraordinary power of God. Collins wrote four letters and Clarke answered as many times.[14] In Clarke's second defense of his attack on Dodwell, he intimates that Collins is little versed in such inquiries or is too stupid to see the validity of his (Clarke's) unanswerable arguments; or rather that, as a man of wit, he raises difficulties merely to perplex readers.[15] This supercilious attitude on the part of the grave and pompous divine naturally vexed his adversary. Collins was too even tempered, however, to descend yet to personal ridicule. In his third letter, he says ironically that people never would have questioned the existence of God if Clarke had not raised the issue in the Boylean lectures but that now they demanded a demonstration.[16] Clarke was incensed and replied that Collins' difficulty was "that he believed too little"; to which Collins answered: "I

[13] Essay concerning the Use of Reason, p. 16.
[14] Clarke's Collected Works (London, 1738), III, 721 ff.
[15] Ibid., p. 783. [16] Ibid., p. 883.

verily think he neither believes *too little* nor *too much;* but that he is perfectly Orthodox, and in all likelihood will continue so."[17] Voltaire's shafts of ridicule against Le Franc de Pompignan were more popular but hardly more effective than Collins' irony. Clarke has the last word and concludes "with hearty wishes that Collins will be very careful to write nothing against the Interest of true Religion and virtue."[18]

In the *Discourse of Free-thinking* Collins, as Robertson remarks, "smilingly claims at least the prophets as great free-thinkers, in their tirades against the Jewish religion."[19] If the Jews were ignorant of the doctrine of immortality, it was necessary for revelation to teach them "that Death signify'd eternal Life in Misery."[20] This irony runs through all his writings to reach its climax in the *Discourse on the Grounds and Reasons of the Christian Religion,* in which his ironical defense of the allegorical interpretation of the prophecies incited Whiston to urge a *Scheme of Gravity for the Direction of those who write about Religion.* Collins answered with a *Discourse concerning Ridicule and Irony in Writing,* published in 1729, the year of his death. Did not the churchmen use ridicule against Hobbes and against ridiculous papish miracles, and yet

Contempt is what they (the solemn and grave), who commonly are the most contemptible and worthless of Men, cannot bear nor withstand, as setting them in their true Light, and being the most effectual method to drive Imposture, the sole Foundation of their Credit, out of the World.[21]

This is entirely in the spirit of Voltaire, who wrote in his *Instruction pastorale:* "Nous avouons qu'après le péché mortel ce qu'un évêque doit le plus éviter, c'est le ridicule."[22] Swift, says Collins, was "one of the greatest droles that ever appear'd upon the Stage of the world," yet he was in favor with the High Church, in spite of his *Tale of the Tub;* Fontenelle ridiculed the pagan oracles; Rabelais, forbidden to speak his mind seriously, did it ironically; the grave William Penn spoke of Swift as "re-

[17] Clarke's *Collected Works,* III, 885 ff.   [18] *Ibid.,* pp. 908, 909.
[19] *Op. cit.,* I, 22.
[20] *Discourse of Free-thinking* (London, 1713), p. 152, note.
[21] *A Discourse concerning Ridicule and Irony in Writing* (London, 1729), p. 7.
[22] XXV, 2.

siding not far from Bedlam"; Archbishop Tillotson ridiculed the mystery of the transubstantiation, calling it "hocus-pocus"; and even Whiston, who "set up for great gravity," is proved by Collins to have used banter against his enemies.[23] Voltaire was well prepared for a lesson in the use of ridicule and irony. He had already mockingly held the train of the high priest in his play *Œdipe*. Collins represented the deistic spirit at the time of Voltaire's visit to England, and the latter's references to Swift and to Bedlam and to "hocus-pocus" may well have been memories of conversations in the distant past, used to give an English flavor to such works as the *Examen important de milord Bolingbroke*. For Voltaire found his method of attack in England, and developed that "ironie perpétuelle qui exaspérait le Procurateur général."[24]

Collins displayed his competency on metaphysical questions in his defenses of Dodwell against Clarke in 1707 on the subject of the natural immortality of the soul; and on free will and necessity, in his letters to Clarke "from a gentleman of the University of Cambridge,"[25] in his *Discourse on Human Liberty,* both in 1717, and in his late *Dissertation on Liberty and Necessity* in 1729.

On the question of the soul, Voltaire's position is almost identical with Collins', who has given an excellent summary of his ideas in his *Dissertation on Liberty and Necessity:*

> That the Soul is acted upon by Matter is past doubt, tho' we know not the precise manner of the Operation; which is not at all to be wonder'd at, since we are Strangers to many Qualities of Matter and wholly in the dark as to the Substance of the Soul: Our most abstracted Conceptions can't furnish us with an Affirmative Idea of Substance Immaterial; but our Inability to account for Multitudes of Effects from the known Qualities of Matter, is, I think, the sole Reason we impute them to any thing else.

Quotations from Voltaire can be found in any of his metaphysical works, from the earliest to the latest, to show the substantial identity of his views. One short passage from the *Traité sur la tolérance* (1763) will illustrate in part:

[23] *Op. cit.,* pp. 24–50.   [24] Lanson, *Voltaire,* p. 51.

[25] Hahn believes that Collins was the author of these letters. For his reasons see Joseph Hahn, *Voltaires Stellung zur Frage der menschlichen Freiheit in ihrem Verhältnis zu Locke und Collins* (Borna-Leipzig, 1905), p. 46, and note also the typical irony in the last letter. Desmaizeaux, in his *Recueil de diverses pièces,* I, xxxiv, note b, attributes the letters to a young student named Bulkely.

Nous savons que l'âme est spirituelle, mais nous ne savons point ce que c'est qu'esprit. Nous connaissons très imparfaitement la matière, et il nous est impossible d'avoir une idée distincte de ce qui n'est pas matière. Très-peu instruits de ce qui touche nos sens, nous ne pouvons rien connaître par nous-mêmes de ce qui est au delà des sens. . . .

Ainsi nous nous servons du mot *esprit,* qui répond à *souffle,* et *vent,* pour exprimer quelque chose qui n'est pas matière; et ce mot *souffle, vent, esprit,* nous ramenant malgré nous à l'idée d'une substance déliée et légère, nous en retranchons encore ce que nous pouvons, pour parvenir à concevoir la spiritualité pure; mais nous ne parvenons jamais à une notion distincte: nous ne savons même ce que nous disons quand nous pronon-çons le mot *substance.* . . .[26]

This question of the immateriality of the soul is closely connected in Collins' works with the problem of determinism, and Voltaire could hardly have accepted the latter argument without also being strongly influenced by the former.

Joseph Hahn, in his thesis on Voltaire's position on the question of freedom of the will in relation to Locke and Collins,[27] has competently shown Voltaire's debt to Collins on the question of determinism. Voltaire had an early predilection for Clarke, whose sermons he praises and gives incontestable evidence of having read, along with the controversies with Collins and Leibnitz printed with them. This influence is strongest in the *Lettres philosophiques* and in the *Traité de métaphysique* of 1734. This latter work, long considered important as giving Voltaire's true opinions on the ground that it was not meant for publication, is apparently only a sort of introduction to Voltaire's *Éléments de la philosophie de Newton,* worked over in 1736 when Voltaire was in exile in Holland, and printed against his wishes in 1738,[28] of which the first part on metaphysics is avowedly the opinions of Clarke, Locke, and other disciples of Newton. In the dedicatory epistle to Mme. du Châtelet, Voltaire writes: "je dirai fidèlement soit ce que je recueillis en Angleterre de la bouche de ses disciples, et particulièrement du philosophe Clarke, soit ce que j'ai puisé dans les écrits même [*sic*] de Newton, et dans la fameuse dispute de Clarke et de Leibnitz."[29] In 1734, as Hahn has pointed out, Vol-

---

[26] XXV, 81–82.
[28] XXII, 397; *Avertissement de Beuchot.*
[27] *Op. cit.*
[29] *Ibid.,* p. 402.

taire believes firmly in free will, but already by 1737 and 1738, in
his letters to Frederick and in his *Éléments de la philosophie de
Newton,* Collins' speculations have begun to trouble him seriously, and his confidence in Locke and in Clarke is beginning to
wane.[30] In the *Éléments de la philosophie de Newton* (1738), he
writes:

> De tous les philosophes qui ont écrit hardiment contre la liberté, celui
> qui sans contredit l'a fait avec plus de méthode, de force et de clarté, c'est
> Collins, magistrat de Londres, auteur du livre *De la Liberté de penser,* et
> de plusieurs autres ouvrages aussi hardis que philosophiques.[31]

He adds that Clarke's bitterness in his replies shows how keenly
he felt the force of his adversary's reasoning. In the *Philosophe
ignorant* in 1766, he has completely adopted Collins' position, and
concludes: "L'ignorant qui pense ainsi n'a pas toujours pensé de
même, mais il est enfin contraint de se rendre."[32] Lanson's comment is to the point: "En réalité, il a moins changé d'avis qu'il ne
pensait: il a surtout osé se mettre d'accord avec lui-même."[33] But
this was more than Locke had dared to do on the same subject.
"I cannot make freedom in man," writes Locke, "consistent with
omnipotence and omniscience in God, though I am as fully persuaded of both, as of any truths I most firmly assent to."[34]
Collins would admit no such contradiction, and this was one of
his ideas to which Voltaire surrendered. In the article "Liberté,"
in 1771, he writes:

> Ou je me trompe fort, ou Locke le définisseur a très bien défini la li-
> berté "puissance." Je me trompe encore ou Collins, célèbre magistrat de
> Londres, est le seul philosophe qui ait bien approfondi cette idée, et Clarke
> ne lui a répondu qu'en théologien.[35]

In the dialogue of the same article, another idea appears which
Hahn shows to have been borrowed from Collins:

> Vous voilà bien malade d'être libre comme votre chien . . . vous avez
> mille fois plus de pouvoir de penser que lui; mais vous n'êtes pas libre
> autrement que lui.[36]

[30] Hahn, *op. cit.,* pp. 22–27.
[31] XXII, 413.
[32] XXVI, 57.
[33] Lanson, *Voltaire,* p. 67.
[34] Hahn, *op. cit.,* p. 39.
[35] XIX, 578.
[36] *Ibid.,* p. 580.

Collins had written:

> But these larger powers and larger weaknesses, which are of the same
> kind with the powers and weaknesses of sheep, cannot contain liberty in
> them, and plainly make no perceivable difference between them and men,
> as to the general causes of action, in finite intelligent and sensible beings.[37]

Although the influence is admitted and inescapable, it is interesting to note that Voltaire avoids textual borrowing.

The third idea which Hahn demonstrates to have passed from
Collins to Voltaire concerns the question of moral responsibility,
of reward and punishment. Both Locke and Clarke had refused
to follow out to a logical conclusion the theory of determinism.
Clarke complained in his remarks upon Collins' *Philosophical
Inquiry* that Collins had tried to subvert all religion and to re-
move all the justice of reward and punishment.[38] Collins de-
molishes this argument skilfully:

> If man was not a necessary agent, determin'd by pleasure and pain, there
> would be no foundation for rewards and punishments, which are the
> essential supports of society. For if men were not necessarily determin'd by
> pleasure and pain, or if pleasure and pain were no causes to determine
> mens wills; of what use would be the prospect of rewards to frame a man's
> will to the observation of the law, or punishments to hinder his transgres-
> sion thereof? . . . If man was not a necessary agent determin'd by pleas-
> ure and pain, he would have no notion of *morality,* or motive to practise
> it: the distinction between morality and immorality, virtue and vice would
> be lost; and man would not be a moral agent.[39]

Collins is not worried about future rewards and punishments, nor
"how any Creature is accountable for the perfection that God
never gave him." He is destroying the entire theological conception of sin, original or otherwise. As Voltaire did after him, "Il
laïcise la métaphysique; il la détache de la théologie dont il ne
garde qu'un *minimum* qu'il ne voit pas d'avantage à éliminer, le
concept ou le mot de Dieu."[40] It was again late in life that Voltaire surrendered to Collins on this point. In his diatribe *Il faut
prendre un parti,"* in 1772, he writes:

[37] *A Philosophical Inquiry concerning Human Liberty* (London, 1717), p. 56.
[38] Clarke's *Works,* III, 735.   [39] *Human Liberty,* pp. 87–88, 90.
[40] Lanson, *Voltaire,* p. 70.

Un destin inévitable est donc la loi de toute la nature, et c'est ce qui a été senti par toute l'antiquité. La crainte d'ôter à l'homme je ne sais quelle fausse liberté, de dépouiller la vertu de son mérite, et le crime de son horreur, a quelquefois effrayé des âmes tendres; mais, dès qu'elles ont été éclairées, elles sont bientôt revenues à cette grande vérité que tout est enchaîné, et que tout est nécessaire.

L'homme est libre, encore une fois, quand il peut ce qu'il veut; mais il n'est pas libre de vouloir; il est impossible qu'il veuille sans cause. Si cette cause n'a pas son effet infaillible, elle n'est plus cause. Le nuage qui dirait au vent: Je ne veux pas que tu me pousses, ne serait pas plus absurde. Cette vérité ne peut jamais nuire à la morale. Le vice est toujours vice, comme la maladie est toujours maladie. Il faudra toujours réprimer les méchants: car, s'ils sont déterminés au mal, on leur répondra qu'ils sont prédestinés au châtiment.[41]

And Voltaire proceeds to ridicule, as did Collins, the so-called liberty of indifference.

In answer to the question of what use his discourse was, Collins replied: "First, the usefulness of truth in general; and secondly, the usefulness of the truths I maintain towards establishing laws and morality, rewards and punishments in society."[42] As an important result of his agreement with Collins, Voltaire "ne construit pas une métaphysique des mœurs; il esquisse une morale tout expérimentale et positive. Il n'y a ni bien ni mal absolus, ni idées morales innées."[43] He could hardly have remained in the metaphysical clouds when Collins had brought the question to earth as a practical principle of social attitude and of penology, to the applications of which the world today is only too slowly approaching.

The influence of English thought on the metaphysical elaborations of Voltaire has been often treated. The apparent division of this influence into two phases has not always been sufficiently emphasized, with the result that Voltaire has too readily been accused of inconsistency and double-mindedness. It is evident from the *Lettres philosophiques*,[44] as well as from Voltaire's notebooks, that he was little interested in the critical deists as such during his stay in England. He found diversion in Swift, Pope,

[41] XXVIII, 532–533.   [42] Preface, p. v.
[43] Lanson, *Voltaire*, p. 67.
[44] Collins and Toland are mentioned only once, and as mere names; XXII, 127.

and Bolingbroke, but he was seriously studying Newton, Locke, and Clarke, whom he especially admired. "Je me souviens," he writes in his *Métaphysique de Newton,* "que dans plusieurs conférences que j'eus, en 1726, avec le docteur Clarke, jamais ce philosophe ne prononçait le nom de Dieu qu'avec un air de recueillement et de respect très-remarquable."[45] This is the man he was accusing in 1766 of having answered Collins "avec mauvaise foi."[46] In the earlier period of Voltaire's interest in metaphysics, Hahn has found textual borrowings from Clarke,[47] but none from Collins.

It is probable that Voltaire knew Collins before 1736 mainly through Clarke's answer to his discourse and from the interchange of letters between the two men, published in Clarke's collected works, where he also may have found and read the letters between Clarke and Leibnitz. Whether from the English, or from the French translation in 1727, the influence of Clarke's *Traités de l'existence de Dieu et de ses attributs,* etc., is apparent in Voltaire's *Lettres philosophiques, Poème sur le désastre de Lisbonne,* and *Candide.*[48] Voltaire's copy at Leningrad is amply annotated, and the comments are very hostile to Clarke and to the Christian revelation. It is impossible to fix the date of these annotations, but they were probably done much later than the period in question, and when Voltaire had definitely adopted the critical attitude of Collins and his associates.[49] For it is only in his later writings that he treats Collins' material at length, and surrenders completely to his views. In 1720, Desmaizeaux had published a *Recueil de diverses pièces sur la philosophie, la religion, etc., par Leibnitz, Clarke, Newton (A. Collins) et autres auteurs célèbres,* reprinted in 1740, in which he included a translation of Collins' *Philosophical Inquiry concerning Human Liberty.* It seems likely that Voltaire found this book in 1736, when he was in exile in Holland, for his first mention of Collins other than as a mere name appears in the *Métaphysique de Newton,* upon which Vol-

---

[45] XXII, 403.   [46] XXVI, 57.
[47] *Op. cit.,* p. 46.
[48] See Morize, *Candide,* p. 18, n. 2; p. 54, n. 1, etc.
[49] "The Private Library of Voltaire at Leningrad," *PMLA,* XLIII (1928), 1007–1008.

taire was working at that time. In his copy of the 1720 edition he
has marked and made notes in the sections by Clarke, Leibnitz,
and Newton,[50] but there is neither marker nor note in the translation of Collins' work. It was apparently only after 1760, when
he had decided "qu'il faut prendre un parti," that he considers
Collins a critical deist and an enemy to Christianity, and his
works give evidence that he then refreshed his memory and
thoroughly digested Collins' treatise.

In considering Collins' attacks against the Bible and established
religion in connection with Voltaire, one must bear in mind again
that fifty years separated the works of the two men, and that they
were writing to entirely different audiences. The general ideas of
Collins' attack, especially on the prophecies, are very largely to
be found in Voltaire's works. As early as 1734, Voltaire wrote,
concerning the *Pensées* of Pascal; "De toutes les prophéties qu'il
rapporte, il n'y en a pas une qui puisse s'expliquer honnêtement de
Jésus Christ."[51] This was exactly Collins' contribution to English
deism. Both men were writing in much the same spirit, and Collins' style was excellent enough not to revolt Voltaire, as did the
cumbersome works of Bolingbroke and other English deists.
Moreover, Voltaire was already familiar with the metaphysical
works of Collins. In his very brief notice on Collins in the *Lettres
. . . sur Rabelais, etc.,* in 1767, Voltaire mentions four of Collins'
most important works: "Ses *Recherches philosophiques* sur la
liberté de l'homme, sur les fondements de la religion chrétienne,
sur les prophécies littérales, sur la liberté de penser,"[52] of which
the second and third are Collins' two late works on the prophecies. These, too, are the four works by Collins now in Voltaire's
library. Our problem here is to discover where Voltaire stands in
relation to Collins' criticisms of the Bible.

Collins naturally wrote nothing antibiblical in his letters to
Locke nor in his controversies with Samuel Clarke. In 1707, however, in his *Discourse concerning the Use of Reason,* he gives
some instances of the necessity of the use of reason to give author-

[50] With the aid of Clarke, who wrote in defense of Newton, he was especially concerned in disabusing Mme. du Châtelet in regard to Leibnitz.
[51] XXXIIII, 417.   [52] XXVI, 485.

ity to revelation. He was undoubtedly thinking of Clarke's *Divine Attributes,* when he drew up his list of God's attributes as found in the Pentateuch:

> God (a) rests; (b) repents; (c) is capable of anger; (d) is ignorant of the State of Adam; (e) is cheered with wine; (f) comes down to earth to see how things are; (g) stands before Moses on the Rock of Horeb; (h) has a face; (i) a finger with which he writes, and (j) back parts. Again (k) he is invisible; (l) he is a spirit.[53]

Reason, says Collins, teaches us to conform the former set of attributes to the latter, which are known anyway by the light of nature. Collins adds some of the evidence to show that Moses could not have written the Pentateuch. Voltaire praises Clarke's *Divine Attributes* as the work of a great philosopher[54] and at the same time condemns repeatedly the attributes assigned to God in the Pentateuch. In his *Dieu et les hommes,* he writes: "Dieu se promener! Dieu parler! Dieu écrire sur une petite montagne! Dieu combattre! Dieu devenir homme! Dieu-homme mourir du dernier supplice! idées dignes de *Punch.*"[55] Collins would not have dared to carry matters so far, and Voltaire never follows Collins' order of attributes although he has used them all in various parts of his criticism, especially in *La Bible enfin expliquée.* In this work he attributes to Collins the thought that "Dieu avait plus de soin du derrière des Israélites que de leurs âmes. . . . C'est parler avec peu de respect."[56] The sally is purely Voltairean, and Voltaire attributes the same idea to Swift in the *Examen important de milord Bolingbroke.*[57] Again, he attributes it to "un auteur connu" in *Dieu et les hommes.*[58] The author is certainly neither Collins nor Swift. It is almost as certainly Voltaire.

Very much in the spirit of Toland is Collins' work of 1709: *Priestcraft in Perfection: Or, a Detection of the Fraud of inserting and continuing this Clause (The Church hath power to decree Rites and Ceremonies, and Authority in Controversies of*

---

[53] London, 1707; pp. 18–19.
[54] *Nouveaux Mélanges* (1765), XX, 229, and elsewhere.
[55] XXVIII, 244.   [56] XXX, 119, n. 3.
[57] XXVI, 205.   [58] XXVIII, 171.

Faith) in the Twentieth Article of the Articles of the Church of England. The conclusions and inferences alone concern this study, and may be summed up as follows:

(1) The uncertainty of tradition works only toward making the word of God of none effect; (2) the uncertainty of the evidence of the gravest divines presents the same weakness; (3) "If men may be impos'd on so easily in such a Country as ours, how much more easily may they be impos'd on in the more ignorant and dark Corners of the Earth, especially before Printing was invented, when all kind of Literature was wholly in the hands of Ecclesiasticks"; (4) it is a supposition that all priests are talented in alterations, etc.; (5) such discoveries help us to rediscover true religion; (6) "How great a value we Protestants ought to set upon the Holy Scriptures, those inestimable Treasures of Wisdom and Knowledge, since there is nothing but uncertainty to be met with anywhere else; and since we are assur'd by the Spirit of Truth itself, that they alone are able to make us wise unto Salvation."[59]

The third article reminds one especially of Toland, and of Voltaire's gratuitous attribution to him:

> Toland assure qu'il est visible que tous ces livres ne furent écrits que longtemps après par quelque prêtre oisif, comme il y en a tant eu, dit-il, parmi nous aux XIIe, XIIIe, et XIVe siècles.[60]

The sixth article also is entirely in the spirit of Toland and resembles very little the general tone of Collins in his other works.[61] The influence of Toland's *Amyntor* is apparent, and Voltaire often confused his deists. Tempting as the suggestion is, it seems more than doubtful that Voltaire read this pamphlet carefully enough to borrow from it in 1776, and nowhere does he concern himself with the articles of the English Church. He was here again giving a random authority for a common deistic argument.

In 1713, appeared Collins' epoch-making work, the *Discourse of Free-thinking,* which gave the word "freethinking" "a universal notoriety, and brought it into established currency in con-

[59] London, 1710; p. 45 ff.　　[60] XXX, 84.
[61] Collins wrote later a small pamphlet on the same subject, and published an *Historical and Critical Essay on the thirty-nine Articles,* in 1724.

troversy, with the normal significance of deist."[62] The work is an attack on the historical foundations of Christianity rather than on the Bible. It has been treated critically by the method often used, and in this case advised, by Leslie Stephen, that is, by reading and basing judgments on the replies to the book by Swift and Bentley, rather than by reading the book itself. Stephen speaks of Bentley as the pulverizer of Collins,[63] a mere dabbler, and this opinion has been followed by Sayous[64] and in modern dictionary articles. Robertson has found, however, that Bentley attacks Collins' scholarship with "insolence and bad faith" and confutes only "one mistranslation which was only a joke or a printer's error, and one misspelling of a Greek name."[65] Collins, moreover, was treated as an atheist, and in the first uproar had to fly to Holland to avoid arrest. An impartial reading of the two works shows that Robertson is much nearer the truth than Stephen, and the very fury of the replies and the dignity of their authors show plainly the importance of Collins' work in the history of English deism. Voltaire mentioned this work in 1738, and again in 1767,[66] but at his death, his library contained only the translation by de Crouzas, and in the 1766 edition.[67] There are no notes in the volume.

Collins' first section attempts to prove that it is every man's right to think freely, that thinking freely is the only means to arrive at perfection through the sciences, that any other course would lead to absurdities, that there can be no rational restraint upon thinking, and that the progress made in England against the devil and witchcraft is one of the numerous benefits of freethinking. The second section maintains that it is our duty to think freely on those points of which men are denied the right to think freely; such as, of the nature and attributes of God, the truth and author-

[62] Robertson's *Short History of Freethought*, I, 7. See also Sayous, *Les déistes anglais*, p. 102.

[63] *English Thought in the Eighteenth Century*, I, 205 ff.

[64] *Les déistes anglais*, pp. 93 ff. His whole treatment of Collins is outrageous.

[65] *Op. cit.*, II, 135. See also *Nouvelles littéraires* (La Haye, 1715), I, 345.

[66] XXII, 413; XXVI, 485.

[67] *Discours sur la liberté de penser*, . . . *trad. de l'anglais* . . . *par M. de Crouzas, nouv. éd. corr.* (Londres, 1766), 2 vols. in 12. Voltaire possessed only the first volume of text, without the editor's augmentations and examination.

ity of the Scriptures, and of the meaning of the Scriptures. In this section especially there is so much in common with Toland that the charge was made that he had had a hand in it, to which he replied that he "never clubbed brains." The influence of each man's thought on the other is, however, unmistakable. In the third and last section, Collins answers the common objections to freethinking in religious matters.

In order to have a right opinion in religious matters, says Collins, it is not only a necessity but the sole duty of man to think freely, since there is no other remedy for the great evil of superstition. To support his argument against superstition, Collins quotes from Horace, Cicero, and Virgil, using from the last named the three lines which may be found ten years earlier in Toland:

> Felix qui potuit rerum cognoscere causas,
> Atque metus omnes et inexorabile Fatum
> Subjecit pedibus, strepitumque Acherontis avari.

In 1737 when Voltaire, in his correspondence with the young Prince Frederick, showed his preoccupation with metaphysical questions and his acquaintance with Collins' arguments against the freedom of the will, he wrote to Frederick:

> La partie de la philosophie la plus utile aux hommes, celle qui regarde l'âme, ne vaudra jamais rien parmi nous tant qu'on ne pourra pas penser librement. Un certain nombre de gens superstitieux fait grand tort ici à toute vérité. Si Cicéron vivait, et qu'il écrivît de Natura deorum, ou ses Tusculanes; si Virgile disait:
>
> > Félix qui potuit rerum cognoscere causas . . . etc.,
>
> Cicéron et Virgile courraient grand risque.[68]

The lines were too commonly used, and the idea too general to establish proof of direct influence, but the circumstantial evidence points to Collins as Voltaire's immediate inspiration.

Collins continues:

> The infinite number of Pretenders in all Ages to Revelations from Heaven, supported by miracles, containing new Notions of the Deity, new

[68] Discourse of Free-thinking (London, 1713), p. 37; Toland, Letters to Serena pp. 60–61; Voltaire, Œuvres, XXXIV, 266; cf. also XVIII, 541.

Doctrines, new Commands, new Ceremonys, and new Modes of Worship, make thinking on the foregoing Heads absolutely necessary.[69]

And he ingeniously quotes orthodox divines writing against new sects. He then points out the inconsistency of the missionaries, who would have the heathen think freely on their own religion, but not on Christianity, once they had embraced it. Why should not the King of Siam send missionary *talapoins* to England and propose that the English think freely concerning their own religion? For there can be no changing of religious belief nor indeed any religious belief at all, but by means of freethinking. Collins suggests certain zealous English divines that England would be well rid of as missionaries, and doubts not that the King of Siam would benefit by a like riddance of a certain number of *talapoins*.[70] He adds: "The Talapoins of Siam have a Book of Scripture written by Sommonocodom, who, the Siamese say, was born of a Virgin, and was the God expected by the Universe."[71] Collins refers for this statement to Tachard's *Voyage au Siam,* where probably Voltaire also found similar material. But in the use to which this common material was put, Voltaire owed much to Collins and to other English deists.

Not only was it the design of the Gospel to set all men upon freethinking, continues Collins, but the abuses of the clergy and their contradictions concerning the authority and sense of the Scriptures make freethinking an absolute necessity. Paul went frequently into the synagogues of the Jews and reasoned with them, but William Penn would be held a madman if he entered St. Paul's during the time of divine service to reason with the Court of Aldermen. Moreover, writes Collins, Christ particularly commands us to search the Scriptures and to beware of false doctrines; to use our reason against all the priests on earth, who were his enemies.[72] Among the contradictions of the priests is the dispute over the essence of God and over his attributes. Tertullian thought that God was a material being, but English divines who today hold this opinion are called atheists by other English divines.[73] The second point of argument divides the Cal-

[69] *Discourse of Free-thinking,* p. 40.   [70] *Ibid.,* p. 43.   [71] *Ibid.,* pp. 52–53.
[72] *Ibid.,* p. 45.   [73] *Ibid.,* pp. 47, 48.

vinists from the Arminians, the Jansenists from the Jesuits, and
the Thomists from the Molinists, etc., as well as his Grace of
Canterbury from his Grace of Dublin.[74] As for the authority of
the Scriptures, "the Brahmins, Persees, Bonzes, Talapoins, Der-
vizes, Rabbis, and all other Priests who build their Religion on
Books, must from the nature of things vary about Books in
the same Religion, about the Inspiration, and Copies of those
books."[75] In his criticism of the books of the Christian Gospel,
Collins used Fabricius' *Codex,* to which he refers, as well as
Grabe's *Spicilegium,* both of which we have found to have been
Voltaire's sources. Collins spends very little time on this argument, evidently considering Toland's *Amyntor* as sufficient unto
the day.

Even though the divine authority of the books of the Bible
were established, continues Collins, the tremendous diversity of
interpretation among divines forces freethinking upon the laity.
To prove this point, he quotes several pages on the difficulty of
interpretation from the polemic works of the Right Reverend
Bishop Taylor, particularly on the difficulty of knowing whether
a passage should be interpreted literally, figuratively, spiritually,
or anagogically, or by several of these methods at once.[76] In the
rest of this section of Collins' work, he plays off one divine
against another, showing the mass of contradictory statements
concerning the Trinity and the necessity of believing in this doctrine of the Trinity, the manner of the Resurrection, predestina-
tion, the eternity of hell torments, the fixing of the Sabbath Day,
the divinity of the Episcopacy, the doctrine of original sin, lay
baptism, usury, and even freethinking. The mass of quotations
from right reverends and learned doctors was far more effective
for Collins' purpose than would have been quotations from
Toland, or Fontenelle, or even Van Dale. Only one obscure cler-
gyman condemns usury, which must therefore, says Collins ironically, be considered a great Christian virtue.[77] Bentley casts some
disparaging remarks upon the accuracy of Collins' citations, but
without proof, and expresses himself as disgusted with the title

74 *Ibid.,* pp. 49, 51, 52. 75 *Ibid.,* p. 56.
76 *Ibid.,* pp. 57–61. 77 *Ibid.,* p. 74.

of Reverend: "The author indeed has made me sick of it, by his
flat insipid Drollery in tacking it to every name he mentions, six
times together perhaps in as few lines."[78] This was where, in
England, the shoe especially pinched. The material, however, was
not adapted to Voltaire's purposes, and it is not surprising to find
that he nowhere concerns himself with these squabbles and contradictions of English divines. In many of the questions in dispute he was greatly interested, for example in the variations in
the interpretations of the Trinity, but his sources are more elaborate and more explicit. In his *Lettres philosophiques,* Voltaire
treated the various sects in England with no little irony, especially the Quakers, whose government in Pennsylvania he often
praises. But he has never used Collins' anecdote, taken from Le
Clerc's *Bibliothèque choisie:*

> A Gentleman ask'd a Proprietor of New Jersey in America (where
> there are few Inhabitants besides Quakers) Whether they had any Law-
> yers among them? Then, Whether they had any Physicians? And lastly,
> Whether they had any Priests? To all which the Proprietor answer'd in
> order, No. O happy Country! replies the Gentleman, That must be a
> Paradise.[79]

Voltaire wrote in 1772:

> Je vous dirai, sans me répéter, que j'aime les quakers. Oui, si la mer ne
> me faisait pas un mal insupportable, ce serait dans ton sein, ô Pensylvanie,
> que j'irais finir le reste de ma carrière, s'il y a du reste.[80]

Approval of the society of the Quakers, if not of their doctrine,
was a part of the deist creed.

In the third and last section of the *Discourse of Free-thinking,*
Collins answers many objections, but principally the objection
that freethinkers are irrational, infamous, and wicked people. To
this, Collins answers, first, that freethinkers must have the most
understanding, and that they must therefore necessarily be the
most virtuous people; and secondly, that they have in fact been
the most understanding and virtuous people in all ages.[81] Under
the first head, Collins claims that the clergy are too busy over reli-

---

[78] *Remarks upon a late Discourse of Free-thinking* (London, 1713), p. 5.
[79] *Op. cit.,* p. 108.   [80] XX, 312.
[81] *Op. cit.,* p. 120.

gious squabbles to turn their attention to the vice on the streets of London, and that it is the obvious advantage of any sect to tolerate vice and wickedness.[82] Moreover, the freethinker cannot secure an easy remission of his sins, and hesitates much longer than the Christian before committing them.

As instances of his second point, Collins cites a long list of free-thinkers: Socrates, Plato, Aristotle, Epicurus, Plutarch, Varro, Cato the Censor, Cicero, Cato of Utica, Seneca, Solomon, the Jewish Prophets, Josephus, Origen, Minutius Felix, Synesius, Lord Bacon, Hobbes, and Tillotson. This discussion comprises nearly a third of Collins' book, and is representative of the usual criticism against Christianity. Much of the same material may be found in Voltaire. Justin Martyr deemed Socrates a Christian, and Erasmus, reading his words spoken just before taking the poisonous draught, "can hardly forbear crying out, 'Sancte Socrates, ora pro nobis.' "[83] Against Celsus, who maintained that Christ had borrowed from Plato, Origen shows that Christ could not read.[84] Origen was the most learned of the early Christians, but was not made a saint, which requires ignorance and zeal.[85] Epicurus was virtuous above all philosophers, especially in friendship, that greatest of all virtues, which is not once mentioned by name in the New Testament.[86] Cato the Censor wondered "how one of our priests can forbear laughing when he sees another."[87] Seneca wrote that death puts an end to all our miseries, and yet early impostors forged letters between him and Paul, and Jerome listed him among the saints.[88] Solomon writes against the immortality of the soul, an idea unknown among the Jews.[89] The Old Testament prophets wrote with the greatest liberty against the established religion of the Jews, and were bolder against the priests than any man would dare be in Collins' day.[90] Josephus was the most learned and polite author of the Jews, but it is regretta-

---

[82] *Discourse of Free-thinking*, p. 116.

[83] *Ibid.*, p. 125. Voltaire, in his *Anecdote sur Bélisaire* quotes these very words from Le Vayer's *La Vertu des Païens*, which was very probably Collins' source. (XXVI, 112.)

[84] *Discourse of Free-thinking*, p. 127.   [85] *Ibid.*, p. 162.

[86] *Ibid.*, p. 129.   [87] *Ibid.*, p. 135.

[88] *Ibid.*, p. 147.   [89] *Ibid.*, p. 151; p. 152, note.

[90] *Ibid.*, p. 154.

ble that his subject was "such an illiterate, barbarous, and ridiculous people," "cross-grained brutes," in dealing with whom God had to "use craft rather than reason."[91] Moreover, Josephus appears to doubt certain miracles, such as that of the Red Sea. Minutius Felix, "like a true modern latitudinarian Christian," explains to the heathen why the Christians had neither temples nor altars.[92] The passage is given both in English and Latin, and was used later by Toland,[93] but Voltaire, in his dictionary article, "Autels," begins his quotation[94] several sentences before that of the English deists, plainly showing that, though they were his inspiration, they were not his sole source. On Synesius, the unbelieving Christian bishop, Collins gives details not found in Toland's "Hypatia," nor in Voltaire's various accounts.[95] Collins ends cleverly with an encomium of Archbishop Tillotson, "whom all English Free-Thinkers own as their Head, and whom even the enemies of Free-Thinking will allow to be a proper Instance to my Purpose."[96] Even as late as 1766, Voltaire himself invoked Tillotson, in defense of La Barre:

> Le grand archevêque Tillotson, le meilleur prédicateur de l'Europe, et presque le seul qui n'ait point déshonoré l'éloquence par de fades lieux communs ou par de vaines phrases fleuries comme Cheminais, ou par de faux raisonnements comme Bourdaloue, l'archevêque Tillotson, dis-je, parle précisément de notre eucharistie comme le chevalier de la Barre.[97]

Again, in his *Avis au public sur les Calas et les Sirven,* he quotes from Tillotson certain passages which Collins has used, and quotes moreover in the original English:

> Better it were that there were no reveal'd religion; and that human nature were left to its own principles mild and mercifull and conducive to the happiness of society, than to be acted by a religion which inspires men with so wild a fury.[98]

Voltaire, too, was seeking the most orthodox and noteworthy authority possible. Collins' work went to press anonymously with

---

[91] *Discourse of Free-thinking,* p. 157 and note.   [92] *Ibid.,* p. 162.
[93] *Coll. of Pieces,* II, 144. Passage marked in Voltaire's copy.
[94] XVII, 495.   [95] *Op. cit.,* p. 165.
[96] *Ibid.,* p. 171.   [97] XXV, 510.
[98] *Ibid.,* p. 535; and Collins, *op. cit.,* p. 174.

the closing lines: "For I think it Virtue enough to endeavour to do Good, only within the bounds of doing your self no Harm."[99] His subsequent forced trip to Holland may have done him no harm, but it had evidently not been planned.

As was the case with Collins' work on determinism, Voltaire avoided textual borrowings, but the influence, for that reason, cannot safely be minimized. The accumulated evidence makes it nearly certain that Voltaire read Collins' *Discourse of Free-thinking* in the late thirties during the period of his metaphysical researches, along with Newton, Locke, and Clarke. The influence was again general rather than detailed, early rather than late. The copy left in his library is a translation by M. Crouzas, reëdited in 1766,[100] after Voltaire had collected from other sources most of his antireligious material. In his later works, when the victory had been won and freedom of thought was taken for granted, he defends rather the freedom of the press, and at length only once, in his *Questions sur les miracles,* in 1765, when he is aroused by the tyranny of the magistrates at Geneva. He stresses again the beneficence of English liberty:

> Conservons toujours les bienséances, dit-il, mais donnons un libre essor à nos pensées. Soutenons la liberté de la presse, c'est la base de toutes les autres libertés, c'est par là qu'on s'éclaire mutuellement. Chaque citoyen peut parler par écrit à la nation, et chaque lecteur examine à loisir, et sans passion, ce que ce compatriote lui dit par la voie de la presse. Nos cercles peuvent quelquefois être tumultueux: ce n'est que dans le recueillement du cabinet qu'on peut bien juger. C'est par là que la nation anglaise est devenue véritablement une nation libre.[101]

During the later period of more serious antibiblical documentation, similarities of thought are expected and suggest rather than prove direct influence. In the historical part of Collins' work, although many details that Voltaire used can be found, it is certain that he derived them from other sources. In Grabe and Fabricius, the two men had common sources for the apocryphal works, and as for the doctrine of the mortality of the soul among the Jews, which Collins was one of the first to popularize in Eng-

---

[99] *Op. cit.,* p. 178.
[100] See above, note 67.
[101] XXV, 419.

land, Voltaire drew his material chiefly from Warburton.[102] The many citations from English divines did not ordinarily find their way into Voltaire's works. But in spirit and method the men show very great similarity, attacking the later miracles with ridicule and irony, belittling the ancient Jewish nation, showing the confusions and contradictions in the early history of the Church, the precariousness of the accepted canon, and the impossibility of a uniform interpretation of the Scriptures.

Collins published little between the *Discourse on Human Liberty* in 1717, and the *Discourse on the Grounds and Reasons of the Christian Religion,* which first appeared in 1724.[103] This work set the English ecclesiastical world into a turmoil which had not abated when Voltaire arrived in England and which continued many years after his departure. Thirty-five replies appeared to this attack by Collins on the authority of the prophecies within the space of two years.[104] Most of these replies were written in the common abusive strain, but to those which admitted seriously the difficulties of the question and applied thought to them, Collins answered two years later in his *Scheme of Literal Prophecy considered.* Besides the many replies from Whiston, who was directly concerned in Collins' *Grounds and Reasons,* there appeared *The Moderator between an Infidel and an Apostate* (Collins and Whiston), by Thomas Woolston, which proved to be a continuation of the attack rather than a reply, and *A Discourse proving the Resurrection of Christ, and shewing that it is a sufficient Demonstration of Christianity,* a work which shows to what a pass the Christian apologists had come at the hands of the deists. Woolston was soon to attack this last remaining demonstration. Warburton considers Collins' *Grounds* the most plausible attack ever published against Christianity, and that the replies might have been left to confute each other.[105] Even Leslie Stephen admits, once, that Collins here had at almost every point

---

[102] XXVI, 393 ff. Warburton's *Divine Legation of Moses* was in a measure a reply to Collins.

[103] Voltaire possessed the 1737 edition.

[104] See Thorschmid's volume on Collins, and the foreword to Collins' *Scheme of Literal Prophecy considered,* 1726.

[105] Robertson's *Short History of Freethought,* II, 136.

the better of the dispute, and that Chandler's *Literal Scheme,* which Collins answers in particular in his second work, was crazy.[106]

Collins' method is to establish the thesis held by many divines that the fulfilment of prophecies is alone the demonstration of the truth of the Christian religion, and then to show the utter weakness of this proof. Christianity is founded on Judaism, the New Testament on the Old. The evangelists and apostles urge the fulfilment of prophecy as proof of the truth of Christianity, among whom Peter especially was not convinced by miraculous attestations, but by sure and demonstrable proofs from prophecy alone. If these proofs are valid, Christianity is invincibly established on its true foundation. But if these proofs should be proved invalid, then Christianity is a cheat, and the miracles can never save it. But that proof from the literal fulfilment of the Old Testament prophecies will not hold water, is evident from an impartial comparison of the two Testaments, as well as on the authority of Origen, Erasmus, Simon, Le Clerc, Grotius, etc., and finally of the ill-fated Whiston, who is the scapegoat of the entire controversy. Collins comments on five principal prophecies commonly considered to have been fulfilled, and shows the necessity of having recourse to the allegorical or typical method of interpretation. This method he deals with at some length and reduces to absurdity, showing allegory to be equivalent to nonsense. In the Boylean lectures, Whiston had shown the dangers and weaknesses of allegorical interpretation. Such a method, wrote Whiston, "exposes the Christian religion to the laughter of infidels," and is "one of the most ill-grounded and pernicious things that ever was admitted by Christians."[107] In condemning the absurd allegorical scheme, Whiston is forced to admit that literal fulfilment is untenable with the Old Testament as it now stands, and proposes to establish the true text and free it from corruptions. Collins, in the second part of his work, ridicules Whiston's scheme of restoring the Old Testament, and charges Whiston

---

[106] *English Thought in the Eighteenth Century,* I, 217. In detailed criticism, Stephen is often fair, but forgets his admissions in his summaries and generalizations.

[107] Collins, *Grounds and Reasons* (London, 1737), p. 88.

with working against Christianity in admitting that its very foundation is full of incredible corruptions, thereby destroying completely the authority of divine inspiration. Such is the scheme and method of Collins' *Grounds and Reasons of the Christian Religion.*

What was Voltaire's reaction to this book and to this controversy which was reëchoing in England at the very time of his visit? The first intimation of his knowledge of it occurs in 1734, six years after his return to France, in a passage quoted above, in which he states that of the prophecies mentioned by Pascal, not one can be honestly explained as referring to Jesus.[108] In 1767, he includes the two works of Collins on the prophecies among the latter's important works against Christianity, but nowhere else in his works does he connect Collins' name with the prophecies. Whiston is several times mentioned as a "bon géomètre et très savant homme, qui s'est rendu ridicule par ses systèmes," and in regard to "ses calculs comiques sur la population de la terre par la famille de Noé." Again, "notre Whiston n'était chrétien que parce qu'il était arien,"[109] but never does Voltaire mention Whiston either in regard to the prophecies.

This mysterious silence is wilful, for Voltaire had Collins' works on the prophecies in his library, and used and annotated them. Voltaire's chief method of attack on the prophecies, however, was to debit impertinences on the Old Testament prophets, such as Ezekiel, in the treatment of whom he shocked Mme. du Deffand.[110] Several times he attacks the validity of the prophecy of Immanuel in Isaiah, but in general he deals with them rarely and briefly. Collins' work was a vital part of the English deistic movement and loses much of its interest and value if taken from its setting. In his second book on the prophecies, Collins quotes from Pascal: "La plus grande des preuves de Jésus Christ, ce sont les prophéties."[111] Voltaire, as we have seen, would have liked to demolish Pascal's position in his *Remarques* in 1734,[112] but did

[108] XXXIII, 417. See above, pp. 3, 37.
[109] XXII, 138; XXIV, 581; XXVI, 197, etc.
[110] XLI, 90, 151.
[111] *Scheme of Literal Prophecy considered* (London, 1727), p. 344.
[112] XXXIII, 417.

not dare. When he did dare, many years later, other writers had taken up Collins' ideas, and from 1768 to 1770 d'Holbach published several volumes translated from, or inspired by, Collins' works. Voltaire's only note in d'Holbach's translation, *Examen des prophéties,* was "livre dangereux" on the title-page—never too dangerous, however, to be used, especially if the use could be adequately concealed. For Voltaire did not fail to use Collins' main argument, of which he was so early persuaded.

An approach to Collins' material is found in Voltaire's article "Prophéties" (1766):

> On sentira la nécessité indispensable d'avoir l'esprit ouvert pour comprendre les prophéties, si l'on fait attention que les Juifs, qui en étaient les dépositaires, n'ont jamais pu reconnaître Jésus pour le messie, et qu'il y a dix-huit siècles que nos théologiens disputent avec eux pour fixer le sens de quelques-unes, qu'ils tâchent d'appliquer à Jésus. Telles sont: celle de Jacob: Le sceptre ne sera point ôté de Juda, et le chef de sa cuisse, jusqu'à ce qui doit être envoyé vienne; —celle de Moïse: Le Seigneur votre Dieu vous suscitera un prophète comme moi, de votre nation et d'entre vos frères; c'est lui que vous écouterez; —celle d'Isaïe: Voici qu'une vierge concevra et enfantera un fils qui sera nommé Emmanuel; —celle de Daniel: Soixante et dix semaines ont été abrégées en faveur de votre peuple, etc. Notre objet n'est point d'entrer ici dans ce détail théologique.
>
> Observons seulement qu'il est dit dans les Actes des apôtres qu'en donnant un successeur à Judas, et dans autres occasions, ils se proposaient expressément d'accomplir les prophéties; mais les apôtres même en citaient quelquefois qui ne se trouvent point dans l'écriture des Juifs; telle est celle-ci alléguée par saint Matthieu: Jésus vint demeurer dans une ville appelée Nazareth, afin que cette prédiction des prophètes fût accomplie: Il sera appelé Nazaréen.[113]

But Voltaire's list differs materially from the five prophecies which Collins picked out to refute, and he is unwilling to enter into mere theological detail. Instead, and very characteristically, he devotes the following two pages of his article to a discussion of the prophecy of the Star of Bethlehem which he had picked up in some of his favorite apocryphal readings, and which he compares to a similar prophecy concerning Zoroaster. He was

[113] XX, 283.

much more concerned to appear learned[114] than to appear to borrow or copy from the common run of English deists.

The principal prophecy the literal sense of which Collins undertook to confute as a connection between the Old and New Testaments, and the only prophecy that Voltaire discusses similarly in detail, was the Immanuel prophecy from Isaiah. Collins' account begins as follows:

> St. Matthew after having given an account of the conception of the virgin Mary, and of the birth of Jesus, says, "all this was done that it might be fulfill'd, which was spoken by the prophet, saying, 'Behold a virgin shall be with child, and shall bring forth a Son, and they shall call his name Immanuel.' " But the words, as they stand in Isaiah, from whom they are suppos'd to be taken, do, in their obvious and literal sense, relate to a *young woman* in the days of Ahaz, king of Judah, as will appear by considering the context.[115]

Collins continues to prove his point, and gives an amazing list of authorities, beginning with Grotius and Huetius, with footnote references to the passages in question. Even Whiston had admitted that the prophecy was not applicable in its literal sense according to the present text of Isaiah.[116] And Collins cites Erasmus as father of the idea that the Hebrew word "Alma" might mean young woman as well as virgin.

Voltaire's treatment of the same subject, with all the facts taken from Collins, illustrates well the differences between the two men in their respective treatment of the prophecies, and helps to clear up the mystery of his silence in regard to Collins. Voltaire throws the odium of the discussion upon the Jews, while with careful irony, Collins has reserved for Whiston the climactic position among the authorities. Again, Voltaire stresses certain impertinences which Collins does not take the trouble to mention. Voltaire's most detailed treatment of the subject is found in the second section of the article "Prophéties," in the *Questions sur l'Encyclopédie* (1771):

[114] In *L'A, B, C*, at the mention of the names of Confucius and Zoroaster, the interlocutor says: "Vous me paraissez bien savant: quels sont donc ces préceptes de Zoroastre et de Confutzée?" (XXVII, 363.)

[115] *Grounds and Reasons*, pp. 32–33.   [116] *Ibid.*, p. 41.

C'est particulièrement dans le prétendu *Rempart de la Foi* du rabbin Isaac que l'on interprète toutes les prophéties qui annoncent Jésus-Christ en les appliquant à d'autres personnes.

C'est là qu'on assure que la Trinité n'est figurée dans aucun livre hébreu, et qu'on n'y trouve pas la plus légère trace de notre sainte religion. Au contraire, ils allèguent cent endroits qui, selon eux, disent que la loi mosaïque doit durer éternellement.

Le fameux passage qui doit confondre les juifs et faire triompher la religion chrétienne, de l'aveu de tous nos grands théologiens, est celui d'Isaïe: "Voici: une vierge sera enceinte, elle enfantera un fils, et son nom sera Emmanuel; il mangera du beurre et du miel jusqu'à ce qu'il sache rejeter le mal et choisir le bien. . . . Et avant que l'enfant sache rejeter le mal et choisir le bien, la terre que tu as en détestation sera abandonnée de ses deux rois. . . . Et l'Eternel sifflera aux mouches des ruisseaux d'Egypte, et aux abeilles qui sont au pays d'Assur. . . . Et en ce jour-là le Seigneur rasera avec un rasoir de louage le roi d'Assur, la tête et le poil des génitoires, et il achèvera aussi la barbe. . . . Et l'Eternel me dit: Prends un grand rouleau et y écris avec une touche en gros caractère, qu'on se dépêche de butiner, prenez vite les dépouilles. . . . Donc je pris avec moi de fidèles témoins, savoir Urie le sacrificateur, et Zacharie, fils de Jeberecia. . . . Et je couchai avec la prophétesse; elle conçut et enfanta un enfant mâle; et l'Eternel me dit: Appelle l'enfant Maher-salal-has-bas. Car avant que l'enfant sache crier mon père et ma mère, on enlèvera la puissance de Damas, et le butin de Samarie devant le roi d'Assur."

Le rabbin Isaac affirme, après tous les autres docteurs de sa loi, que le mot hébreu *alma* signifie tantôt une vierge, tantôt une femme mariée; que Ruth est appelée *alma* lorsqu'elle était mère; qu'un femme adultère est quelquefois même nommée *alma;* qu'il ne s'agit ici que de la femme du prophète Isaïe, que son fils ne s'appelle point *Emmanuel,* mais *Maher-salal-has-bas;* que quand ce fils mangera du beurre et du miel, les deux rois qui assiégent Jérusalem seront chassés du pays, etc.

Ainsi ces interprètes aveugles de leur propre religion et de leur propre langue combattent contre l'Eglise, et disent obstinément que cette prophétie ne peut regarder Jésus-Christ en aucune manière.

On a mille fois réfuté leur explication dans nos langues modernes. On a employé la force, les gibets, les roues, les flammes; cependant ils ne se rendent pas encore.[117]

There is no question but that Voltaire's ironical use of the Jewish rabbis and their treatment of the prophecies was far more effective in France than would have been an explanation of the Collins-Whiston controversy. But what he gains in effectiveness,

[117] XX, 288–289.

he loses in veracity. For the *Rempart de la foi,* or the *Liber de Capite Fidei,*[118] by Isaac Abrabanel, is an orthodox defense of the teachings of Maimonides, nor is the word Christ or Christian to be found in the whole work. The mystery is explained by turning to the works of the mystifying Baron d'Holbach. In 1768 and in 1770, d'Holbach published in translation Collins' two works on the prophecies,[119] and in 1770 he also published a work entitled *Israël vengé, ou Exposition naturelle des prophéties hébraïques que les Chrétiens appliquent à Jésus, leur prétendu Messie.* This work was given as a translation by Henriquez of a Spanish work by Orobio de Castro, or Isaac Balthazar. It is to this Isaac that Voltaire refers in 1771 as his authority on the prophecies. But the work is just another of the many literary cheats perpetrated by d'Holbach, Voltaire, and other *philosophes* of the eighteenth century.[120] D'Holbach was merely putting into another form and under another name what he had learned from Collins. In other works, Voltaire gives chapter references to the *Rempart de la foi*[121] for material quoted which occurs nowhere in the genuine book by Isaac Abrabanel, and proceeds immediately thereafter to discuss the opinions of the Rabbi Orobio.[122] The latter is found to have summed up very neatly the main deistic arguments against the Christian religion; for d'Holbach was translating Annet, Toland, and Woolston as well as Collins, and did not miss the chance to use his gleanings wherever he could. D'Holbach is thus an important intermediary between Voltaire and the English deists, notwithstanding the fact that Voltaire possessed copies of Collins' works on the prophecies in the original English.

In the *Sermon des cinquante*[123] and in many other works Vol-

---

[118] Amsterdam, 1638. French translation, Avignon, 1884.

[119] See *Catalogue de la Bibliothèque nationale,* under d'Holbach.

[120] A note on the work in Barbier's *Dictionnaire des ouvrages anonymes* questions the existence of the Orobio manuscript, and the writer states: "Je sais avec certitude que le baron d'Holbach a refait en grande partie l'ouvrage, s'il n'est pas entièrement de lui, ce que je suis porté à croire." D'Holbach included in his *Bon sens du curé Meslier* passages from Bolingbroke which were not published until many years after the death of the curate.

[121] XXIX, 519.

[122] *Lettres . . . sur Rabelais, etc.,* XXVI, 518, 519.

[123] XXIV, 447.

taire discusses this same prophecy from Isaiah, often in such a way as to cast opprobrium on the customs and manners of the ancient Jews. In the *Extrait des sentiments de Jean Meslier* and elsewhere, he deals more exclusively with the prophets Ezekiel and Hosea as more fruitful in obscenities.[124] The allegorical and typical treatment of the prophecies, which Collins ironically pretends to defend against Whiston, Voltaire treats with the utmost contempt. In the *Examen important de milord Bolingbroke,* he writes:

> Il se trouva avec le temps des disciples qui raisonnèrent un peu: on prit le parti de leur dire que tout l'Ancien Testament n'est qu'une figure du Nouveau. Le petit morceau de drap rouge que mettait la paillarde Rahab à sa fenêtre pour avertir les espions de Josué signifie le sang de Jésus répandu pour nos péchés, etc. . . . Plaisante et folle imagination, de faire de toute l'histoire d'une troupe de gueux la figure et la prophétie de tout ce qui devait arriver au monde entier dans la suite des siècles.[125]

Collins speaks of the red cloth of Rahab in his chapter, "Typical or Allegorical reasoning defended against Mr. Whiston,"[126] but it is difficult to link definitely the two passages. Voltaire had only to read Dom Calmet or numerous other Church writers to find a target for his ever ready critical wit. On the subject of Rahab, however, he quotes Collins gratuitously in *La Bible enfin expliquée,* a work in which one would be surprised to find a *bona fide* quotation or attribution:

> Collins soutient que Josué sembla se défier de Dieu en envoyant des espions chez cette femme, et que puisqu'il avait avec lui Dieu et quarante mille hommes pour se saisir d'un petit bourg dans une vallée, et que la palissade qui enfermait ce petit bourg tomba au son des trompettes, on n'avait pas besoin d'envoyer chez une gueuse deux espions qui risquaient d'être perdus.[127]

This passage has all the earmarks of being Voltaire's own and original commentary. In any case, Collins did not write it.

Likewise, on the subject of the prophecies, although Voltaire

[124] XXIV, 324–325. See also *Examen important de milord Bolingbroke,* XXVI, 217–219. We shall see that Tindal was the source for these remarks.
[125] XXVI, 244, 245.   [126] *Op. cit.,* p. 198.
[127] XXX, 122.

had read widely on the subject and used much scholarly material, yet much of his commentary is his own, whether he attributes it to the Jewish rabbis or to the English deists. Furthermore, he stressed the personal failings of the prophets rather than the lack of support which the prophecies gave to the demonstration of the truth of Christianity. There was no question of authority in Catholic France, while in England the protestant divines were obliged to abandon one authority after another before the attacks of such men as Collins. Their very divisions served to defeat them and presented an easy mark for a man of Collins' wit and attainments. Voltaire showed here great good sense and adaptability in refusing to follow servilely the English deistic movement.

Voltaire read Collins' two books on the prophecies in the original English, as the notes in his copies testify. But these very notes, probably made late in life, indicate that he was interested chiefly in points beside the main issue. In the *Discourse on the Grounds and Reasons of the Christian Religion* (London, 1737), there are nine markers, on four of which there are autograph remarks, and three of which indicate the presence of stickers or tiny bits of paper pasted over passages that interested him. On a marker in the preface, he wrote "remarque singulière: aucun philosophe grec n'a dit du mal d'un autre."[128] Five markers concern the authenticity of the Pentateuch, the Septuagint version of the Bible, and the Samaritan Pentateuch.[129] A note on one of these markers, "profètes hérétiques," refers to Collins' claim that most of the prophets were of the Samaritan schism. Another note is in English: "remember the apostles quoted the Greek often, not alway." A seventh marker, with a sticker, indicates Collins' remark that Grotius could "neither find the Messias in the Old Testament, nor the Pope in the New."[130] Voltaire, in all his criticisms of Grotius, does not appear to have used this note. The eighth marker bears the words "cum duo erunt unum," referring to the time when Jesus said he would come again.[131] And lastly a marker and sticker indicate Whiston's Arian creed, "the Father is the One God."[132]

[128] *Op. cit.,* pp. xxii–xxiii.
[129] *Ibid.,* pp. 122–123, 160–161, 171, 175, 185.
[130] *Ibid.,* p. 213.   [131] *Ibid.,* p. 222.   [132] *Ibid.,* p. 244.

The *Scheme of Literal Prophecy considered* (London, 1727) contains only two markers, and these are equally irrelevant to Collins' main thesis. The first indicates Cicero's contempt for the Sibylline books, which he thought should be used for the putting down of old, rather than for the setting up of new, religious fancies.[133] The second marker concerns either Bishop Chandler's tirade against the Roman Church,[134] or Whiston's remarks that the book of *Canticles* is a strange and unedifying book which should be discarded from the canon, and that true original Christianity, far from being established, is not even tolerated.[135] Collins' second work was essentially controversial, and it seems doubtful if Voltaire spent much time over it. Collins spent many pages proving the untrustworthiness of Jewish tradition, and defending the integrity of Grotius. Voltaire takes glee, as we have seen above, in setting off the Jewish tradition against the Christian, and he attacked Grotius under the name of Bolingbroke.[136] He welcomed a man of Collins' standing into the ranks of philosophical unbelievers, but borrowed directly from the English volumes very little, for his few trifling notes were put to little specific use. The definite influence came through the translations of d'Holbach, under the pseudonym of Rabbi Isaac. Voltaire thus concealed his English source and gave no credit to Collins.

The comparison of Collins with Voltaire has served to bring out and to emphasize several important aspects of the problem of Voltaire's relations to the English critical deists. At the time of Voltaire's visit to England, he showed little interest in the deistic movement, and read Collins' metaphysical works probably in translation and chiefly in connection with Clarke, Locke, and Newton. Not until a decade later did the force of Collins' arguments begin to make themselves felt, and it was only some forty years later that Voltaire declares himself definitely and finally convinced. Yet the Collins' influence was extremely important in the shaping of Voltaire's attitude toward the metaphysical and

---

[133] *Op. cit.*, pp. 48, 49. [134] *Ibid.*, p. 430.
[135] *Ibid.*, p. 431.
[136] XXVI, *Lettre de milord Bolingbroke à milord Cornsbury*, pp. 301–305.

moral problems of life. Through this influence, he denied the freedom of the will and finally admitted that this problem had no bearing on the question of morality. His scheme of morality contained nothing of the metaphysical, and, following Collins' skepticism concerning the immortality of the soul, nothing of the theological, except in so far as Voltaire taught what he evidently did not believe, the doctrine of future rewards and punishments. This last trait in Voltaire modern freethinkers would consider a weakness, but in recompense, rather than call Voltaire an amateur in metaphysics with Lanson,[137] they would say to his credit that he was one of the first great popularizers to separate social and moral problems from the entanglements of metaphysics and theology, just as they credit Collins with originality in the modern conception and statement of the case of determinism.

In the realm of purely critical deism, we are reminded once more that Voltaire's early interest in the prophecies, which may have been founded on mere echoes of the deistic controversy, had been quickly discouraged. His active participation in biblical criticism came late in life when his English days were long-distant memories. When he read Collins' works, both in the original English and in translation,[138] he made a wise selection from the material offered, in view of the different circumstances in which he wrote, but very effectively concealed his source. There is also some connection between Collins' use of ridicule and irony and similar methods used by Voltaire, as pointed out by Lanson, but here we shall find much more similarity between Voltaire and the next deist under consideration, Thomas Woolston.

[137] Lanson, *Voltaire,* p. 73.

[138] He gives bare mention of d'Holbach's translations, in a letter to d'Alembert in 1771 (XLVII, 543).

CHAPTER IV

VOLTAIRE AND THOMAS WOOLSTON: THE ARGUMENT AGAINST MIRACLES

AT the close of his *Scheme of Literal Prophecy considered,* Collins promised his correspondent other religious treatises then in manuscript. "I shall begin," he writes, "with a 'Discourse upon the Miracles recorded in the Old and New Testament'; which is almost transcrib'd for your use."[1] The reason that this work was never published was very probably because Thomas Woolston, in 1727, began his publication of six discourses on the miracles of our Savior. Collins' mild irony and ridicule would have seemed very flat in comparison with the methods of his much more rabid successor and continuator. Whether Collins' eight octavos in manuscript were destroyed or still exist is not known. In his will he left them to his friend Desmaizeaux, who in an unguarded moment sold them for fifty guineas to Collins' widow. Desmaizeaux repented and sent back the money to the widow, but did not get the manuscripts. The charge was later made that she betrayed them into the hands of the Bishop of London. D'Israeli has reported several interesting letters in this regard between Mrs. Collins and Desmaizeaux in his *Curiosities of Literature.*[2] The loss is unfortunate, but in regard to the New Testament miracles, Woolston had already begun to fill the gap.

Thomas Woolston had a well-marked influence upon Voltaire. Direct borrowings from his discourses on the miracles appear in nearly every work that Voltaire wrote against Christianity, from the *Sermon des cinquante* to the *Bible enfin expliquée* and *l'Établissement du christianisme.* Many times Voltaire quotes him by name and gives his original phrases in English, the better to persuade his readers that such blasphemies could

---

[1] London, 1726 (1727), p. 419. [2] London, 1840, pp. 380-382.

actually have existed in print. More often, Voltaire uses his favorite arguments without mentioning the source, and often enough, too, he parades Woolston under the name of some other English deist. All English deists, Toland, Collins, Bolingbroke, Gordon, were to him just so many Woolstons, all equally rabid in their attacks on the Christian religion. Sometimes he even appears apologetic in repeating such blasphemies as Woolston's,[3] but he wanted to prove to his French readers that a man could write such things and still live peacefully on, undisturbed by the thunderbolts of "the God of the Old and New Testaments." He knew, moreover, something of Woolston's life. He contested the commonly accepted opinion that Woolston died in prison, and related other interesting anecdotes.

Thomas Woolston[4] was born at Northampton in 1669, and was thus Toland's senior by one year. In 1685 he entered Sidney College, Cambridge, where he took both degrees in the arts, and was later received bachelor of divinity. He took orders and became a fellow of the college, where he lived quietly for many years studying divinity and acquiring a reputation for learning and piety. In 1705 he published his first work, *An Old Apology for the Truth of the Christian Religion against the Jews and Gentiles, revived.* In this work he adopted from Origen, his favorite Father, the method of allegorical and typical interpretation of the Scriptures. Moses in the Old Testament is the type of Christ in the New. Woolston preached this dangerous doctrine at Cambridge to the surprise of his audience, but his intentions were thought good and his character greatly respected. For fifteen more years he studied quietly without publishing. But in 1720 he began a series of publications which he continued unabated until his imprisonment in 1730 for his discourses on the miracles. His purpose was ostensibly to defend the early allegorical Fathers, but developed into ever more bitter attacks on the "literal clergy" and the literal word. In 1721 he lost his fellowship for overstaying his leave, in spite of the endeavors of Whiston and

---

[3] See XX, 86 ff.

[4] For a detailed account of Woolston's life see *The Life of the Reverend Mr. Thomas Woolston* (London, 1733), attributed to Thos. Stackhouse. The work appears much too sympathetic to Woolston to have been written by Stackhouse.

other friends to have it continued. From that time on he resided in London, where he might have lived in comparative opulence if he had not insisted on paying, himself, all the expenses for the printing and selling of his books. In 1730 he was sentenced to a year's confinement and a fine of one hundred pounds, which he was unable to pay. The main obstacle to his release, however, was his refusal to retract or to promise to write no more. He enjoyed the freedom of the Rules of the King's Bench, and though technically a prisoner when he died in 1733, he lived and died in his own house, as related by Voltaire. Even during his imprisonment, he was well known as a man of great temperance, patience, and humanity, and died with great fortitude. His earliest biographer wrote:

A few minutes before his Death he uttered these words, "this is a Struggle which all Men must go through, and which I bear not only patiently but with Willingness." He then immediately closed his Eyes and Lips with his own Fingers, seemingly with a Design to compose his Face with Decency, without the Help of a Friend's Hand, and then expired.[5]

He was buried in St. George's churchyard in Southwark. It was generally considered that he died under persecution for religion, and Clarke, before his death, and Whiston, with whom he had fallen out, and who had himself lost his seat at Cambridge for his religious opinions, had worked for his freedom.[6]

The difficulty in dealing with Woolston's life and works lies in the fact that even his contemporaries could not decide whether or not he was sincere in his defense of the allegorical and typical method of interpretation of the Scriptures. The possibility of his sincerity in defending the Christian religion is admitted by nearly all later critics. The orthodox divines either could not believe that he was not sincere, or thought it expedient not to admit that a fellow divine of such learning and standing could have fallen so scandalously from grace. They preferred to treat him as a victim of mild insanity, a charge which Woolston himself naturally resented, but dared not resist. The most he could do was to admit to Whiston, who long persisted in believing him sincere, that he

[5] *Life of Woolston*, p. 29.   [6] *Ibid.*, pp. 18, 19.

hardly knew whether he was a Christian or not.[7] Leslie Stephen
is uncertain; he writes: "Whether Woolston intended it or not,
the reader would probably consider allegorical as equivalent to
fictitious."[8] He speaks often of the "mad Woolston," and of an
intellect disordered from reading Origen. Even Sayous, who
attacked Toland's sincerity so bitterly, says: "If Woolston's pre-
tentions were not a comedy, they were at least an illusion that
does not bear examination."[9]

Among those who doubted the sincerity of his allegories, the
Reverend Thomas Stackhouse wrote, in 1730, in *A Fair State of
the Controversy between Mr. Woolston and his Adversaries:*

> These and many more conclusions which follow upon the wild notion
> of Miracles wholly mystical and allegorical, without any literal meaning,
> are such gross and shocking Absurdities, that nothing, one would think,
> but either great Weakness of Understanding or great Disorder of Mind,
> strong Affectation of Singularity, or even strong Prejudices against the
> Christian Religion, could lead a man into.[10]

He concludes that Woolston was "an Enemy of Christianity, a
Blasphemer of the holy name of Jesus."[11] Skelton, in his *Deism
Revealed,* 1749, writes of Woolston:

> His pitiful trick of refuting the miracles, under pretense of allegorizing
> them, is so stale and barefaced, his style so low and rude, and his attempts
> to reason so absurd and senseless, that I could not help looking on him as
> a very despicable fellow, who was on the shift for bread.[12]

This judgment is manifestly unfair in its closing sentences, but
we are forced to agree with its main point. In France, Voltaire
was not fooled, as we shall presently see, and Tabaraud decides
that Woolston was purposely attacking Christianity, on evidence
which shows a careful consideration of his works, early as well
as late. For Woolston must be read completely and chronologically for an adequate understanding of his purpose and method.

In his early works, Woolston is seemingly very zealous in support of religion, in spite of his diatribes against the "hireling

[7] *English Thought in the Eighteenth Century,* I, 231.
[8] *Ibid.,* p. 228.   [9] *Les déistes anglais,* p. 126.
[10] *Op. cit.,* p. 52.   [11] *Ibid.,* p. 294.
[12] London, 1749, II, 358.

priests." He writes very much as a Second Day Adventist, to whom reason and rational criticism mean nothing, yet he scoffs under cover at the idea of a second coming. It is only in his *Moderator between an Infidel and an Apostate,* in 1725, that he confirms early suspicions, and shows himself a deist in his outburst of admiration for Collins, to whom he refers as Mr. "Grounds."[13] From this point on, it becomes increasingly evident that his allegorical method is merely a veil with which he attempted (and with what success!) to cover his attacks on the literal word and on the clergy that preached it. Tabaraud remarks justly: "Enfin, il déchira entièrement le voile dans le *Modérateur entre un incrédule et un apostat,* où il établit que, pris à la lettre, les miracles ne prouvent point que Jésus-Christ soit le Messie."[14] It was only by such methods that Woolston could attack so virulently the literal word and keep so long out of prison, even in "tolerant England."

On the influence of Woolston's discourses on Voltaire, Tabaraud writes:

> C'est dans ses diatribes que Voltaire a fait une ample récolte pour les nombreux écrits dont il a inondé la France, pendant la dernière moitié de sa longue carrière.[15]

But we shall endeavor to prove that he was wrong concerning Voltaire's treatment of the discourses on the miracles:

> Voltaire, en recueillant ce qu'ils contiennent de plus propre à décrier ceux du Nouveau-Testament, s'est appliqué à leur donner un travestissement burlesque, qui enchérit sur les impiétés de l'auteur anglais.[16]

Voltaire merely quoted Woolston, sometimes with seeming trepidation, and even left out many of Woolston's crudest remarks. If he had used Woolston to the full, he would not have been classed by Sayous as a moderate in comparison with the extremists, Diderot, d'Holbach, and others.[17]

As a conclusion to this brief summary of Woolston's life and character, and as an introduction to a study of his works, it is

---

[13] *Moderator,* pp. 138–144.
[15] *Ibid.,* p. 200.
[17] *Les déistes anglais,* p. 208.

[14] *Biog. Univ.* (Paris, 1828), LI, 199.
[16] *Loc. cit.*

fitting to give Voltaire's notice concerning him in his *Lettres . . .
sur Rabelais, etc.*, in 1767, reserving a detailed discussion until
we take up the question of his discourses on the miracles. This
notice is no mere dictionary summary, but shows actual knowledge, as will be shown, of Woolston's text. Several details seem
to have been taken from the life of Woolston attributed to Stackhouse. The notice follows:

> Le trop fameux Thomas Woolston, maître ès arts de Cambridge, se
> distingua, vers l'an 1726, par ses discours contre les miracles de Jésus-
> Christ, et leva l'étendard si hautement qu'il faisait vendre à Londres son
> ouvrage dans sa propre maison. On en fit trois éditions coup sur coup, de
> dix mille exemplaires chacune.
>   Personne n'avait encore porté si loin la témérité et le scandale. Il traite
> de contes puérils et extravagants les miracles et la résurrection de notre
> Sauveur. Il dit que quand Jésus-Christ changea l'eau en vin pour les con-
> vives qui étaient déjà ivres, c'est qu'apparemment il fit du punch. Dieu
> emporté par le diable sur le pinacle du temple, et sur une montagne dont
> on voyait tous les royaumes de la terre, lui paraît un blasphème monstru-
> eux. Le diable envoyé dans un troupeau de deux mille cochons, le figuier
> séché pour n'avoir pas porté de figues quand ce n'était pas le temps des
> figues, la transfiguration de Jésus, ses habits devenus tout blancs, sa con-
> versation avec Moïse et Elie, enfin toute son histoire sacrée est travestie en
> roman ridicule. Woolston n'épargne pas les termes les plus injurieux et les
> plus méprisants. Il appelle souvent notre Seigneur Jésus-Christ: *the fellow,*
> ce compagnon, ce garnement; *a wanderer,* un vagabond; *a mendicant
> friar,* un frère coupe-chou mendiant.
>   Il se sauve pourtant à la faveur du sens mystique, en disant que ces
> miracles sont de pieuses allégories. Tous les bons chrétiens n'en ont pas
> moins eu son livre en horreur.[18]
>   Il y eut un jour une dévote qui, en le voyant passer dans la rue, lui
> cracha au visage. Il s'essuya tranquillement, et lui dit: *C'est ainsi que les
> Juifs ont traité votre Dieu.* Il mourut en paix en disant: *'Tis a pass every
> man must come to;* c'est un terme où tout homme doit arriver. Vous trou-
> verez dans le *Dictionnaire portatif* de l'abbé Ladvocat, et dans un *Nouveau
> Dictionnaire portatif,* où les mêmes erreurs sont copiées, que Woolston est

---

[18] The manuscript abridgment of Woolston's *Discourses* in Voltaire's possession
contained the following statement by the anonymous translator: "Nous négligerons
aussi l'esprit de haine contre l'ordre ecclésiastique que je n'extrairay sûrement pas, non
plus que toutes les resveries allégoriques des pères, qu'il n'a vraisemblablement rapor-
tées que comme son prétexte, pour les rendre ridicules et dont je croy qu'il faisait le
cas qu'elles méritent."

mort en prison, en 1733.[19] Rien n'est plus faux; plusieurs de mes amis l'ont vu dans sa maison: il est mort libre chez lui.[20]

In 1705, at the age of thirty-five, Woolston published his first work, which resumes subjects on which he had been preaching for some time in Cambridge, to the considerable surprise of his audience. The title-page gives not only the title but the intent and scope of the book: *The old Apology for the Truth of the Christian Religion against the Jews and Gentiles revived: wherein is shewn against the Jews, that Christ is the Prophet like Moses, doing all those Signs, Wonders and Judgements before and upon the Emperors and Empire of Rome, which Moses wrought upon Pharaoh and Egypt, until the Heathen Emperors and the Gentiles, like Pharaoh and the Egyptians, were drown'd and overwhelm'd in the Red Sea; and against the Gentiles, that God in Christ Jesus did manifest his Divine Authority to the Emperors and the Gentiles in the best and properest manner that can be imagined; and that they were very inexcusable for Persecuting the Church, and no sooner departing from Idolatry to the Worship of him.*[21] Woolston assures us that studies in the allegorical and prophetical sense of the Scriptures will show God's Providence in all history since Christ's appearance. He explains even the most insignificant details of the Old Testament as types or allegories. His authorities are the allegorizing Fathers. When these authorities fail him, he appeals to "plain reason," which means to him the wildest fancy he can invent to support his thesis. The thesis is "the Fitness and Necessity of God's Manifestation of his Power to the Civil Authority, when he is revealing a new Religion."[22] So plain reason proves that Pilate must have sent a letter concerning Christ to Tiberius and the Roman Senate, because it was fitting for God to act thus, even though it is admitted that the extant letter is a forgery.[23] The Romans had wished to deify Tiberius and his wife, but Tiberius judged that

[19] Neither dictionary states definitely that Woolston died in prison. He died in his own house, but was technically a prisoner. Voltaire was misled by the account of his death in the *Life of Woolston* referred to above, pp. 28, 29.

[20] XXVI, 485–486.

[21] *The old Apology revived*, etc. (London, 1705).

[22] *Ibid.*, p. 366.   [23] *Ibid.*, pp. 35 ff.

Rome was superstitious enough and had already enough gods. So what could have been more fitting, says Woolston, than that Pilate's letter (the contents of which he imagines) should have arrived at this moment; for

Tiberius, . . . with all the readiness imaginable would send it to the Senate to puzzle and surprise them with it; and no doubt as it was his Customary way, sent an Epistle along with it; signifying "that, since they were the judges of the Gods, and had been importunate with him to accept of that honour, there was news from Pilate of a God of the Jews, to whom divine Worship they might see to be due for far better Reasons than he could pretend to!"[24]

The Senate naturally thought he was mocking and refused to deify Christ, just as Pharaoh had been obdurate before the miracles of Moses. Not only in this main thesis, but in many other details, Woolston shows himself subversive beneath his constructive disguise, and clever, rather than naïve. If he had been sincere in his apology, and in his overzealous defense of allegorical interpretation, he would not have dwelt so imaginatively on Christ's deification; he would not have taken pains to show that Pilate's letter and the Sibylline oracles were manifest forgeries; he would not have quoted Tertullian to the effect that every man had to worship God as he pleased,[25] that the Christian *myths* were greater than the Roman *myths,* and that since Christ was no more fabulous than Romulus, the Romans might just as reasonably believe in him.[26] Moreover his allegories and types are so far-fetched and so unreasonable, even in comparison with a serious Dom Calmet, that they put the allegorical method of interpretation to ridicule, as Woolston plainly intended they should. He quotes the wildest ones he can find from Origen and other Fathers, and adds many of his own which are even more ludicrous. The lice which Moses produced before Pharaoh were a type of the lice among the soldiers in Trajan's army. It follows that there were lice in all their quarters, and from the expression "There is Rome where the Emperor is," it may be seen that there were lice before Tiberius and the Roman Senate, just as there

[24] *The old Apology revived*, pp. 69, 70.   [25] *Ibid.*, p. 282.
[26] *Ibid.*, p. 55.

were before Pharaoh.[27] In the plague of the frogs, the frogs are types of the Jews, "let them take it as they will";[28] and "Ammianus Marcellinus very appositely to the purpose now before us, speaking of the Jews, calls them 'Tumultuating and stinking Jews.' "[29] Woolston's audiences must have been hypnotized, if they continued to think that his intentions were good.

Of this early work, Voltaire makes no mention, although he left a copy, unannotated, in his library at Leningrad. He was too busy contesting the seriously advanced types of Dom Calmet and other Church writers in France to bother with Woolston's fancies. He ridicules Calmet's typical interpretations of Ezekiel and of the Song of Solomon, and adds: "Mais il faut avouer qu'une morale saine et pure est encore plus préférable."[30] More often, however, he treats the typical arguments with silence. Woolston says of Exodus that it is "one of the most amazing pieces of History, either sacred or profane; which some think hardly to be credited, much less equall'd or parallel'd."[31] The pillar of the cloud was to him typical of Christ, who said: "I am the light of the world"; and he concludes:

This great Light of the World, Jesus Christ, this Candle of the Lord, set as I may say, in those two Candle-sticks, (to which they are compared) the Law and the Prophets will give us light into the darkest Corners of the World, both with respect of Time and Place, and enable us to see the Wisdom and Providence of God therein. This may seem strange and almost incredible; but I am fully ascertain'd thereof, and don't doubt but time will manifest the Truth of it.[32]

Woolston's motto seems to have been: "Destroy the letter and let time do the rest." As a comparison of method, we have seen Toland trying to rationalize this miracle, while Voltaire remarks: "Cette colonne de nuée était inutile pendant le jour, et ne pouvait servir qu'à empêcher les Juifs de voir leur chemin."[33] Voltaire is thus seen to have preferred Woolston's methods of ridicule to Toland's serious attempt at sound biblical criticism.

Unlike Jean Meslier, Woolston did not wait until his death to

[27] Ibid., p. 133.   [28] Ibid., p. 113.   [29] Ibid., p. 125.
[30] XVIII, 523.   [31] Op. cit., p. 280.   [32] Ibid., p. 382.
[33] XXX, 80.

declare his hatred of the clergy and his own compromising situation. His disguise was so perfect, however, that after his removal
to London in 1720 he could dwell among sheep suspected but
comparatively unmolested for ten more years, and publish tracts
to his heart's content. His first, which were in Latin, continued
or resumed the matter in his long *Apology:* one dissertation to
prove that Pilate did write a letter concerning Christ, but the letter reported by the Fathers was a forgery; and two letters
addressed to Whitby, Waterland, Whiston, and other preachers
of the letter, in defense of Origen, accusing them of appealing to
the Fathers as the best interpreters of the Scriptures, and at the
same time of holding doctrines directly contrary to the sense of
those same Fathers. Woolston did not want to allow them to
ride two horses at once, and it mattered little in the long run if
he deprived them of both. Perhaps surprised at the gullible reception accorded his tracts, he turned to English again, and wrote a
defense of the Quakers. In 1721 he continued with a defense of
the Fathers and Apostles for their allegorical interpretation of
the Law of Moses, followed by two letters on the same subject, in
which it was noted that he was much more bitter against the
literal clergy than zealous for the Fathers.[34] Only he could defend
the latter in such a way as to convict them of forgeries and nonsense. In 1722 he published a treatise on the exact fitness of the
time in which Christ was manifested in the flesh, a treatise composed and delivered twenty years previously at Cambridge.[35] We
have seen what "fitness of time" meant to Woolston in his treatment of Pilate's letter to Tiberius. In 1723 and 1724 he is much
more violent against the hireling preachers, ministers of the letter, in his four *Free Gifts to the Clergy,* which together with his
own answer, were published separately in pamphlet form.

From these five pamphlets, it becomes evident that Woolston's abuse of religion was founded, like Toland's and Collins', upon a hatred of a corrupt clergy. The essential difference
between them is that Woolston was a divine and had to write as

[34] *Life of Woolston,* p. 9.
[35] *Loc. cit.* "This Piece may be justly numbered among our most curious Tracts of
Divinity."

a divine. Curiously enough, he found himself able to sign his works and write much more abusively than his comrades in arms. From now on, his allegories are aimed solely at the literal clergy, and his language is much more abusive. His only authority is the Fathers, but unfortunately, he admits, there is a great diversity of opinion among them, much of which Daillé[36] missed. So Woolston mounts his fiery chariot and goes up to Mount Thabor to have the opinion of Elias on matters in dispute. "The Oracles of God are Ambiguities, Ænigmas, Parables and Amphiboles, which outwardly carry an Appearance of one Sense, but the true Sense is hidden and involv'd with Tropes and Figures."[37] Elias is very hard on the hireling clergy. The Jews had a tradition that on his coming he would purify bastards. Elias explains that "the bastards to be purified are those, who are born of Spiritual Fornication, such as are the Clergy at this day, who are Sons of an adulterous Woman, the Whore of Babylon."[38] They, and not the pope, are the Anti-Christ, they who are "the warmest Advocates for the Divine Right of their Incomes."[39] Like Swift's *Tale of the Tub,* of which there are many echoes, Woolston's mockeries fall on Protestant and Papist alike: "Was it not enough for us to shake off the Rags of Popery, but we must divest ourselves of the Ornaments of Christianity?"[40] Each *Free Gift* ends with insults and taunts, with the hope of a reply, which he had finally to write himself.

With the *Moderator*[41] and the two supplements which follow it, Woolston enters the dispute over the prophecies in the guise of a modern Origen, with which Father he had in common both great learning and a keen sense of the difficulties of literal interpretation of the Scriptures. The *Moderator,* as Tabaraud has pointed out, is very important for an understanding of Woolston's position in English critical deism. In the dedication "To the Most Reverend Father in God, William, Lord Archbishop of Canterbury," Woolston laments the ill-success of ecclesiastical answers to Collins' attacks on the messiahship of our Jesus, and

[36] Woolston knew thoroughly Daillé's *Use of the Fathers.*
[37] *Second Free-Gift,* 1723, pp. 23–24.   [38] *Third Free-Gift,* 1723, p. 60.
[39] *Ibid.,* p. 5.   [40] *Second Free-Gift,* p. 59.
[41] London, 1725.

especially of the trifling reply of the Bishop of Litchfield. He shows a keen appreciation of both the spirit and methods of English deism.

> "Nay, what is most lamentable," he writes, "those very Treatises which are sincerely meant for the Defense of Christianity, are unfortunately turn'd to its Disadvantage by our Adversaries, who are always picking up one Thing or other out of them, with which they insult the Authors, and wound our Religion to the Quick."[42]

Disappointed by the absence of answers to his own treatises, Woolston can nevertheless rejoice in Collins' victory over the ministers of the letter:

> He has so disturbed the Clergy with this double game of literal and allegorical Interpretations, that they know not where to have him, nor upon what Principle to oppose him, because of the unhappy Consequences that follow on them.[43]

Under the pretense, which had now become even more barefaced, that Collins was the Celsus necessary to make Origen famous,[44] Woolston is able to abuse the Fathers and their allegories and types, in order that he himself as the greatest "Typist, Mystist, Hieroglyphist, Oneirocrite,"[45] that ever lived may come to their defense. His only regret is that Collins did not find such allegorical whims as did he, that he did not sufficiently attack the traditions of the ancient Jews nor ridicule the second coming.[46] He ends his *Moderator* with an exhortation to Collins to continue his work to a greater victory, promising him that people will say

> this is the great C———s, who . . . vanquished many Thousands of our Babylonish Preachers, and had gain'd a compleat Victory over all the gods of the Universe if the alone great, wise, and good God of the Creation, had not, just before his Triumph, rais'd a superior Army of Prophets, Apostles, Fathers, Mystists, Oneirocrites, Hieroglyphists, Mythologists, Enigmatists, and Parabolists, to his Conviction and Conversion.[47]

It has seemed necessary to defend Woolston at some length from the supposition that he did not intentionally write against

---

42 *Moderator*, p. v.   43 *Ibid.*, p. vi.   44 *Ibid.*, p. 119.
45 *Ibid.*, p. 77.   46 *Ibid.*, p. 138.   47 *Ibid.*, pp. 143, 144.

the Christian religion. We are convinced that such was his intention, and that to him belongs the credit or the infamy. If much
reading of Origen had made him mad, yet his madness was on
the side of deism rather than of religious fanaticism. Origen at
least did not ridicule the literal word in order the better to establish his allegories, and this was Woolston's ever increasing tend-
ency. His senseless typifying of the details of the Immanuel
prophecy was just as much ridicule as Voltaire's more open variety. As a zealous allegorist, Woolston could explain the virgin
birth in a mystical sense, that the virgin was "pregnant with
Divine Reason to bring forth the Man-Child of the Logos of the
Law and the Prophets," but only as a deist could he, with Voltaire, dwell on the suspicions of Joseph, and on the story of the
soldier Panther from the Toldos Jeschut.[48] One wonders once
again whether Leslie Stephen read Woolston in the original, or
whether he was content with the opinions of some of Woolston's
overcredulous opponents. In this case, he would better have taken
Voltaire's opinion that the mystical interpretation was only a
subterfuge.

Voltaire's library today contains none of these works published
between the *Old Apology* and the *Discourses on the Miracles*.
And however much the former work may have influenced him
in a general way, there is nothing in his works to suggest special
interest or textual borrowing.

Woolston is now ready to attack the miracles reported in the
Gospels. Collins had tried in vain to rule them out as proofs of
the truth of the Christian religion. His attack on the prophecies
had been too successful, and the apologists were therefore turning
to the miracles as a last means of refuting the deists, and especially to the resurrection as the solid and final proof of the truth
of their religion. Collins had promised works on the miracles,
but Woolston was the first in the field. With the obvious intention of tantalizing and irritating the clergy, he begins with
minor miracles, but promising always greater efforts. In his six
separately published discourses, each dedicated to a different
bishop, he treats fifteen miracles fully, and refers to several

[48] *Ibid.*, pp. 53, 54.

others. The miracle of Cana in his fourth discourse started legal proceedings against him, but he was able to publish his climactic sixth discourse on the resurrection before he was silenced. Voltaire is an uncertain authority for the tremendous sale of these discourses.[49] In his *Lettres . . . sur Rabelais, etc.,* he says there were "trois éditions coup sur coup, de dix mille exemplaires chacune,"[50] but in his dictionary article, "Miracles," each edition has increased to twenty thousand copies, and he adds: "Il est difficile aujourd'hui [1771] d'en trouver chez les libraires."[51] In fact, the discourses were reprinted separately, some of them reaching a sixth edition. Although it was reported that many copies were sent to the American colonies, they are today extremely rare in America.[52] The discourses with their separate pagination were commonly bound in one volume, but Voltaire's copy was divided into two, the first containing the first four discourses, and the second, the fifth and sixth discourses and Woolston's two defenses of his discourses. Voltaire also possessed d'Holbach's translation, dated *dix-huitième siècle,*[53] on the title-page of which he wrote, as usual in d'Holbach's works, *livre dangereux;*[54] and a manuscript "Extrait" in French,[55] of the nature of the underground manuscripts described by M. Lanson.[56] A few markers and marginal notes prove some use of the manuscript, but nothing indicates any use of d'Holbach, except perhaps of the anonymous *Life of Thomas Woolston* mentioned above, with which d'Holbach prefaced his translation. On the other hand, the English

[49] But the author of *The Life of Woolston* states that Woolston could have lived comfortably from the profits of the sales, if he had not insisted on defraying the expenses of his publishers. See p. 23.

[50] XXVI, 485.   [51] XX, 86.

[52] Copies may be found in the Andover-Harvard Theological Library, and d'Holbach's translation is in the Boston Public Library. Professor Kaye, of Northwestern University, very kindly loaned me his personal copy. The first discourse in this volume is a sixth edition, the second a fourth edition, the others third or second editions. Voltaire's copy shows nothing beyond a third edition.

[53] The British Museum Catalogue gives 1780 as a tentative date. But the work must have appeared at least several years earlier, before Voltaire's death in 1778.

[54] "The Private Library of Voltaire at Leningrad," *PMLA,* XLIII (1928), 1003.

[55] Extrait d'un livre intitulé Discours sur les miracles de iesus, traduit de l'anglois: (bound with the MS of Dumarsais' *Examen de la religion chrétienne*); 79 closely written pages, with a page of explanation by the abridger.

[56] "Questions diverses sur l'histoire de l'esprit philosophique en France avant 1750," *R.H.L.,* XIX (1912), 307.

original is full of markers and stickers, and Voltaire, in his many quotations from the original English, is always careful to give the correct page references.

Voltaire's use of Woolston's discourses on the miracles, from the point of view of content as well as method forms an important part in the study of the English influence. First, we must dispose of the prefaces. Voltaire was astounded by their temerity:

> Ce qu'il y a de plus étrange encore, c'est que chacun de ses discours est dédié à un évêque. Ce ne sont pas assurément des dédicaces à la française; il n'y a ni compliment ni flatterie: il leur reproche leur orgueil, leur avarice, leur ambition, leurs cabales; il rit de les voir soumis aux loix de l'Etat comme les autres citoyens.[57]

In truth, Woolston's discourses are not noted for their delicacy. That his irony was directed against the established religion and its defenders was no bar to Voltaire's appreciation.

In the first preface, addressed to the Bishop of London, Woolston writes:

> That scurvy Writer of the *Scheme of literal Prophecy,* etc., which your Lordship must have heard of, would insinuate, that they are only atheistical Priests, who for fear of their Interests in the Church set Persecutions on foot: But after your Lordship has published a strenuous *Defence* of Christianity to the Purpose of our Present Controversy, I'll have no such Suspicions of you.[58]

The Bishop had accused Woolston of incredulity, for which Woolston demands reparation for what he has suffered in reputation and property. In the second discourse, Woolston addresses himself to the Bishop of Litchfield with subtle and provocative irony. He promises to ride the clergy gently and treat only the less ridiculous miracles, lest he be dismounted before he has reached the end of his course. In the third discourse, he advises the Bishop of St. David's, who had answered his miracle of the money-changers, not to burn his fingers on it, for "it's a hot one."[59] The fourth preface is addressed "to the Right Reverend Father in God, Francis, Lord Bishop of St. Asaph," to whom he suggests "an Act of P————t to turn the Clergy to grass," to

[57] XX, 89.   [58] *First Discourse,* p. vi.   [59] *Third Discourse,* p. vii.

the advantage of both religion and the public good.[60] This bishop was the former Mr. Hare who had been Collins' teacher at Cambridge, and who was said to have secured his promotion through his attacks on Toland. Hare had himself written a book on the difficulties and discouragements of studying the Bible. Woolston tells him that Swift should have a bishopric for his *Tale of the Tub*, and that he himself was waiting for Canterbury. In the sixth preface, Woolston, who had now some experience with the courts, explains to the Bishop of Oxford that lawyers drink quietly together after their disputes, but that religious controversialists call each other names.[61] He begs him to persuade the Bishop of London to stay home in Lent, for he fears he is possessed with the devil. These prefaces were certainly not "à la française." The first sounds much like Voltaire's sarcasms addressed to the Bishop of Puy whom he immortalized. But Voltaire, even while he is using Woolston's material against the Christian religion, is at the same time careful to defend himself from the charge of abusing the French clergy. His attitude is well expressed in the *Homélie sur l'interprétation du nouveau Testament*, in a paragraph in which he has used an expression from Woolston and is evidently thinking of him:

> Ne choquez jamais la superstition dominante, si vous n'êtes assez puissants pour lui résister, ou assez habile pour échapper à sa poursuite. . . . Rejetons donc toute superstition afin de devenir plus humains; mais en parlant contre le fanatisme, n'irritons point les fanatiques: ce sont des malades en délire qui veulent battre leurs médecins. Adoucissons leurs maux, ne les aigrissons jamais, et faisons couler goutte sur goutte dans leur âme ce baume divin de la Tolérance, qu'ils rejetteraient avec horreur si on le leur présentait à pleine coupe.[62]

Voltaire no doubt envied Woolston's peaceful burial in St. George's churchyard. But it may be doubted whether the French bishops cared for these gentle phrases any more than the English for Woolston's outrages.

---

[60] *Fourth Discourse*, p. vii. A sticker marks this passage in Voltaire's copy at Leningrad, and another, the same metaphor occurring again in Woolston's *Defense*, I, 23.

[61] Cf. "Voltaire's English Notebook," *Mod. Phil.*, XXVI (February, 1929), 321.

[62] XXVI, 354.

Voltaire kept up amicable relations with the French clergy and with the Jesuits as long as it was good policy for him to do so. His actual break with them was caused by particular quarrels soon after his establishment at Ferney.[63] But since Voltaire, for the purposes of documentation, was reading such anticlerical authors as Woolston during these very years, as his borrowings indicate, Woolston should properly be counted in as a direct influence in his attacks against the clergy. It is noteworthy that Voltaire is particularly violent in works which he attributes to Englishmen, and that his most devastating anticlerical pages occur in the *Examen important*[64] of the much abused Bolingbroke, in which the Woolston influence is markedly strong.

Woolston's first miracle is of the merchants chased from the temple. He finds that "the literal History of many of the Miracles of Jesus, as recorded by the Evangelists, does imply Absurdities, Improbabilities, and Incredibilities."[65] Like the Fathers, he sets out to explain their mystical meaning. But unlike the Fathers, his obvious intent is to destroy the literal word, and his allegories curiously enough redound to the discredit of the "hireling clergy" with great regularity. The literal Jesus was merely an impostor, so Woolston believes only in the spiritual Messiah. It is hard to understand how one abject and unimposing man could, with a whip, chase out of the temple a troup of men who had no respect for him, and be allowed to upset the temple. Voltaire has picked up all the savory details and we will let him speak from the *Examen important de milord Bolingbroke:*

Il entre dans le temple, c'est-à-dire dans cette grande enceinte où demeuraient les prêtres, dans cette cour où de petits marchands étaient autorisés par la loi à vendre des poules, des pigeons, des agneaux, à ceux qui venaient sacrifier. Il prend un grand fouet, en donne sur les épaules de tous les marchands, les chasse à coups de lanières, eux, leurs poules, leurs pigeons, leurs moutons, et leurs bœufs même, jette tout leur argent par terre, et on le laisse faire! Et si l'on croit le livre attribué à Jean, on se contente de lui demander un miracle pour prouver qu'il a droit de faire un pareil tapage dans un lieu si respectable. C'était déjà un fort grand miracle que trente ou quarante marchands se laissassent fesser par un seul homme, et per-

---

[63] G. Desnoiresterres, *Voltaire et J.-J. Rousseau*, pp. 268 ff.
[64] XXVI, 296–299.   [65] *First Discourse*, p. 4.

dissent leur argent sans rien dire. Il n'y a rien dans *Don Quixote* qui approche de cette extravagance.[66]

And Voltaire adds of his own:

> Tous ces miracles semblent faits par nos charlatans de Smithfields. Notre Toland et notre Woolston les ont traités comme ils le méritent.[67]

In his *Dieu et les Hommes,* he adds another detail from Woolston:

> Cet acte qui paraît si ridicule à milord Bolingbroke, à Woolston, et à tous les francs-pensants, serait aussi répréhensible que si un fanatique s'ingérait parmi nous de fouetter les libraires qui vendent auprès de Saint-Paul le livre des *Communes prières.*[68]

As late as 1777, in *l'Établissement du christianisme,* an addition is made, and *auprès de Saint-Paul* is followed by *dans Pater-Noster-Row,* both terms serving merely to add to the English atmosphere.[69] It may well be noted here that neither Toland nor Bolingbroke ridiculed this miracle nor any other Gospel miracle, also that Voltaire refers constantly to remarks that he has falsely attributed to Bolingbroke in his *Examen important.* Voltaire uses this material on at least three other occasions, including his article "Miracles,"[70] where he transposes Woolston book in hand, and the *Sermon des cinquante* (1762),[71] where the Woolston material first appears in detail in Voltaire's works.

Woolston's second miracle of the first discourse concerns the casting out of devils into swine. He points out the inhumanity of letting men possessed with devils live and wander among the tombs. But stranger still there were no pigs in the land, nor were they allowed to be kept or eaten under the Jewish law.[72] Moreover a miracle, to be credible, should work for some good end,

---

[66] XXVI, 224–225. The details follow closely those in Woolston's discourse, and it has not been thought necessary to juxtapose the two texts. See *First Discourse,* pp. 22–31, and especially the citation from Origen, page 24, which is marked in Voltaire's copy in the Leningrad library.

[67] Woolston, yes, but not Toland nor Bolingbroke.

[68] XXVIII, 198–199.

[69] XXXI, 63. Annet's *Life of David,* so thoroughly used by Voltaire (see *infra*), was printed in Paternoster Row.

[70] XX, 86.   [71] XXIV, 450–451.

[72] *First Discourse,* p. 33.

and there was no bounty nor justice in destroying the pigs.[73] English judges of the last age would have had Jesus hanged as a sorcerer, and the Jews would have been excused if they had put him to death as a thief. Christians would call Mahomet a wizard if any such miracle had been attributed to him.[74] This miracle Voltaire calls "le plus beau," "le plus plaisant de tous," and he has used it at least twenty-six different times, a record for his Woolston material. It appears at least once in every one of his important deistic works, nor is there any detail of his attack that appears more regularly. After an introduction on Woolston in his article "Miracles," he writes:

> Si on l'en croit, le diable envoyé par Jésus-Christ dans le corps de deux mille cochons est un vol fait au propriétaire de ces animaux. Si on en disait autant de Mahomet, on le prendrait pour un méchant sorcier, *a wizard,* un esclave juré du diable, *a sworn slave to the devil.*[75]

Voltaire was thus using his English in 1771. In his *Conseils raisonnables à M. Bergier,* he adds:

> Le prix de deux mille cochons a toujours surpassé celui de dix mille moutons. Noyer ces bêtes ou les empoisonner, c'est la même chose. Que feriez-vous d'un homme qui aurait empoisonné dix mille moutons?[76]

But he has not repeated here the point that he found "le plus plaisant." In his *Examen,* he writes:

> Le plus beau de tous, à mon gré, est celui par lequel Jésus envoie le diable dans le corps de deux mille cochons, dans un pays où il n'y avait point de cochons.[77]

This last phrase is a sort of refrain which enters into most of his references to the miracles. Repetitions of the incident grow tiresome in the various letters which compose the *Questions sur les miracles.*[78]

Of the transfiguration, the third miracle of the first discourse, Woolston is unhappily only too sure that infidels could easily find

[73] *Ibid.,* p. 34.   [74] *Ibid.,* pp. 38, 39.
[75] XX, 86. Voltaire gives in a note the correct reference to the *First Discourse,* p. 38. Stickers on these pages manifest Voltaire's direct use of the material.
[76] XXVII, 46; *First Discourse,* p. 34.   [77] XXVI, 225.
[78] XXV, 364, 385, 397, etc.

solid objections and unanswerable difficulties in the literal word. There is no miracle and no transfiguration in the shining ("rubicund") countenance nor in the raiment which appeared as white as snow in the reflection of the sunlight. Any ventriloquist can throw his voice, and our theologians wouldn't like to have Jesus regarded as a juggler.[79] If he had desired witnesses to this miracle, as he should have done the better to increase faith, he should not have gone on the mountain to hide the miracle among the clouds.[80] Voltaire treats the various details of this miracle for different purposes, using Woolston's material some dozen times. In his *Lettres . . . sur Rabelais, etc.,* he writes:

> La transfiguration de Jésus, ses habits devenus blancs, sa conversation avec Moïse et Elie, enfin toute son histoire sacrée est travestie en roman ridicule.[81]

Usually the miracle merely enters as one of the list, with emphasis on "les habits blancs," the mystical sense of which is discussed in connection with the wine of Cana. But in his lists, Voltaire shows that he did not like Woolston's point that raiment shining white in the sun is no miracle. For example, in his *Conseils raisonnables,* he adopts another interpretation: "ses habits sont devenus tout blancs pendant la nuit."[82]

The second discourse begins with the cure of the woman with the bloody issue. Woolston finds it impossible to determine whether this issue was a heavy menstruation or just a nosebleed.[83] If it was the woman's normal period, it shouldn't have been suppressed.[84] And if, as the preachers of the literal word claimed, it was a cure by the imagination, then there was no miracle. The miracle must be explained in a mystical sense. The woman is the Church, and the bloody issue means the "hireling priests"; or, if you please (for Woolston is not very particular which way you take it), the priests are the doctors that the woman spent all her

---

[79] *First Discourse,* pp. 41, 42.   [80] *Ibid.,* p. 45.

[81] XXVI, 485. Voltaire here again uses Woolston's quotations from the Church Fathers, especially the marked note on page 48.

[82] XXVII, 40; see also, XXVIII, 199.   [83] *Second Discourse,* p. 10.

[84] *Ibid.,* p. 12. Woolston points out that the woman lived twelve years with her curse, but died soon after the cure.

money on in a vain search for a cure.[85] Christ will fulfil the mystical sense at his second coming, which Woolston hopes will be soon. Voltaire does not use this miracle, even in his customary and summary lists. This was probably not due to his sense of decorum, but rather because the main point of Woolston's remarks was in the mystical explanation, which Voltaire did not bother with.

The same is true of Woolston's next miracle, that of the woman bowed over with the palsy.[86] The divines would flout such a simple miracle, he says, if told by any impostor, archheretic, or popish exorcist, just as the infidels, Jews, and Mahometans do of this miracle of the New Testament.[87] There is nothing remarkable about it except the part played by Satan, and the fact that it was accomplished on the Sabbath day.[88] We must explain the eighteen years by Augustine's mystical arithmetic. The woman typifies the clergy "bow'd down to the letter," or the Church bound by Satan, and the Sabbath should be used "to release man from his Bondage and Servility to irrational principles."[89] Moreover, devils were unknown to the world before Christ came, on the authority of Arnobius, but at that age one would think that "Hell first broke loose," and that they "accompanied the Jews in their Dispersion," and "the Apostles in their Travels."[90] Voltaire kept this idea, and was fond of saying that the chief mission of the apostles was to cast out devils,[91] but he never used the other details of Woolston's exposition.

The sixth miracle, the last of the second discourse, is of Jesus and the Samaritan woman. On this occasion, writes Woolston, Jesus palmed himself off on the credulity of a simple woman as the true Messiah, like a strolling gypsy fortune teller.[92] However, he "squeez'd no money for his prophetic art," as do the modern priests.[93] If the disciples marveled, it must have been at his conversation with a whore,[94] or that he was entertained two days by the adulterous woman and the men of Sychar.[95] The discussion

---

[85] Ibid., pp. 18–24.
[86] There are no markers in these pages in the Leningrad copy.
[87] Ibid., p. 28.
[88] Ibid., pp. 31, 35.
[89] Ibid., p. 39.
[90] Ibid., p. 40.
[91] Cf. XXVI, 239.
[92] Second Discourse, pp. 50–52.
[93] Ibid., p. 55.
[94] Ibid., p. 61.
[95] Ibid., p. 55.

ends with some obscenities on the ass on which Jesus rode into Jerusalem, and on his temptation by the devil.[96] Voltaire used all these details. His fullest treatment is in his article "Miracles," in which he devotes some four pages to Woolston. This work first appeared in the *Questions sur l'Encyclopédie* in 1771, and deals with ten of Woolston's fifteen miracles. Here he gives page references to the discourses, instead of his usual references to the Gospels:

> Il dit la bonne aventure à la Samaritaine comme un franc bohémien: cela seul suffisait pour le faire chasser, comme Tibère en usait alors avec les devins. Je m'étonne, dit-il, que les bohémiens d'aujourd'hui, les *gypsies*, ne se disent pas les vrais disciples de Jésus, puisqu'ils font le même métier.[97] Mais je suis fort aise qu'il n'ait pas extorqué de l'argent de la Samaritaine, comme font nos prêtres modernes, qui se font largement payer pour leurs divinations.
>
> Je suis les numéros des pages. L'auteur passe de là à l'entrée de Jésus-Christ dans Jérusalem. On ne sait, dit-il, s'il était monté sur un âne, ou sur une ânesse, ou sur un ânon, ou sur tous les trois à la fois.
>
> Il compare Jésus tenté par le diable à saint Dunstan qui prit le diable par le nez, et il donne à saint Dunstan la préférence.[98]

Voltaire is not bashful in repeating that "il fréquente des femmes de mauvaise vie,"[99] but his usual treatment of this section is to stress the temptation on the mountain, mingling in an incident that is not Woolston's, but with which it becomes firmly connected in his mind. For once, in the *Examen,* he is interested in the typical sense:

> Quand les chrétiens disaient: Jésus est prédit par le patriarche Juda, car le patriarche Juda *devait lier son ânon à la vigne, et laver son manteau dans le sang de la vigne;* et Jésus est entré dans Jérusalem sur un âne, donc Juda est la figure de Jésus: alors les Juifs riaient encore plus fort de Jésus et de son âne.[100]

But this is not taken directly from Woolston, and the miracle is not one that enters regularly into Voltaire's lists, perhaps because

[96] *Second Discourse,* pp. 64, 65.

[97] A sticker marks this passage in Voltaire's copy, p. 52.

[98] XX, 86, 87. A sticker on page 65 of the *Second Discourse* marks the reference to Dunstan.

[99] XXVIII, 202.   [100] XXVI, 241.

of its distinct phases, and the difficulty in finding a "bon mot" summary.

Woolston had been persecuted for citing in his *Moderator,* "an untoward Saying of St. Jerome." In this second discourse he continues his punning with "a worse Intimation of St. John of Jerusalem":

> According to him it may be questioned, whether the Hosannahs of the People were of any more Respect to Jesus, than the Huzzahs of a Mob would be to the Bishop of L———n, if to shew his Meekness and Lowliness, he should ride upon an Ass, in his *Pontificalibus* through this city. But I have here a momentous Controversy to decide about the Beast he rode on. St. Matthew seems to say, he rode upon both Ass and Colt together. St. Mark and St. Luke say, he rode upon the Colt, on which Man never before sat. The Bishop of Litchfield says, he rode upon the Ass (on which Man had before sat) and the Colt ambled after. St. Cyril and St. Chrysostom say, he rode upon the Colt, and the She-Ass trotted after. St. John the Evangelist says, he rode upon a Mule, or an "onasion" Ass-like Creature of the neuter Gender.[101]

This passage pleased Voltaire mightily. He rarely omits some allusion to the ass on which Jesus entered Jerusalem. In the *Histoire de l'établissement du christianisme,* for example, he introduces Woolston's money-changers miracle with the words: "Jésus étant arrivé sur son ânesse, ou sur son ânon, ou sur tous les deux à la fois, entre dans le parvis du temple, etc."[102] It is difficult, too, to disconnect this passage of Woolston's from Voltaire's mockery on the subject of the coat of arms of "l'évêque du Puy":

> Cet écusson représente un homme monté sur un quadrupède; vous doutez si cet animal est la monture de Balaam, ou celle du chevalier que Cervantes a rendu fameux. L'un était un prophète, et l'autre un redresseur des torts; vous ignorez qui des deux est le patron de mon cher confrère.[103]

The details are original and originally treated, but the spirit, if not the idea, is entirely that of Woolston's dedications to the English bishops, on which Voltaire later commented and must then have known well.

The third discourse contains only two miracles, of which the

---

[101] *Second Discourse,* pp. 63, 64. Marked in Voltaire's copy.
[102] XXXI, 63.   [103] XXV, 2.

fig tree, which bore no figs when it was not the time of figs, is one of Voltaire's favorites. On this occasion, Woolston represents Jesus as peevish and impatient.[104] If he was hungry, why did he not get fed by angels as in the desert?[105] Since it was not the season of figs, he should not have destroyed somebody's property like a malignant witch.[106] Since the tree withered the next day, it is probable that he took "his carpenter's axe to it on the sly at night."[107] This concise account pleased Voltaire so much that he used it some twenty-four times, in every one of his critical works between 1762 and 1777. In his article "Miracles," he treats the subject as follows, giving original phrases and correct page references:[108]

A l'article du miracle du figuier séché pour n'avoir pas porté des figues hors de la saison; c'était, dit-il, un vagabond, un gueux, tel qu'un frère quéteur, *a wanderer, a mendicant, like a friar,* et qui, avant de se faire prédicateur de grand chemin, n'avait été qu'un misérable garçon charpentier, *no better than a journey-man carpenter.*[109] Il est surprenant que la cour de Rome n'ait pas parmi ses reliques quelque ouvrage de sa façon, un escabeau, un casse-noisette. En un mot, il est difficile de pousser plus loin le blasphème.[110]

In the *Sommaire historique des quatre évangiles,* in 1776, which is largely Woolston material, Woolston is "les critiques," and as an apostate is very naturally connected with Meslier:

Les critiques s'élèvent avec violence contre le miracle que fait Jésus en séchant le figuier qui ne portait pas des figues avant la saison. Dispensons-nous de rapporter les railleries de Woolston et du curé Meslier, et contentons-nous de dire avec tous les sages commentateurs que, sans doute, Jésus désignait par là ceux qui ne devaient jamais porter des fruits de pénitence.[111]

The fig tree appears in all the lists, whether two are mentioned or ten. Special treatment is accorded in the *Traité sur la tolérance.* Here Woolston's miracles are reviewed to discover whether or

---

[104] *Third Discourse,* p. 5.   [105] *Ibid.,* p. 6.
[106] *Ibid.,* pp. 7, 8.   [107] *Ibid.,* p. 15.
[108] A sticker marks these lines (*ibid.,* p. 8), which are very carefully quoted and translated.
[109] Voltaire's note here is "Troisième discours, page 8."
[110] XX, 87.   [111] XXX, 308.

not Jesus was tolerant. The money-changers and the fig tree might suppose intolerance, while the recommendation of fidelity to the adulterous woman and the partaking of joys at a wedding are perfectly innocent.

Un figuier n'a pu donner des figues vers le commencement de mars, on l'a séché: est-ce une raison pour faire sécher nos frères de douleur dans tous les temps de l'année?[112]

It is interesting to watch Voltaire's *clichés,* whether from Fabricius or Woolston, undergo modifications as they pass through this *Traité.* In the *Questions sur les miracles,* Voltaire explains that some miracles must be understood in the opposite sense of the literal word:

Lorsqu'il est dit que Jésus sécha le figuier vert, cela veut dire qu'il fit reverdir un figuier sec: car ce dernier miracle est utile, et le premier est pernicieux.[113]

Voltaire seems not to have found his material from Woolston once for all. New details, new turns of thought appear continually. He must have slept on Woolston's volume along with the Pentateuch, Ariosto, and the codex of Fabricius.

The second and last miracle of the third discourse is the miraculous cure at the pool of Bethesda. Woolston suggests that John must have been trying to blast his master's reputation when he wrote this old wives' tale.[114] In all the Roman histories and in Josephus there is no mention of an angel descending to the pool.[115] How often and when did the angel descend? before the coming of Jesus?[116] A race to the pool is an odd and merry way of conferring divine mercy—like scrambling for pennies ("Homines sunt Lusus Deorum"). Only one was cured, and the rest must have emerged like drowned rats.[117] Either John is bantering us, or the man was just lazy and was finally shamed out of it.[118] If he had been paralytic, he would have been a fool to wait

---

[112] XXV, 85.
[113] *Ibid.,* p. 413. Woolston quotes the passage from Augustine; *Third Discourse,* p. 10. The passage is not marked in Voltaire's copy.
[114] *Third Discourse,* p. 35.   [115] *Ibid.,* p. 38.
[116] *Ibid.,* p. 41.   [117] *Ibid.,* pp. 43–44.
[118] *Ibid.,* pp. 34, 45.

thirty-eight years at the pool. He "might as well have waited for the Falling of the Sky, that he might catch Larks."[119] And if Christ had such great healing power as reported, he should have cured them all.[120] Woolston ends by advising the Bishop of St. David's that infidelity is a grand subject for burlesque and banter, and challenges him to a match of wits.[121] It is difficult to understand why Voltaire used the detail of this miracle only twice. He shows that he knew it well and it was one of Woolston's cleverest.[122] It was perhaps too long for his purposes. In his article "Miracles," he writes of Woolston:

> Il s'égaye sur la piscine probatique de Bethsaïda, dont un ange venait troubler l'eau tous les ans. Il demande comment il se peut que ni Flavius Josèphe, ni Philon, n'aient point parlé de cet ange; pourquoi saint Jean est le seul qui raconte ce miracle annuel; par quel autre miracle aucun Romain ne vit jamais cet ange et n'en entendit jamais parler.[123]

The method becomes a commonplace with Voltaire, who wonders why Sanchoniathon never speaks of Moses and the Jews, nor the Egyptians, and rarely the Romans, why the eclipse and the comet were not mentioned by Roman contemporary historians, why Josephus mentions Jesus only in an obvious intercalation. In the *Examen,* he says of the early Christians:

> Ils étaient si peu de chose que ni Flavius Josèphe, ni Philon, ni Plutarque, ne daignent en parler; et si Tacite en veut bien dire un mot, c'est en les confondant avec les Juifs et en leur marquant le plus profond mépris.[124]

Woolston's method is closely joined here to Woolston's detail. The Bethesda miracle, however, does not appear in Voltaire's usual lists.

The first miracle of the fourth discourse is of sight restored to a man by an eye salve, made of dirt and spittle. This is no real miracle, says Woolston, because human means were used.[125] Although England had such chance-doctors, yet "none of the odd and unaccountable Medicaments are to be compared with

---

[119] *Third Discourse,* p. 48.   [120] *Ibid.,* p. 50.   [121] *Ibid.,* p. 71.
[122] There are no markers to indicate especial interest.
[123] XX, 87.   [124] XXVI, 240.
[125] *Fourth Discourse,* p. 10.

Jesus' Balsam for sore Eyes."[126] "If I was, what I am not, an Infidel, I should think . . . that Jesus was a juggling impostor."[127] Let the divines explain the clay and spittle, they who insist that the miracles are to be tried, condemned, or approved by our reason and senses. They must see that the authority of Jesus goes with them.[128] Woolston then gets more deeply embroiled than ever with his mystical explanations which are to save the day for Christianity. Like the rest of the cures, this miracle is barely treated by Voltaire.[129] One short sentence bearing on it appears in the *Sermon des cinquante* in the middle of a list: "Il guérit un aveugle, et cet aveugle voit des hommes comme si c'étaient des arbres";[130] but other sources are responsible for this note on blindness.

The second miracle of the fourth discourse is the wedding of Cana, the first of all the miracles of Jesus. Woolston complains that he is too grave to treat it as ludicrously as he ought. He had long before promised it to his readers, and is still using the literary trick of suspense. With legal proceedings undoubtedly in mind, he brings a Jewish Rabbi to the rescue, and lets him tell of the "extravagant and voluptuous wedding at Cana."[131] Jesus and his mother were lovers of good fellowship and were easily persuaded to join the party. The guests were evidently already "more than half-Seas over,"[132] and Jesus and his mother were soon all "cut," as is witnessed by his waspish, snappish reply to her, "Woman, what have I to do with thee," "a witless Sentence, such as Fuddlecaps utter by halves when the wine's in, and the Wit's out."[133] He called Mary a woman, not a virgin, and indeed she "cohabited with the old carpenter."[134] A sober and prudent philosopher or magician would never have made the wine, and the miracle resembles an imposture, because Jesus had to use

---

[126] *Ibid.*, p. 11.   [127] *Ibid.*, p. 14.

[128] *Ibid.*, pp. 15, 16.

[129] A reference to Moore, the famous apothecary, mentioned by Woolston (p. 6) helps Voltaire's English atmosphere in the *Examen important* (XXVI, 217).

[130] XXIV, 451.   [131] *Fourth Discourse,* p. 30.

[132] *Ibid.*, p. 31. Woolston gives the Greek word which Voltaire copied in several references to the miracle.

[133] *Ibid.*, p. 32.   [134] *Ibid.*, p. 34.

water, with which he probably mixed spirituous liquors,[135] for the "company was too stitch'd to tell the difference."[136] Does this miracle, asks Woolston, show God's love of mankind, according to Chandler's test of true miracles? Indeed, the priests could make a good penny if they could only curse vineyards like fig trees and make water into wine as they do wine into blood.[137] The literal word is too difficult. With St. Augustine, we must be inebriated with spiritual wine.[138] As for the sentence "Woman, what have I to do with thee?" "if we cast away the interrogation, and look upon the Sentence, as ellyptical, like an infinite number of prophetical ones, the Sense paraphrastically, and agreeably to the rest of the Mystery, arises thus":[139]—but why should one be more interested than Voltaire in Woolston's mystical vagaries. It should have been now most apparent even to the most gullible that under the guise of defending the mystical sense, Woolston was having a beautiful time with the literal word and at the same time was reducing the allegorical method to ridiculous absurdity. However much or little he may deserve commendation, he was certainly most devilishly clever.

This treatment of the Cana miracle pleased Voltaire only slightly less than his favorite miracle of the pigs. He uses the detail over a score of times, and never fails to put it in his Woolston lists. Among many long passages concerning the miracle, the fullest is again in the article "Miracles"; Voltaire misses very little:

L'eau changée en vin aux noces de Cana excite, selon lui, le rire et le mépris de tous les hommes qui ne sont pas abrutis par la superstition.

Quoi! s'écrie-t-il, Jean dit expressément que les convives étaient déjà ivres, et Dieu, descendu sur la terre, opère son premier miracle pour les faire boire encore!

Dieu fait homme commence sa mission par assister à une noce de village. Il n'est pas certain que Jésus et sa mère fussent ivres comme le reste de la compagnie: 'Whether Jesus and his mother themselves were all cut,

---

[135] Voltaire has left a marker at the corresponding page of his abridged manuscript of Woolston's *Discours*, which reads here: "il mit la main à l'œuvre et fit de la ponche en mettant un peu d'eau de vie dans de l'eau." Many of his references to the Cana miracle include this feature.

[136] *Fourth Discourse*, p. 37.   [137] *Ibid.*, p. 42.
[138] *Ibid.*, p. 45.   [139] *Ibid.*, p. 50.

as were others of the company, it is not certain.' Quoique la familiarité de
la dame avec un soldat fasse présumer qu'elle aimait la bouteille, il
paraît cependant que son fils étaient en pointe de vin, puisqu'il lui répon-
dit avec tant d'aigreur et d'insolence, *waspishly and snappishly:* Femme,
qu'ai-je affaire à toi? Il paraît par ces paroles que Marie n'était point
vierge, et que Jésus n'était point son fils; autrement, Jésus n'eût point
ainsi insulté son père et sa mère, et violé un des plus sacrés commande-
ments de la loi. Cependant il fait ce que sa mère lui demande, il remplit
dix-huit cruches d'eau, et en fait du punch. Ce sont les propres paroles de
Thomas Woolston. Elles saisissent d'indignation toute âme chrétienne.

C'est à regret, c'est en tremblant que je rapporte ces passages; mais il y
a eu soixante mille exemplaires de ce livre, portant tous le nom de
l'auteur, et tous vendus publiquement chez lui. On ne peut pas dire que
je le calomnie.[140]

Voltaire has not only taken great care to quote carefully with
references, but he explains with equal care that these are not his
words. He never had to overstate Woolston. Many times, when
he cannot be so careful with his references, he rather under-
states. However deep was his regret in relating these passages, he
may very truthfully have trembled, and with reason. The case
of the Chevalier de la Barre was not many years old. Voltaire
was genuinely astonished at English freedom. He did not understand that the English were too slow-minded to perceive Woolston's trickery.

In his *Histoire de l'établissement du christianisme*, Voltaire
adds details for a new purpose, showing his adaptability:

Il changea seize cent vingt pintes d'eau, qui étaient là à point nommé
dans de grandes cruches, en seize cent vingt pintes de vin.[141] On peut
observer que ces cruches, à ce que dit le texte, étaient là pour les purifi-
cations des Juifs, selon leur usage. Ces mots ne marquent-ils pas évidemment que ce ne peut être Jean, né Juif, qui ait écrit cet évangile?[142]

Voltaire's usual interest in this miracle lay in the words,
"Femme, qu'y a-t-il entre vous et moi?"[143] and in the lack of
dignity displayed by Jesus, who was one with God, in changing

---

[140] XX, 87, 88.

[141] Woolston writes, page 39: "twelve or eighteen Firkins of English Measure,
enough to intoxicate the whole Town of Cana of Galilee."

[142] XXXI, 72. This bit of internal criticism is merely suggested by Woolston.

[143] *Fourth Discourse*, p. 34, marked in Voltaire's copy with a sticker.

water into wine for villagers who were already drunk.[144] In the ninth letter of the *Questions sur les miracles,* "dans le style du prêtre Needham," which is not only full of Woolston detail, but is very close to the Woolston style, Voltaire develops a mystical interpretation of his own which will be treated in a later paragraph on method.

The third miracle of the fourth discourse concerns the healing of the paralytic, than which, writes Woolston, "no Tale more monstrously romantick can be told."[145]

> It is such an Accumulation of Absurdities, Improbabilities, and Incredibilities, that a Man of the most easy Faith, if he at all think, can't digest. It's not credible, I said, to suppose, the People of Capernaum, where Jesus dwelt, and was known and little admired, would at all press to see or hear him: And if the occasion of their Concourse was to behold his Miracles; it is less reasonable to think they would tumultuate to their own disappointment; but rather make way for the diseased, for the satisfaction of their own Curiosity, to come to him: And if they did mob it to their own disappointment, about the door of the House; it was next to impossible for the poor Man and his Couch to be heav'd over their Heads, and rais'd to the top of it: More unreasonable yet to think, the master of the House would suffer the Roof of it to be so broken up: But most of all against Reason to suppose, Jesus would not give forth the healing word, and prevent all this Labour, or by his divine Power disperse the People, that the Paralytick might have present and easy access to him.[146]

Woolston is here dealing with circumstances of the cure, rather than the cure itself, and shows the same blissful lack of the historic sense that we find in Voltaire. But Voltaire evidently considered this miracle as a cure and treated it with absolute silence.[147] Of Woolston's four miracles concerning cures, he treated only one of them, and then very casually, whereas every other of Woolston's fifteen miracles can be found unmistakably at least three times in Voltaire's works, and always at least once in detailed form. The thirty-five years that intervened between the writings had seen considerable progress in the medical sciences. The English deists of the early years of the eighteenth

---

[144] XXV, 379, 385; XXVI, 186, 224, 544; XXVII, 92, 231, etc.
[145] *Op. cit.,* p. 62.   [146] *Ibid.,* pp. 61, 62.
[147] He put no markers or stickers in these pages.

century considered medicine as a craft only little less harmful than priestcraft. Woolston used the cures of the Gospels to ridicule the balsams and pills of the English doctors and apothecaries. Voltaire, who continually made use of pills and quack medicines, could hardly enter into the spirit of the deists on this point. Moreover, the argument against miraculous cures was much more effective in Protestant England where the age of miracles was admittedly over than in France where such cures were still of daily occurrence. By omitting these miracles from his treatises, Voltaire again showed adaptability and good sense in the use of his sources.

In his *Fifth Discourse,* Woolston comments on the three miracles of Jesus' raising the dead, the daughter of Jairus, the son of the widow of Naim, and Lazarus. Both Woolston and Voltaire group these miracles together, and emphasize the raising of Lazarus. Two of the miracles are recorded by only one evangelist, says Woolston, and the greatest is postponed to John, the last authority, and is therefore the most fabulous because the last recorded.[148]

Matthew, Mark and Luke, who knew as much of this Sham Miracle as John, had not the Confidence to report it; because, when they wrote, many Eye-witnesses of the Fraud were alive to disprove and contradict them; therefore they confined their Narratives to Jesus's less juggling Tricks, that had pass'd more current.[149]

Nothing is said of the three people after their resurrection, and such silence in history is shocking to the credibility of the miracles.[150] Jesus should have made a more careful choice of his subjects, two of whom were insignificant.[151] Why did he not rather "tack on" the head of John the Baptist?[152] None of the three was long dead. Jesus himself admits that the daughter of Jairus was "but asleep," hence there was no miracle. The widow of Naim's son was a corpse for burial, but if this was not a mistake, it was a manifest fraud.[153] Lazarus was indeed buried four days, but if these days were counted like the three days of Jesus' entomb-

---

[148] *Fifth Discourse,* pp. 6–11.
[150] *Ibid.,* p. 33.
[152] *Ibid.,* pp. 25–26.
[149] *Ibid.,* p. 52.
[151] *Ibid.,* p. 21.
[153] *Ibid.,* pp. 27–28.

ment, the time is less than two days, and his body could hardly be said to stink. Moreover, his face was covered by a napkin, which suggests fraud. It is likely that Lazarus was constantly fed during the time that he remained in the cave.[154] Why did Jesus weep, when he knew that he could raise his friend? and why did he call to him in a loud voice, when the dead can hear the whisper of the Almighty? It seems probable that Lazarus, the accomplice in the imposture, was deaf. The napkin over the face prevented witnesses from seeing the change from decomposition to life.[155] Moreover, only the most credulous believed in Jesus after this miracle, while the chief priests were so enraged at the imposture that Jesus was forced to flee with his disciples into the wilderness. They took counsel together how to put him to death, and later crucified him as a deceiver and blasphemer.[156] But the story is so full of absurdities, says Woolston, "that, if the Letter alone be regarded, St. John, who was then above a hundred, when he wrote it, had lived beyond his Reason and Senses."[157] Woolston includes his severest attacks against the letter of the miracles in a satirical invective, supposedly written by his old friend, the Jewish Rabbi, which he publishes regretfully, lest it be handed about clandestinely and without the antidote of his allegorical interpretation, supported by long passages from the Fathers.[158] This interpretation he makes little less ludicrous than his "ingenuous" (but truly ingenious) confession of faith against the charge of infidelity. Upon the authority of the Fathers, he believes that "the Ministry of the Letter is Antichristian," that their opposition to allegorical interpretation is "the sin of Blasphemy against the Holy Ghost," and that the spirit and power of Jesus will soon enter the Church and drive them out, as Jesus did the money-changers.[159] Woolston's deism is gradually coming to the fore. At the end of his discourse, he writes, in the spirit of Toland and Collins:

I am delightfully ravish'd and transported with the Forethought and Contemplation of the Happiness of Mankind, upon the Extinction of

---

[154] *Fifth Discourse*, pp. 29–30.
[156] *Ibid.*, pp. 42, 47, 48, 51.
[158] *Ibid.*, pp. 42–55.

[155] *Ibid.*, p. 30.
[157] *Ibid.*, p. 38.
[159] *Ibid.*, pp. 67–69.

Ecclesiastical *Vermin* out of God's House; when the World will return to
its *Primogenial* and *Paradisaical* State of Nature, Religion and Liberty;
in which we shall be *all taught of God,* and *have no need* of a foolish and
contentious *Priest,* hired to harangue us with his Noise and Nonsense.[160]

The pretense must, however, be still maintained, and Woolston
ends with an invocation to the "spiritual Messiah."

Voltaire mentions the raising of the dead vaguely in the *Conseils raisonnables à M. Bergier.*[161] But in his article "Miracles," he
deals with Woolston's fifth discourse at length and book in hand.
The historical argument interested him especially. Speaking still
of Woolston by name, he writes:

C'est aux morts ressuscités par Jésus-Christ qu'il en veut principalement.
Il affirme qu'un mort ressuscité eût été l'objet de l'attention et de l'étonne-
ment de l'univers; que toute la magistrature juive, que surtout Pilate, en
auraient fait les procès-verbaux les plus authentiques; que Tibère ordon-
nait à tous les proconsuls, préteurs, présidents des provinces de l'informer
exactement de tout; qu'on aurait interrogé Lazare qui avait été mort
quatre jours entiers, qu'on aurait voulu savoir ce qu'était devenue son
âme pendant ce temps-là.

Avec quelle curiosité avide Tibère et tout le sénat de Rome ne l'eussent-
ils pas interrogé; et non-seulement lui, mais la fille de Jaïr et le fils de
Naïm? Trois morts rendus à vie auraient été trois témoignages de la
divinité de Jésus, qui auraient rendu en un moment le monde entier chrétien. Mais, au contraire, tout l'univers ignore pendant plus de deux siècles
ces preuves éclatantes. Ce n'est qu'au bout de cent ans que quelques
hommes obscurs se montrent les uns aux autres dans le plus grand secret
les écrits qui contiennent ces miracles. Quatre-vingt-neuf empereurs, en
comptant ceux à qui on ne donna que le nom de *tyrans,* n'entendent
jamais parler de ces résurrections qui devaient tenir toute la nature
dans la surprise. Ni l'historien juif Flavius Josèphe, ni le savant Philon, ni
aucun historien grec ou romain ne fait mention de ces prodiges. Enfin
Woolston a l'imprudence de dire que l'histoire de Lazare est si pleine
d'absurdités que saint Jean radotait quand il l'écrivit: "Is so brimful of
absurdities, that saint John when he wrote it, had liv'd beyond his senses."
(Page 38, tome II.)[162]

Supposons, dit Woolston, que Dieu envoyât aujourd'hui un ambassa-
deur à Londres pour convertir le clergé mercenaire, et que cet ambassa-
deur ressuscitât des morts, que diraient nos prêtres?[163]

---

[160] *Ibid.,* pp. 70, 71.   [161] XXVII, 40.
[162] Voltaire's reference is correct, and in his copy, a sticker marks the passage.
[163] XX, 88, 89; see *Fifth Discourse,* p. 47, for proof of textual translation of the
last paragraph.

Voltaire's summary is masterful, and gives evidence of no little command of the English language, both in understanding the essential points and in translation. However, he omits many of Woolston's absurdities in order to enlarge on the details of the curiosity of Tiberius and on the early obscurity of the Gospels, which we have seen to be very much in the Woolston spirit, but which do not occur in the fifth discourse. Woolston's argument here is rather to bemoan the loss of the works of Celsus and Porphyry, which the Fathers could not answer, and which would undoubtedly prove this miracle to have been a manifest imposture.[164] Voltaire gives two correct references to Woolston's work, one of which appears in the body of the text, where Voltaire wanted it well understood that the words were not his. The article "Miracles" is of especial importance, because elsewhere Voltaire, in accordance with his usual practice, is content to give only the Scripture references which he found at the bottom of Woolston's pages.

Woolston reached the climax of his criticism of the miracles in the sixth discourse, in which he treats solely of the resurrection of Jesus. With the prospect of imprisonment before him, he addresses a most ironical dedication to the Bishop of Oxford, and then calls in his "old friend, the Jewish Rabbi,"[165] whom he has instructed to refrain from all the facetiousness which the nature of the subject offers. Many of the clergy had retreated before the onslaughts of the deists, and had foolishly reposed all proof of the truth of Christianity on the miracle of the resurrection. This miracle Woolston attempts to prove to be "the most . . . barefaced Imposture ever put upon the World."[166] The rabbi promises that he will turn Christian if the resurrection is proved. The apostles and the chief priests had entered into a covenant that the tombstone be sealed, in order that the prophecy of rising from the dead in three days might be manifestly fulfilled before witnesses, and that the nation might thereby be satisfied as to the messiahship of Jesus. But instead of waiting for the expiration of the

165 Voltaire wrote "lettre d'un prétendu rabin" against this passage in his manuscript version of Woolston's work.
166 *Sixth Discourse,* p. 27. A sticker marks this epithet in Voltaire's copy.

three days, Jesus' body was slipped out in the morning of the day before. The apostles had to get the body while they could, even by a barefaced infringement of the covenant of the seal.[167] The soldiers on guard, who numbered probably only three or four, were either bribed or given the wink by Pilate. The Evangelists admit that they were asleep; and well they might be after the festivities and reveling of the Feast of the Passover. If they had not been drunk of their own accord, the apostles had made them so.[168] Nor was the resurrection made manifest later. Jesus appeared only to his disciples, who were known deceivers, like Lazarus, and liars. He should have appeared publicly and thereby silenced all unbelievers for all time.[169] Christ appeared in ever varying forms and shapes, so that he was often not recognized at first by those who so recently had been so familiar with him. The disciples, who were strangely enough unmolested, told the story of the fraud until they believed it themselves.[170] But the world might have enjoyed great happiness under the Christian religion if the resurrection had been disproved, for that was the foundation of a most confused superstructure of wild doctrines and opinions. God's providence is shown in the common lay disbelief, and the world at last is to be cured of credulity and turn to the religion of nature.[171] If the resurrection was to have been credited, "better and more plausible Tales should have been invented," rather than such a "Robinson Crusoe romance."[172] Woolston appeals again to "that Happiness of the state of Nature, Religion, and Liberty, which may be looked for upon the coming of the Messiah, the allegorical accomplisher of the Law and the Prophets."[173] To him, the belief in the resurrection is the true miracle, yet such belief is the interest of the priests, the comfort of the superstitious, and the fear of the wise.[174] In regard to the

[167] *Ibid.,* pp. 10–15. [168] *Ibid.,* pp. 19, 20.
[169] *Ibid.,* pp. 22–25. [170] *Ibid.,* pp. 33–36.
[171] *Ibid.,* p. 38.
[172] *Ibid.,* pp. 29–31. Voltaire's copy contains a marker between pages 28 and 29. There is a sticker also on page 32 over the passage which relates the "prediction of his own resurrection" by "one Dr. Emms, one of the French prophets."
[173] *Ibid.,* p. 38. Voltaire put a sticker at the beginning of this discussion, page 37, over a passage cited from Justin Martyr which reads: "They who lived according to the Law of Nature, were true Christians."
[174] *Ibid.,* p. 26.

clergy, the rabbi, though he has proved that Christ is not risen, is too wise "to make the inference of Paul, that 'their Preaching is vain.' "[175] It is difficult to distinguish between Woolston and his rabbi, as indeed there was actually no distinction. After the rabbi's letter, Woolston promises that he who refutes the rabbi's arguments shall be by his consent the next Archbishop of Canterbury. The Divines, he says, "must give up their Religion as well as their Church, or go along with me to the Fathers for their mystical Interpretation of the whole Story of Jesus' Resurrection."[176] His quotations in support of the mystical interpretations are particularly numerous. Even Augustine grants that the three days and three nights of Christ's burial must be interpreted in a mystical sense to mean the three ages of the world.[177]

Woolston informs his readers that he had planned another discourse on the immaculate conception, and on the loaves and the fishes, but he found himself too grave for such subjects, and his rabbi too gay and wanton. Instead, he promises, if God spare him life and liberty, to treat many passages from Jesus' life which do not bear the examination of the letter, in order to confound the ecclesiastics, who "in all ages past have been the *Bane* of Society and the *Pest* of Mankind, as appears from the Wars and Persecutions, they have rais'd in the World; and from that Strife, Variance and Discord, they have occasion'd in Citys and Familys."[178] In defending himself from blasphemy, Woolston writes: "If any of our School of Free-Thinkers should say of his Opponent that he's profane and blasphemous, he would be reprimanded for want of Wit, Temper and good Manners."[179] He ends his discourse with an attack against his persecutors:

Mr. Atkinson's Argument for the Persecution of me, is much the same with that, which John Calvin used for the Persecution of that great Philosopher Servetus; the Injustice and Cruelty of whose death and sufferings is a greater Reproach to the Name of Calvin, than the Martyrdom of any Protestant can be to the Memory of any Popish Prelate.[180]

With such views, it is no wonder that Woolston was Voltaire's favorite deist.

[175] *Sixth Discourse,* p. 39.   [176] *Ibid.,* p. 43.   [177] *Ibid.,* p. 47.
[178] *Ibid.,* p. 64.   [179] *Ibid.,* p. 67.   [180] *Ibid.,* pp. 70–71.

Woolston's material on the resurrection was again not entirely adaptable to Voltaire's purposes. Rather than follow Woolston's absurdities, Voltaire chose to stress the historical argument, the failure of contemporary historians to mention the natural prodigies that accompanied the resurrection, the contradictions concerning the date, and the proof by Halley that there was no comet visible during those years. In England the debate on the miracles had centered about the impossibility of fraud in connection with the bodily resurrection, and it was to combat this argument that Woolston stresses the pact between the apostles and the chief priests, and reproduces the opinion of the Jews from Celsus to modern times. His handling of the miracle is often recognizable in Voltaire only through its position at the end of his usual summaries of the discourses, where the treatment is limited to a single sentence, as in the treatise *De la paix perpétuelle:* "vous n'ignorez pas que ce Dieu, ayant été pendu publiquement, ressuscita secrètement."[181] Even in the article "Miracles," the resurrection is treated in one short paragraph, with one leading quotation:

Il (Woolston) blasphème l'incarnation, la résurrection, l'ascension de Jésus-Christ, suivant les mêmes principes. Il appelle ces miracles l'imposture la plus éffrontée et la plus manifeste qu'on ait jamais produite dans le monde. "The most manifest, and the most bare-faced imposture that ever was put upon the world."[182]

In England, Woolston's discourse led to Sherlock's famous *Trial of the Witnesses* and to much argument concerning the sealing of the tomb, but that was many years ago and Voltaire preferred his own methods. The shading off from the Woolston miracles to his favorite method of treatment is illustrated in the *Epître aux Romains:*

Jésus prêche des paysans; Jésus garçon de la noce change l'eau en vin pour des paysans déjà ivres. Jésus est emporté par le diable sur une montagne. Jésus chasse les diables, et les envoie dans le corps de deux mille cochons, dans la Galilée, où il n'y eut jamais de cochons. Jésus dit des

injures atroces aux magistrats. Le préteur Pontius le fait pendre. Il manifeste sa divinité sitôt qu'il est pendu; la terre tremble, tous les morts
sortent de leurs tombeaux, et se promènent dans la ville, aux yeux de
Pontius. Il se fait une éclipse centrale du soleil en plein midi, dans la
pleine lune, quoique la chose soit impossible. Jésus ressuscite secrètement,
monte au ciel, et envoie publiquement un autre Dieu, qui tombe en plusieurs langues de feu sur les têtes de ses disciples. Que ces mêmes langues
tombent sur vos têtes, pères conscripts, faites-vous chrétiens.[183]

Voltaire uses the word "pendu" advisedly, for he finds that crucifixion was unknown among the Jews at that time.[184] In the
Examen important, he follows Woolston's argument:

Il fut exécuté publiquement, mais il ressuscita en secret. Ensuite il
monta au ciel en présence de quatre-vingts de ses disciples, sans qu'aucune
autre personne de la Judée le vît monter dans les nuées: ce qui était pourtant fort aisé à voir, et qui aurait fait dans le monde une assez grande
nouvelle.

But in general Voltaire was much better documented on the
miracles of the resurrection than Woolston, and his arguments
carry much more weight in modern criticism.

Voltaire had at his command throughout his critical works
certain groups of ideas which appear again and again, with variations in treatment and stress to fit the subject in hand, and in
fairly well-defined order. In his attacks on the New Testament,
he begins customarily with the historical background and versions of the advent of Jesus,[185] and then enters immediately upon
the discussion of the miracles as treated by Woolston, which he
follows up with a discussion of the contradictions of the Evangelists and the nonsensical parables of Jesus, attributed to Meslier. These groups are ordinarily followed by the miracles of
Paul and the early apostles and by his apocryphal gleanings from
Fabricius. A neat and concise combination of several of the
groups mentioned above is found in *Dieu et les hommes:*

Jésus est né d'une vierge; les ancêtres de son père putatif remontent à
David par deux généalogies entièrement différentes. Lorsqu'il naquit dans

---

[183] XXVII, 92.   [184] XXIV, 282.

[185] Herod and the massacre of the Innocents and the Panther story from the *Tol-
dos Jeschut* was common material which Voltaire admits getting from Basnage's
Histoire des Juifs. Voltaire also remarks that the original Hebrew was translated into
Latin by Wagenseil (XIX, 219). Cf. Basnage, *op. cit.,* l. V, ch. 15.

une étable, trois mages ou trois rois vinrent du fond de l'Orient l'adorer dans son auge. Le roi Hérode, qui se mourait alors, ne douta pas que Jésus ne fût un roi qui le détrônerait un jour, et fit égorger tous les enfants des villages voisins, comptant que Jésus serait enveloppé dans le massacre. Ses parents, selon les évangélistes, qui ne peuvent mentir, l'emmenèrent en Egypte; et, selon d'autres, qui ne peuvent mentir non plus, il resta en Judée. Son premier miracle fut d'être emporté par le diable sur une montagne d'où l'on découvrait tous les royaumes de la terre. Son second miracle fut de changer l'eau en vin dans une noce de paysans lorsqu'ils étaient déjà ivres. Il sécha par sa toute-puissance un figuier qui ne lui appartenait pas, parce qu'il n'y trouva point de fruit dans le temps qu'il ne devait pas en porter: car ce n'était pas le temps des figues. Il envoya le diable dans le corps de deux mille cochons, et les fit périr au milieu d'un lac, dans un pays où il n'y a point de cochons, etc., etc. Et, quand il eut fait tous ces beaux miracles, il fut pendu.[186]

Woolston's material is predominant and easily distinguishable. Voltaire's wit was never studied nor labored. He chose from Woolston's miracles those that could be quickly summed up in a "bon mot," such as the fig tree and the swine. Moreover, he has closely amalgamated to the Woolston lists a contribution of his own, that of the temptation on the mountain. Although it is not mentioned in Woolston's discourses, it is nearly always present in Voltaire's adapted lists and lends something to the rapidity of the shafts.

Voltaire found Woolston's miracles more adaptable than any other group of ideas in his repertoire. Except for the *Philosophe ignorant* and the *A, B, C,* which are essentially metaphysical, the material is found in every one of his critical works on religion between 1762 and 1777. It is also found in shorter or polemical works such as the *Dialogue du douteur et de l'adorateur,* the *Dîner du comte de Boulainvilliers,* the *Homélie du Pasteur Bourn,* the *Instruction à Frère Pédiculoso,* the *Banissement des jésuites de la Chine,* and in various "Catéchismes" of the *Dictionnaire philosophique.*[187]

The chronology and extent of Voltaire's use of Woolston must

[186] XXVIII, 220, 221.
[187] Page references: XXV, 130; XXVI, 544; XXVII, 13, 231, 308; XVIII, 78, 168. The list is used again as a marginal note to Abbadie's *Vérité de la religion chrétienne,* where Voltaire used Woolston to combat Abbadie in the privacy of his own library. See "The Private Library of Voltaire at Leningrad," *PMLA,* XLIII (1928), p. 1006.

next be treated. The Woolston material does not appear in the *Sermon du rabbin Akib,* in 1761, the subject of which is a Jewish defense against Christian charges and therefore directly in line. Nor are there clear evidences to be found in the *Extrait de Jean Meslier,* early in the following year. The material definitely appears then for the first time in the *Sermon des cinquante,* where an entire page is devoted to six Woolston miracles.[188] Since so many opportunities were offered and not taken in the *Sermon du rabbin Akib,* the internal evidence from the use of the Woolston material would fix the date of the *Sermon des cinquante* after November, 1761.[189] In 1763, the material is found in the *Catéchisme de l'honnête homme,*[190] and the famous *Traité sur la tolérance,* in which latter work a page of the Moland edition is devoted to comments upon four of Woolston's miracles.[191] In 1765 the *Questions sur les miracles* abounds with references to the same miracles. The work is directed against the Jesuit Needham, who was supposed to have made eels from paste, just as Jesus turned water into red wine by the use of spirituous liquors and cochineal. In this one work there are at least ten distinct references to the Cana miracle, four to the money-changers, and three to the fig tree.[192] Also, Voltaire here first gives Woolston's name to his reading public.[193] In 1767 there are two references in the *Questions de Zapata*[194] and considerable use, as would be expected, is made in the *Examen important de milord Bolingbroke,*[195] where Woolston is also often mentioned by name, although Bolingbroke himself ignored him entirely. In the same year appeared the account of Woolston in the *Lettres . . . sur Rabelais, etc.*[196] Skipping the less important uses,[197] several pages are devoted to Woolston and his miracles in *Dieu*

---

[188] XXIV, 450, 451.

[189] Beuchot believes the work to have first been published in 1762.

[190] XXIV, 530, 532.   [191] XXV, 85, 86.

[192] *Ibid.,* pp. 364, 369, 375, 376, 379, 385, 395, 397, 404, 405, 413, 417, etc.

[193] *Ibid.,* pp. 361, 364. Voltaire early mentioned Woolston's *Discourses* in an abandoned draft of his *Lettres philosophiques* (Lanson edition, II, 264).

[194] XXVI, 186.   [195] *Ibid.,* pp. 224, 225, 226, 240, 241.

[196] *Ibid.,* pp. 485, 486.

[197] See list in note on the preceding paragraph.

et les hommes,[198] in 1769. Although the material appears scantily in the original *Dictionnaire philosophique*[199] of 1764, the most satisfactory treatment of all appeared in 1771, in the *Questions sur l'Encyclopédie,* article "Miracles."[200] In 1776 and 1777, in the *Sommaire historique des quatre évangiles,*[201] and in the *Histoire de l'établissement du christianisme,*[202] several pages are devoted to Woolston's criticisms, with some new phrases which give evidence of a renewed acquaintance with the discourses. Chronologically, the use of the Woolston material coincides with that of the Fabricius material, covering the last fifteen years of Voltaire's life. The latter material is used more extensively, but the former more often.

Even more important to Voltaire than the Woolston material, it may well be believed, was the Woolston spirit, once stripped of its flimsy subterfuge; for the material itself furnished him with only a small part of his ammunition. Woolston was the wittiest of the English deists. Shaftesbury and Collins had preached the use of wit and ridicule in religious controversies, but their reverend successor had far excelled them in practice. Yet Tabaraud is wrong in charging Voltaire with exaggerating Woolston's impious language.[203] From the foregoing treatment of the two men, it is evident that Woolston was even more given to burlesque than Voltaire, and much more evidence could be gathered. The latter showed much good sense in his choice of material, and left out many of the *grossièretés* in which Woolston's works abound. Woolston sinned in this respect, however, no worse than Swift, whose amicable relations with the Church surprised Voltaire.[204] From the point of view of pure satire, Woolston's works compare favorably with Swift's, but were far too unorthodox to be even considered for their literary merits. It is therefore in no way surprising that Woolston exerted a far greater influence on Voltaire in both subject matter and method than did Swift.

To Woolston, as well as to Voltaire, the established religion

[198] XXVIII, 196, 197, 198, 202, 220, 228.
[199] See above.   [200] XX, 86–89.
[201] XXX, 306–308.   [202] XXXI, 61, 62, 63, 72.
[203] *Biographie universelle,* Paris, 1828, pp. 198–200.
[204] XXVI, 489, 491.

meant superstition and error, and the devil take those who accused them of blasphemy. Prosecuted and forbidden to allegorize any more miracles, Woolston wrote two defenses of his discourses in which he maintains to the end his mystical interpretation against the ministry of the letter. "I have indeed ludicrously treated the Letter of the Scriptures (in my Discourses)," he writes, "which by the said Bishops is falsely called Blasphemy: But should they either ludicrously or sedately write against the allegorical Sense of them, I could prove *that* to be real Blasphemy."[205] Voltaire was fond of replying to his critics that he was a better Christian than they.

Voltaire's copy of this *First Defense* contains markers and stickers which show his predilection for Woolston's spirit and ideas. Two paragraphs especially marked must be quoted at length, so important is their content in the understanding of Voltaire's own attacks on the Christian Church. The first concerns the moral responsibility of so-called infidel writers, such as Woolston and Voltaire:

> The Bishop says, that we Infidels (for I am one it seems) *labour industriously to root out all Sense of Virtue and Religion among us.* This is sad indeed, if true; and very bad men should we be, and deserving of the worst Punishment. But this wants Proof. How does he know that we are for rooting out all Sense of Virtue and Religion amongst men? Does it appear so by our Writings or our Practices? Does he find in our Books any Exhortations to Looseness and Immorality? Nothing of this I am sure. Is he then so well acquainted with Infidels, as to know them to be of more depraved and debauch'd Lives than profess'd Christians? Nor this neither. I have not as yet heard that any of my Disciples have been hang'd, lamenting his Misfortune of reading my *Discourses,* as what encouraged him to Sin, and brought him to the Gallows. No, those unhappy People, hitherto, die in the Faith and Communion of the Church, either of England or of Rome, and hope to be saved through the Merits of our Saviour. Neither do I hear of any Gentleman, old or young, who has given a greater Loose to his Lusts and Passions, since he read my Books. Such News would trouble me.[206]

This passage conforms in spirit to the essential mildness and virtue of Woolston's character. It was Pierre Bayle who launched

---

[205] *Defense of the Discourses on Miracles* (London, 1729), Part I, pp. 19–20.
[206] *Defense,* I, 36–37.

vigorously into eighteenth-century deism the idea of the complete separation of religion and morality. Voltaire undoubtedly
found comfort in Woolston's sincere statement of the problem
and defense of his works. He greatly needed that comfort when
the young Chevalier de la Barre, put to death on charges of sacri-
lege, was found to have in his pocket Voltaire's *Dictionnaire
portatif.* Voltaire himself insisted in his article "Liberté d'imprimer," that the work of Spinoza, "le plus dangereux, le plus
pernicieux de tous," had done no harm to anyone.[207]

The other paragraph which Voltaire marked at length was a
quotation from Dr. Moore's *Mystery of Godliness,* in which the
base conduct of the clergy is given as a cause of infidelity:

> Men are exceedingly tempted to think the whole Business of Religion
> is at best but a Plot to enrich the Priests, and keep the People in awe,
> from observing that they, who make the greatest Noise about Religion,
> and are the most zealous therein, do neglect the Laws of Honesty and
> common Humanity; that they easily invade other Men's Rights; that they
> juggle, dissemble, and lie for Advantage; that they are proud, conceited,
> love the Applause of the People, are envious, fierce, and implacable,
> unclean and sensual, merciless and cruel; care not to have Kingdoms flow
> in Blood, for maintaining their Tyranny over the Consciences of poor
> deluded Souls.[208]

This passage expresses an essential belief or dogma in the cate-
chism of English and French eighteenth-century deism. It very
ably explains one of the greatest causes of "infidelity." If such
charges against the clergy have largely disappeared today, we
have to thank just such men as Woolston and Voltaire. For personal morality, like tolerance, did not well up from within the
Church, but was forced upon it from without.

Several of Voltaire's critical works are very closely allied in
spirit to Woolston's diatribes. In the *Sermon du rabbin Akib,* the
rabbi is much milder than Woolston's, but the method is identical, and the material is so closely parallel that it is surprising to
find no direct influence. The *Questions sur les miracles* is perhaps
the most striking example of similarity of spirit, and here the
Woolston influence is direct. For instance, Voltaire, like Wool-

---

[207] XIX, 587.   [208] *Defense,* I, 39–40.

ston, pretends to take the part of a moderator, though his sympathies are plainly on the side of the freethinker. His transformation of water into red wine by the use of liquors and cochineal[209] is merely one example of his lesson from Woolston. The bantering tone of his mystical explanation of the transfiguration should at least be quoted:

> Je poursuis donc, et je dis qu'il est vrai que l'habit ne fait pas le moine; mais, comme je l'ai prouvé ci-dessus, l'habit est la figure de l'âme. Le vin de Cana était rouge, et les habits de la transfiguration blancs; or, le blanc signifiant la candeur, et le rouge étant la couleur du zèle, il est clair que si vous unissez ensemble ces deux couleurs vous avez un rouge tirant sur le jaune: donc les miracles sont très possibles; donc ils sont non-seulement possibles, mais ils sont très-réels; donc M. Covelle a tort.[210]

Yet Voltaire's use of mystical interpretation is only a little more ridiculous than Woolston's allegorical tirades against the clergy.

The Woolston spirit is especially manifest in works which Voltaire attributes to Englishmen and to which he attempts to give an English flavor. The *Examen important* contains patently more of Woolston than it does of Bolingbroke. *Dieu et les hommes* and *l'Histoire de l'établissement du christianisme* are other examples. In this latter work, among the "doutes" which Voltaire has signed with the names of English deists, he slips up on Woolston and credits him (along with Collins) with certain remarks on the transfiguration which belong to neither author.[211] Worse still, he signs with the name of Gordon his favorite miracle from Woolston on the casting out of the devils into the swine.[212] In this work Voltaire's confusion of the English deists has reached its climax and is evidently purposeful. Yet in spirit they are all magnified into so many Woolstons.

There appear no indications of the time when the manuscript of the abridged version of Woolston's *Discourses* came into Vol-

---

[209] XXV, 405.   [210] *Ibid.*, p. 404.
[211] XXXI, 62.
[212] *Ibid.*, p. 61. Two fortuitous references occur also in the late work, *La Bible enfin expliquée*, XXX, 76 and 133. In the former instance, in which Meslier's reproaches against the Jews are listed, Voltaire writes: "Le curé Meslier, et Woolston après lui." Woolston's works were all published before Meslier's *Testament* appeared, as Voltaire well knew. Moreover, he elsewhere wrongly attributed much the same material to Toland.

taire's possession. Voltaire's marginal note in the manuscript: "Lettre d'un prétendu rabin," may well have inspired the title of his *Sermon du rabbin Akib,* in 1761. First direct use of Woolston's subject matter appears in the *Sermon des cinquante,* published in 1762. Voltaire had the original English work at least by 1767, for his *Examen important de milord Bolingbroke.* His most direct borrowing from Woolston occurs in the dictionary article "Miracles," of 1771. During the entire last fifteen years of his publication, from 1762 to 1777, there is not a deistic article of importance from his pen that did not contain some borrowing from Woolston's *Discourses.* And Woolston's rabid anticlerical, critical spirit is found in slightly milder form in those many works which he wrote under the guise of some real or imaginary English deist.

CHAPTER V

VOLTAIRE AND TINDAL: THE MORAL ARGUMENT

MATTHEW TINDAL is regarded along with Shaftesbury as one of the chief proponents of natural religion. But Tindal contributed much also to the destructive criticism of the deistic movement. Toland had asserted that there was nothing unreasonable in Christianity, Collins had attacked the prophecies and Woolston the miracles. Tindal was now to assert that the Old and New Testament revelations were not divinely inspired, were useless, and often contrary to natural ideas of morality. This latter method of attack was a favorite with Voltaire. Leslie Stephen writes: "In so far as the Christian faith differs from a simple code of morality, it would seem that Tindal's state of mind was pretty much that of Voltaire."[1]

Tindal was born about 1657 and was thus some twelve years Toland's senior. He was educated at a country school and at Oxford, was granted a law fellowship at All Souls' College in 1678, and was admitted as an advocate at Doctor's Commons in 1685, with a pension of two hundred pounds which was regularly paid him to his death. He was at Oxford in 1696 when Toland launched the eighteenth-century campaign with his *Christianity not Mysterious*. But Tindal was very deliberate. His first work to receive marked attention was his *Rights of the Christian Church asserted, against the Romish and all other Priests who claim an Independent Power over it, etc.*, published in 1706, when he was nearly fifty; and he was well over seventy when he published his *Christianity as Old as Creation*, a book which marked the culminating point of deism. His other works were mainly in favor of the freedom of the press and in support of the Whig anticlerical party: in 1704, *Reasons against restraining the Press;* in 1717, an

---

[1] *English Thought in the Eighteenth Century*, I, 144.

attack on Walpole for splitting the party by his resignation; in 1729, a letter in answer to Bishop Gibson, defending Collins and Woolston and the freedom of the press. When Tindal died in 1733, a forged will deprived his nephew of his property and allowed the second volume of his *Christianity as Old as Creation* then in manuscript to fall into the hands of this same bishop, who deliberately burned it[2] and thereby won the argument.

The worst that can be said of Tindal's character by his enemies is that he was gluttonous, though they admit that he was so abstemious in drinking wine that he often got the better of his adversaries in argument. A more favorable account says that "he led a Life conformable to the sublimest Rules of Morality," and that though he suffered the most exquisite torture for eight days before his death, he died with the fortitude and resolution of a Stoic.[3] Considering the calumnies with which many of the deists were confronted, it would seem that he had the better of his adversaries in more than mere argument. Tindal wrote, moreover, with a strong conviction which lends a tone of sincerity and elevation even to his most destructive criticism. Swift wrote angrily against the pernicious works of freethinkers, among whom he classed Tindal when the latter had as yet written only in their defense and against the ambitions of the high clergy. In his *Project for the Advancement of Religion,* the author of the *Tale of the Tub* gives himself away rather seriously: "Hypocrisy," he writes, "is much more eligible than open infidelity and vice: it wears the livery of religion . . . and is cautious of giving scandal."[4] If the deists had confined their attention to religion and left the clergy alone, it may be thought that Swift would not have been so bitter.

Voltaire gives a curious account of Tindal in his *Lettres . . . sur Rabelais, etc.* (1767), in which he stresses Tindal's relations with Pope, who had condemned him in his *Dunciad.* After showing the injustice of counting Bishop Taylor among the infidels, Voltaire writes:

[2] *Ibid.,* I, 135. [3] *The Bee,* No. 25.
[4] See Robertson, *Short History of Freethought,* II, 132, 133 and note.

Mais pour le docteur Tindal, auteur du *Christianisme aussi ancien que le monde,* il a été constamment le plus intrépide soutien de la religion naturelle, ainsi que de la maison royale de Hanovre. C'était un des plus savants hommes d'Angleterre dans l'histoire. Il fut honoré jusqu'à sa mort d'une pension de cent livres sterling. Comme il ne goûtait pas les livres de Pope; qu'il le trouvait absolument sans génie et sans imagination, et ne lui accordait que le talent de versifier et de mettre en œuvre l'esprit des autres, Pope fut son implacable ennemi. Tindal de plus était un whig ardent, et Pope un jacobite. Il n'est pas étonnant que Pope l'ait déchiré dans sa *Dunciade,* ouvrage imité de Dryden, et trop rempli de bassesses et d'images dégoûtantes.[5]

The information concerning Tindal is very scanty and evidently gleaned from a dictionary. But Voltaire welcomed the opportunity to take a dig at Pope. There must have passed in his mind memories of literary squabbles in England, and especially of Pope's "All is well," the easy optimism of the English aristocrat which Voltaire did so much to combat. It may well be imagined that it was the aging Voltaire himself who did not find Pope's works to his taste, covering his frankness with Tindal's name.

Tindal displayed his legal talents in his *Rights of the Christian Church asserted.* The title is explained by Tindal's etymological definition of the Church as a congregation of the faithful in which the laity are chiefly to be considered. His purpose is to prevent the clergy from obtaining independent power in matters of religion. He first attacks the theory of divine right even in the state, for government arises first by common consent. There cannot be two independent powers in the same society, and the religious power, by the use of excommunication, would soon limit temporal power over life and property. Both theoretically and historically, the Church was unfit to exert such power over the liberties and consciences of men. Ammianus Marcellinus, "that wise Heathen," complains that "no Beasts were such deadly Enemies to Men, as the more savage Christians were generally to one another."[6] Theoretically, the independent power of the Church makes all reformation unlawful, perpetuates old corruptions and adds new ones, and denies liberty of conscience. Moreover, the

[5] XXVI, 484–485.
[6] *Rights of the Christian Church asserted* (London, 1709), p. 119.

claim of the clergy to independent power has been the occasion of infinite mischief and corruptions in the Christian world. The prosperity of Holland and the happiness of Denmark arose because the clergy are there bridled. Tindal's method was to turn against the Anglican Church its own arguments against the papists. Citing the Great Schism and the Anglican defection, he attacks the apostolic succession historically; and morally, in that it is a great absurdity to believe that God should delegate absolute power over men's consciences for all time.[7]

In his English notebook, Voltaire showed an interest in this political, anticlerical, whiggish deism, as expressed in Tindal's *Rights,* though it is possible that he may have taken his notes from the *Independent Whig,* by Thomas Gordon and John Trenchard. One of his early entries concerns ordination:

> One greatest error among christians is about the holy ghost. Formerly when a man was made a Lawyer in Jerusalem, he was so by these words, receive the holy ghost. Now one (doth) make use of the same words in making a priest.[8]

Tindal, in discussing ordination, had remarked merely that the word was "applicable also to Lawyers, Physicians, or Men of any other Rank or Order."[9] Voltaire's next entry discusses the indelible character of the clergy:

> T'is a meer fancy to believe the character of a priest is indelible. A lay man is made a clergy man only by designation, t'is an office wich can be revoked, and which was revoked effectually in the old ages of christianity, when a priest wanted church and function.

This might well be a reworking of Tindal's treatment of the subject:

> Nothing can be more senseless than this notion of an Indelible Character; . . . the Custom of degrading or reducing Ecclesiasticks to a Lay-Communion, was in use many Ages before this Notion of I know not what peculiar and indelible Character was thought of, and so could not well be discontinu'd afterwards.[10]

---

[7] Le Clerc spoke a good word for this work, in his *Bibliothèque choisie* (X, 29) and later, in his twenty-first volume, defended Toland against Carroll's preposterous *Spinoza reviv'd.*

[8] "Voltaire's English Notebook," *Modern Philology,* XXVI (February, 1929), 309.

[9] *Op. cit.,* pp. 356–357.   [10] *Ibid.,* p. 352.

Voltaire's wording is here closer to Tindal's than to similar expressions in the *Independent Whig,* or in Hickeringill's *Naked Truth.*[11] Other entries in the notebook which resemble very closely Tindal's thoughts deal with the exaggerated distinction between the clergy and the laity, and the general uselessness of the clergy, when the truths of natural religion are so obvious to all capacities.[12] For other entries of like nature the *Independent Whig* is plainly his source.[13]

Another passage from Tindal's anticlerical work is of especial interest in regard to Voltaire. Tindal explains that the power of excommunication was derived from the Druids, and continues:

> The most material Difference between these Christian and those Heathen *Druids,* is, that one sacrific'd Men to the Deity, but t'other to the Devil; and by burning them alive, make 'em as far as they can taste of Hell, before they send 'em thither: of which to persuade the Spectators, they dress 'em up in a *San-benito,* or a coat all painted with Devils and Flames; and they take their leave of each Sufferer with this most charitable Expression, *Jam animam tuam tradimus Diabolo.*[14]

Fifty years later in his *Candide,* Voltaire used the same detail, the sources of which M. Morize has conclusively traced.[15] It is interesting to note that the detail of the San-benito was early a part of the common cosmopolitan deistic arsenal. Tindal uses it again in his later work.[16]

There are also many passages of Tindal's *Rights* which look forward to his *Christianity as Old as Creation,* to his theory of the "Light of Nature," to his belittlement of Jewish history, and to his odious comparisons of Christianity with other religions, as he has above compared it to the religion of the Druids. For example, he explains that the slavery of the Jews in Egypt made them prone to idolatry. It is evident from Tindal's work that the deists' animosity against the Jews was merely a method to attack the divine inspiration of their revelation. For self-preservation, the English deists rarely paid much open attention to each other, although a mutual influence is often very evident. Tindal quotes

[11] London, 1681, in folio, p. 23.
[12] *Op. cit.,* 309, 318–319.
[13] *Ibid.,* 314.
[14] *Op. cit.,* p. 100.
[15] A. Morize, *Candide,* p. 41 and n. 2.
[16] *Christianity as Old as Creation* (London, 1730), p. 84.

the famous forgery passage from "the author of *Amyntor*,"[17] and finds that the Musselmen have corrupted the Old and New Testaments, by adding the sentiments of Mahomet, less than the Church, by its oral tradition and decrees.[18] Like Toland and Collins, Tindal was obliged to write anonymously to escape persecution.

The *Rights of the Christian Church asserted* caused considerable stir in England. Voltaire possessed a copy, which is still found in his private library at Leningrad. Strangely enough, he wrote on the title-page, "Collins," and never refers to the book as Tindal's. This is proof that he never firmly grasped the history of the English deistic movement. There are no notes in the book in Voltaire's handwriting. His deism differed from English deism in that he felt it expedient in France not to arouse the anger of bigots, hence the comparative mildness of his anticlerical animus. His interest in the clergy, in excommunication, in ordination, etc., was largely historical; but in later years his historical sources became much too elaborate to be charged to Tindal. But he adopted very closely Tindal's views on religion, on the Jews, on the Mahometans, on Christianity. The early passages in the English notebook resemble closely sentences in Tindal on the indelible character of the clergy. In no case, however, is there satisfactory evidence of direct textual borrowing. Many of Tindal's arguments had become commonplaces in deistic literature long before Voltaire became himself a pronounced deist. The influence of this early work may be considered important, but general.

With *Christianity as Old as Creation,* published in 1730, the year following the last of Woolston's discourses on the miracles, English deism is considered by critics to have reached its highwater mark, "that work eliciting," notes Robertson, "first to last, over one hundred and fifty replies, at home and abroad."[19] This criticism must apply principally, however, to constructive deism, which began to wane after Tindal. For if men had begun to see, with Middleton and Hume, how limited was the trust

[17] *Op. cit.,* p. lxxii.   [18] *Ibid.,* p. 321.
[19] Robertson, *op. cit.,* II, 137.

that they could put in the simple and supposedly universal light of nature and reason as a criterion in matters of religion, yet destructive criticism of the divine inspiration, reasonableness, and morality of the foundations of the Christian religion has never abated to any marked degree. Tindal's faith in the sufficiency of the universal light of reason was nothing short of touching, and it was from this angle that he naturally could be the most easily attacked. To him, the Jewish and Christian revelations were "a mere duplicate of the original document written upon the hearts of men";[20] but on one important condition: When revelation, by the light of reason, was apparently unreasonable or immoral (and these defects Tindal was nothing loath to point out) then the "original document" was alone to be trusted. The implication was all too obvious that revelation was not only useless but often pernicious, and Tindal's legal mind must have fully comprehended the implication.

Tindal's theory of a universal natural law and religion can be summed up in one short passage, noted by Voltaire:

> Natural religion, which is of the greatest importance to mankind, and is a perpetual standing rule for men of the meanest, as well as the highest capacity, carries its own evidence with it, those internal inseparable marks of truth; but can that be said of any religion which depends on tradition?[21]

And Tindal proceeds to answer his question in the negative. Voltaire was fond of saying that "le vrai christianisme est la loi naturelle perfectionnée";[22] in his dictionary article "Théisme," he writes:

> Notre religion révélée n'est même et ne pouvait être que cette loi naturelle perfectionnée. Ainsi le théisme est le bon sens qui n'est pas encore instruit de la révélation, et les autres religions sont le bon sens perverti par la superstition. Toutes les sectes sont différentes, parce qu'elles viennent des hommes; la morale est partout la même, parce qu'elle vient de Dieu.[23]

Voltaire is thinking of Tindal, too, in the following passage from the *Profession de foi des théistes:*

[20] Leslie Stephen, *op. cit.,* I, 138.
[21] *Christianity as Old as Creation* (London, 1730), p. 218. Voltaire put a marker in his copy at this page.
[22] XXV, 8.   [23] XX, 506.

Notre religion est sans doute divine, puisqu'elle a été gravée dans nos cœurs par Dieu même, par ce maître de la raison universelle, qui a dit au Chinois, à l'Indien, au Tartare, et à nous: Adore-moi, et sois juste. *Notre religion est aussi ancienne que le monde,*[24] puisque les premiers hommes n'en pouvaient avoir d'autre, etc.[25]

The paragraph continues to the words "le petit peuple juif." Respect for the Chinese as sons of nature, and belittlement of the Jews as idolatrous, barbarous "enthusiasts" unworthy of the special attention of the Supreme Being, were never failing tenets of deists, but especially of Voltaire and Tindal.

Voltaire gave proportionately much less space than Tindal to his constructive deism, but the similarity of their deistic "philosophy" is striking. In Voltaire's copy of *Christianity as Old as Creation,* now in the public library at Leningrad, his page markers are almost entirely confined to chapters XII and XIII, under the significant headings: "That they who, to magnify Revelation, weaken the Force of the Religion of Reason and Nature, strike at all religion; and that there can't be two independent Rules for the Government of Human affairs; That the Bulk of Mankind, by their Reason, must be able to distinguish between Religion and Superstition; otherwise they can never extricate themselves from the Superstition they chance to be educated in." The markers reveal Voltaire's interest in Tindal's assertions that any external revelation must depend on reason, that reason is the final judge, while the Scriptures, as evidence, are secondary,[26] that God as governor of the universe, rather than as king of the Jews, gave laws to all mankind,[27] and that Paul himself said: "Prove all things, hold fast to that which is good."[28] Voltaire's general belief in natural religion goes back at least to the famous *Épître à Uranie,* where he writes:

> Songe que du Très-Haut la sagesse éternelle
> A gravé de sa main dans le fond de ton cœur
> La religion naturelle.[29]

[24] The italics are mine.   [25] XXVII, 55–56.
[26] *Op. cit.,* pp. 166–167.
[27] *Ibid.,* p. 174. A sticker marks this passage, in addition to the page marker.
[28] *Ibid.,* p. 190.   [29] IX, 361.

Evidence of the force of his belief in natural religion is found in a marginal note in a volume in his library: "Je mourrais pour cette religion éternelle, la mère de toutes les autres qui déchirent les entrailles dont elles sont sorties."[30] Tindal was one of many sources for Voltaire's belief, but an important one. Voltaire, however, left England before the appearance of Tindal's *Christianity as Old as Creation*. Many years after his return to France, he still speaks of Newton, Leibnitz, and Locke as partisans of natural religion.[31] Nor does he mention Tindal until late in life. It is probable that he paid no close attention to Tindal's work until he felt free to develop himself the ideas that he found so well expressed there; his religious beliefs, however, developed more in accord with Tindal's than with any other English author's.

We now come to Tindal's long thirteenth chapter, in which we find the answer to his question as to whether traditional religion carries with it the internal and infallible evidences of truth:

> Does not the scripture give very many instances of inspired persons as much governed by their passions as uninspired? Was not Abraham, though a prophet, and so dear to God, that he would not destroy a neighbouring town without acquainting him with it, guilty of an incestuous marriage, his wife being his sister by his father's side? And did he not endeavour to betray her chastity to two kings, in disowning her to be his wife, by which conduct he got from one of them, who entreated him well for her sake, men and maid servants, sheep, oxen, asses and camels; and from the other, a thousand pieces of silver, besides sheep, oxen, men and women servants? and immediately after his faith was counted to him for righteousness, did he not doubt of God's promise, till God spoke to him in a deep sleep?[32]

Thus Tindal begins his attack on the divine inspiration of the Scriptures. The criticism proceeds directly in every case from his apology for the religion of nature and is scattered over many scores of pages, but he is not through until he has touched upon very many of the high points which appear many years later in Voltaire's deistic pamphlets. The points of contact are so numer-

---

[30] "Voltaire's Library at Leningrad," *PMLA,* XLIII (1928), p. 1006.
[31] *Éléments de la philosophie de Newton* (1738), XXII, 419.
[32] *Op. cit.,* p. 219. Marker.

ous, and in the case of the behavior of the prophets so similar, that it is no wonder that the Abbé Guénée, in his *Lettres de quelques Juifs à M. de Voltaire,* calls Voltaire, in regard to Tindal, "a poor copier of a poor writer."[33] The Reverend Philip Lefanu, who translated these letters into English, notes in a foreword that Voltaire "has cast many cruel and ill-grounded aspersions on the Jewish nation and religion," and adds that "to this end he has collected all the antiquated objections of Collins, Tindal, etc., and dressed them up anew for the same purpose for which they were first proposed."[34] He accuses Voltaire of adding little from his own fund, but this is far from the truth. Voltaire added a wealth of patiently collected detail which he exhibited at length especially in his *Bible enfin expliquée,* a work with which the English translator in 1777 was not perhaps acquainted. But more than mere detail and the more grievously to wound his reverend readers, he added his inimitable wit.

The scope of this work will not permit the quoting of the vast amount of detail that Tindal and Voltaire used to show the immorality of Abraham and the absurdity of the biblical story. For comparison with the quotation above, a short passage from Voltaire's *Questions de Zapata* may be chosen:

> Par quel art justifierai-je les deux mensonges d'Abraham, le père des croyants, qui à l'âge de cent trente-cinq ans à bien compter, fit passer la belle Sara pour sa sœur en Egypte et à Gérare, afin que les rois de ce pays-là en fussent amoureux, et lui fissent des présents? Fi! qu'il est vilain de vendre sa femme![35]

Tindal is moderate and brief on David's cruelty, licentiousness, and treachery,[36] and we must leave that discussion until we come to Peter Annet's *David, the Man after God's own Heart.* Tindal repeats Collins' physical attributes of God collected from the Old Testament, and adds many comments of his own:

[33] *Letters of certain Jews to Monsieur de Voltaire* (Dublin, 1777), 2 vols. in 8; I, 328, note.

[34] *Ibid.,* I, 5.

[35] XXVI, 176. The only antibiblical thrust in *Candide* is a veiled allusion to this incident (XXI, 163).

[36] *Op. cit.,* pp. 220, 221. Voltaire wrote on his marker: "crimes de David et de Salomon."

What strange notions must the bulk of mankind, could not their reason direct them, have of the supreme being, when he is said to have rested,
and to be refreshed; and that wine cheereth both God and man?[37] . . .
And must we not think it as unworthy of God to talk to a serpent as to
Satan?[38]

Voltaire is less moderate, at least in the form: "Dieu se promener! Dieu parler! Dieu écrire sur une petite montagne! Dieu
combattre! Dieu devenir homme! Dieu-homme mourir du dernier supplice! idées dignes de *Punch*," he writes, as we have
before noted, in his very English *Dieu et les hommes*.[39]

The details of the story of creation presented an easy mark for
the shafts of the philosophers of Reason, who never tired of
showing the absurdity of the literal interpretation. But the allegorical interpretation involved the doctrine of original sin, and
this Tindal found not only absurd but immoral, and derogatory
to the natural perfection of the supreme being. Tindal takes as
his starting point Clarke's philosophical attributes of God, with
which Voltaire had been so much pleased in his early days, and
applies them logically to the story of creation in order to blast
the theological position. Leslie Stephen remarks that Tindal
played the same rôle in regard to Clarke that Toland had played
in regard to Locke. If Voltaire read Tindal's last chapter, he had
sufficient reason to change his early praise of Clarke and call him
an irritated theologian.[40]

Clarke had stated that the true deists were "ignorant of the
original dignity of human nature."

Had they known [says Tindal] the sacred story of Adam and Eve,
that would have confirmed them in their sentiments. The most they could
perceive by it would be, that the first pair came into the world in every
sense naked, destitute of all that knowledge, experience gave their pos-
terity; and therefore God, the better to support them in this state of universal ignorance, planted a garden for them; that they might live on the
fruit of it: how weak was their reason, how strong their appetites! when
they could not abstain (the sole command given them) from the fruit of
but one tree, in a garden too, where must needs be an infinite variety,
and the choicest fruit!

[37] *Christianity as Old as Creation*, p. 226. A marker and a sticker indicate the exact
passage.
[38] *Ibid.*, p. 228.   [39] XXVIII, 244; cf. XXX, 10, n. 2.
[40] XIX, 578; XXVI, 57.

These philosophers would have been at a loss to conceive, how Eve could entertain a conference with a serpent (incapable of human voice) even before consent had given any meaning to sounds. And they would be apt to ask, why, though custom had made it shameful to go without clothes in those places where clothes are worn; the first pair should nevertheless, though they knew not what clothes were, be ashamed to be seen unclothed by another, and by God himself? so that, when they heard the voice of God walking in the Garden, in the cool of the evening, (a strange representation these philosophers would think of God!) they hid themselves from his presence: Nay God himself, their fig-leave aprons, which they (having, it seems, all things necessary for sewing) sewed together, not being sufficient to hide their shame, made them coats of the skins of beasts, newly created in pairs. . . . And it was upon the woman's saying, the serpent beguiled me, and I did eat; that the Lord said to the serpent, because thou hast done this, thou art cursed above all cattle, and above every beast of the field: Upon thy belly shalt thou go, and the dust thou shalt eat all the days of thy life. . . . Did he all the days of his life go upon his belly, and eat dust? Does not God, continuing the discourse to the serpent, say, I will put enmity between thee and the woman; between thy seed and her seed; it shall bruise thy head, and thou shalt bruise his heels. . . . If a book is to be interpreted thus, especially in relation to historical facts; how can we, these philosophers would say, be sure of its meaning in any one place? . . . They might as well ask, why all other animals should bring forth in pain, for the fault of Eve? . . . Those philosophers might not think the matter a jot mended, by substituting (did the story afford room for it) a devil, instead of a serpent; since they could not see, how an infinitely good God could permit a most malicious cunning spirit to work on the weakness of a woman, just placed in a new world,[41] etc.

This is not only very much in the style of Voltaire's criticism, but one would be inclined to find here the general idea that led Voltaire to include some scandalous verses concerning the indignity of the first pair in his *Mondain*. The details of the parody were probably his own invention, and M. Morize believes them "une transposition d'idées qui, en elles-mêmes, n'ont rien à voir avec Adam et Ève."[42] The evidence is slender, but *Le Mondain* is remarkable among Voltaire's early works as being one of the very few in which he approached the details of critical deism. The inclusion of these verses on the primitive pair was unfortu-

[41] *Op. cit.,* pp. 348–352.
[42] A. Morize, *L'Apologie du luxe,* pp. 135, 143.

nate, and persecution ensued. Voltaire wrote to Thiériot, adding more details to his picture:

> Je trouve qu'on a grande raison de s'emporter contre l'auteur de cet abominable ouvrage, dans lequel on ose dire qu'Adam ne se faisait point la barbe, que ses ongles étaient un peu longs et que son teint était hâlé: cela mènerait tout droit à penser qu'il n'y avait ni ciseaux, ni rasoir, ni savonette dans le paradis terrestre, ce qui serait une hérésie aussi criante qu'il y en ait.[43]

It is possible that these remarks were occasioned by Tindal's ironical suggestion of Adam and Eve's "having, it seems, all things necessary for sewing," but if so, it is a rare instance of Voltaire's borrowing from English biblical criticism before 1762.

Some thirty years after the *Mondain,* in his *Sermon des cinquante,* Voltaire begins his criticism of the Old Testament much after the manner of Tindal:

> Premièrement, sans parler de l'injustice extravagante dont on ose charger l'Etre suprême, d'avoir donné la parole à un serpent pour séduire une femme, et perdre l'innocente postérité de cette femme, suivons pied à pied toutes les horreurs historiques qui révoltent la nature et le bon sens.[44]

At the close of his career, he still has the serpent in mind, in his *Bible enfin expliquée:*

> Une preuve indubitable que la *Genèse* est donnée pour une histoire réelle, c'est que l'auteur rend ici raison pourquoi le serpent rampe. Cela suppose qu'il avait auparavant des jambes et des pieds avec lesquels il marchait. On rend aussi raison de l'aversion qu'ont presque tous les hommes pour les serpents. Il est vrai que les serpents ne mangent point de terre; mais on le croyait, et cela suffit.[45]

In his discussion of original sin, Clarke had said that divine revelation was an absolute necessity for the recovery of mankind. Tindal charges him with entertaining a base conception of God:

> This is supposing, God has left all mankind for four thousand years together, and even the greatest part to this day, destitute of sufficient means to do their duty, and to preserve themselves from sinking into a corrupted and degenerate state; and that it was impossible for them when thus sunk, to recover themselves; and yet that God (their duty being the

---

[43] XXXIV, 171.   [44] XXIV, 439.   [45] XXX, 11, n. 1.

same after, as before the fall,) expected impossibilities from them; viz. either to preserve themselves from thus falling; or if fallen, to recover themselves.[46]

Tindal had only to draw the conclusions that Clarke's philosophy very apparently suggested. Voltaire expresses himself very similarly in his article "Originel (Péché)":

C'est ici le prétendu triomphe des sociniens ou unitaires. Ils appellent ce fondement de la religion chrétienne son *péché originel*. C'est outrager Dieu, disent-ils, c'est l'accuser de la barbarie la plus absurde que d'oser dire qu'il forma toutes les générations des hommes pour les tourmenter par des supplices éternels, sous prétexte que leur premier père mangea d'un fruit dans un jardin.[47]

In certain passages the texts are very similar. For instance, Tindal says that certain sects worshiped the serpent rather than Christ, "for foretelling that Adam, though threatened with certain death on the day he eat the forbidden fruit, should not then die; who accordingly liv'd after that sentence about 900 years."[48] And Voltaire: "Il n'est pas même conté dans la *Genèse* que Dieu ait condamné Adam à la mort pour avoir avalé une pomme. Il lui dit bien: 'Tu mourras très-certainement le jour que tu en mangeras'; mais cette même *Genèse* fait vivre Adam neuf cent trente ans après ce déjeuner criminel."[49] One of Voltaire's hobbies was to figure the ages of the patriarchs.[50] But except for this one passage inspired by Tindal on the opinions of the unitarians, Voltaire's argument against original sin was historical: nothing is said concerning the doctrine in either Testament, nor was any credit given to this strange idea before Augustine.

On the cruelties and immoralities of the Old Testament, we find many ideas in common in Tindal and Voltaire. Several passages must be compared. Tindal condemns the harsh treatment of the Canaanites and the barbarous assassination of a king by Ehud:

Would not people, if, like the children of Israel, they were destitute of an habitation, be apt to think what the Israelites did to the Canaanites, a

[46] *Op. cit.*, pp. 339, 340.   [47] XX, 151.
[48] *Op. cit.*, p. 350.   [49] XX, 152. Cf. XXVI, 341.
[50] Cf. XXVIII, 186.

good precedent; and that they might invade a neighbouring, idolatrous nation, that never did them the least harm; and extirpate not only men and women, but even their innocent infants, in order to get possession of their country? And I question, whether the Spaniards would have murdered so many millions in the Indies, had they not thought they might have used them like Canaanites. How many precedents, besides that of Ehud, (who, on a message from the Lord, stabbed the king to whom his people sent him with a present) did the Popish priests plead from the Old Testament, for the assassination of the two Henries of France?[51]

And Voltaire's *Sermon des cinquante* offers a very close parallel:

> Voilà votre beau pays, leur dit Dieu; égorgez tous les habitants, tuez tous les enfants mâles, faites mourir les femmes mariées, réservez pour vous toutes les petites filles. . . . Que de crimes commis au nom du Seigneur! ne rapportons que celui de l'homme de Dieu, Aod. Les Juifs . . . ont juré obéissance au roi Eglon: un saint Juif, c'est Aod, demande à parler tête à tête avec le roi de la part de Dieu . . . Aod l'assassine, et c'est de cet exemple qu'on s'est servi tant de fois chez les chrétiens pour trahir, pour perdre, pour massacrer tant de souverains.[52]

Aod hid the knife under his mantle, "comme firent depuis Jacques Clément et Ravaillac."[53] Again, Voltaire, in his *Pucelle,* calls Aod "le Ravaillac hébreu."[54] Even the association of ideas is common to the two men, and suggests direct influence.

Tindal asks:

> If men flatter themselves that they are true Israelites and those of a different religion mere Egyptians; will they not be apt to imagine, when they see how the Israelites spoiled the Egyptians by the command of God himself, who made them borrow what they were not to repay; that this might be a good precedent for them?[55]

And Voltaire writes:

> Vous convenez avec nous, leur dit M. Toland, que vous avez volé les Egyptiens en vous enfuyant de l'Egypte, que vous leur avez pris des vases d'or et d'argent, et des habits. Toute la différence entre votre aveu et notre opinion, c'est que vous prétendez n'avoir commis ce larcin que par ordre de Dieu. Mais, à ne juger que par la raison, il n'y a point de voleur qui n'en puisse dire autant.[56]

---

[51] *Op. cit.,* p. 238.
[53] XXVI, 180.
[55] *Op. cit.,* p. 237; cf. p. 316.

[52] XXIV, 442.
[54] IX, 259.
[56] XXVI, 427.

The detail and the application are again similar. We have seen that these words and the method of attack were not Toland's. It seems very certain, however, that Voltaire was thinking of Tindal, and confused the two men either deliberately or unconsciously. We do not expect direct quotations from the works of the English deists, and were surprised to find them in the case of Woolston.

Tindal continues:

> When men find the harlot Rahab celebrated, even in the new testament, for lying to the government, and betraying her country to its most cruel enemies; . . . are they not in danger, if they find it to their advantage, to do the same?[57]
>
> And now . . . to give no other instances, than the transactions of Judah and Tamar, we might approve the strategem, in getting to lie with her father-in-law: . . . she was blessed with twins, from whom the noble house of Judah, with all its kings, and the Messiah himself was descended.[58]

Voltaire, in *Les Questions de Zapata,* writes:

> Comment excuserai-je l'action de la courtisane Rahab, qui trahit Jéricho sa patrie? En quoi cette trahison était-elle nécessaire, puisqu'il suffisait de sonner de la trompette pour prendre la ville? Et comment sonderai-je la profondeur des décrets divins, qui ont voulu que notre divin Sauveur Jésus-Christ naquît de cette courtisane Rahab, aussi bien que de l'inceste que Thamar commit avec Juda son beau-père, et de l'adultère de David et de Bethzabée? Tant les voies de Dieu sont incompréhensibles![59]

In the *Bible enfin expliquée,* Voltaire attributes the same idea to Fréret as against Dom Calmet, and again to Collins.[60] But the authorities in this work are generally given at random, and the evidence points decidedly to Tindal.

Tindal says little concerning Moses except that he seems by the Old Testament to have been often worshiped himself as a god. Voltaire, on the other hand, was particularly interested in Moses, and especially in contesting his authorship of the Pentateuch. In a long note in the *Traité sur la tolérance,* Voltaire gives as authorities that the Pentateuch was written at the time of the kings, "Wollaston, Collins, Tindal, Shaftesbury, Bolingbroke, et

---

[57] *Op. cit.,* p. 237.   [58] *Ibid.,* p. 249.
[59] XXVI, 178–179.   [60] XXX, 121, n. 1.

beaucoup d'autres."[61] L'abbé Guénée, in his *Letters of certain Jews,* demolished this list.[62] He noted that Tindal attacked equally the Jewish and Christian revelations, but that he wrote with an air of moderation, and made no objections to the accepted authorship of the Pentateuch.[63]

It was with regard to Voltaire's objections against the morality of the prophets that Guénée accuses him of having copied Tindal word for word. The similarity of detail and method is indeed striking, and several examples may be given. Tindal notes the curious dialogue between Balaam and his ass, and then continues:

> How many commands did God give his prophets, which, if taken according to the letter, seem unworthy of God, as making them act like mad men or idiots? As for instance, the prophet Isaiah walked for three years together naked for a sign. Jeremiah is commanded to carry his girdle as far as Euphrates, and there to bury it in a hole of a rock; and after many days he is sent to dig it up again . . . Ezekiel is commanded by the Lord to draw Jerusalem on a tile . . . to take an iron pan and set it for a wall between him and the city . . . to lie three hundred and ninety days on one side, and forty days on the other; and then to mix man's dung with his bread. And afterwards the Lord said, I have given thee cow's dung for man's dung. . . . And as St. John was commanded to eat a book; so the prophet was commanded to eat a roll; and likewise to clip his hair, and to dispose of the clippings after a very odd manner; and several other things as strange, too many here to mention. And the prophet Hosea, who was like a priest, was bid to take a wife of whoredoms; (though that by Moses law was forbid a priest) and children of whoredoms; and had three children by his wife, to whom the Lord himself gave names.[64]

Voltaire writes of these four prophets and of Elisha in the chapter "Des prophètes juifs" of his *Philosophie de l'histoire,* and it was from this work that Guénée decided he had copied Tindal. The grouping and order are the same in both texts, but Voltaire added many comparisons in the early part of his chapter from heathen prophets, and has elaborated on the Hebrew prophets, among whom Ezekiel was his favorite.

[61] XXV, 67, n. 5.

[62] Bolingbroke alone thought it was not improbable that the Pentateuch was compiled after the time of Moses. *Works* (Philadelphia, 1841), II, 478.

[63] *Op. cit.,* I, 209–211.   [64] *Op. cit.,* 229, 230.

Il faut être un peu familiarisé avec l'antiquité pour n'être point effarouché des actions et des discours énigmatiques des prophètes juifs. Isaïe . . . marche tout nu dans Jérusalem, pour marquer que les Egyptiens seront entièrement dépouillés par le roi de Babylone. Quoi! dira-t-on, est-il possible qu'un homme marche tout nu dans Jérusalem, sans être repris de justice? Oui, sans doute: Diogène ne fut pas le seul dans l'antiquité qui eut cette hardiesse . . . Jérémie n'avait que quatorze ans quand il reçut l'esprit. . . . Il achète une ceinture de lin, la met sur ses reins, et va la cacher, par l'ordre de Dieu, dans un trou auprès de l'Euphrate: il retourne ensuite la prendre, et la trouve pourrie. . . . Ezéchiel peut surprendre davantage . . . il mange un volume de parchemin; on le lie avec des chaînes. Il trace un plan de Jérusalem sur une brique; il met à terre une poêle de fer; il couche trois cent quatre-vingt-dix jours sur le côté gauche, et quarante jours sur le côté droit. Il doit manger du pain de froment, d'orge, de fèves, de lentilles, de millet, et le couvrir d'excréments humains. . . . Mais Ezéchiel ayant témoigné son horreur pour ce pain de douleur, Dieu lui permet de ne le couvrir que d'excréments de bœufs. Il coupe ses cheveux, et les divise en trois parts; il en met une partie au feu, coupe la seconde avec une épée autour de la ville, et jette au vent la troisième. . . . Le Seigneur ordonne d'abord au prophète Osée, chapitre I, de prendre pour sa femme une prostituée, et il obéit. Cette prostituée lui donne un fils,[65] etc.

Voltaire proceeds to obscene details of his own finding.

Without giving any more detailed similarities, let us quote l'abbé Guénée, who made a careful study of these texts. In a note on his heading "Severity of Elias and Elisha," he writes:

These two facts have been quoted by Tindal, as well as those of Joshua, Michas, and the Bethsamites, and almost all those which have, or shall be mentioned in the course of this letter (on the conduct and writings of the prophets). Mr. de Voltaire only repeats the English Deists's words. In these petty criticisms, he is so far from having the honour of invention, that he has not even that of applying them properly. Could he think that no one would ever read Tindal, or be acquainted with the learned answers given to him? What a part do these oracles of philosophy act, these mighty geniuses, who think themselves born to give light to the universe, when they become every moment, the poor copiers of a poor writer![66]

While accepting Guénée's general thesis and granting that Tindal was a poor writer, we must deny that Voltaire was a poor copier.

La Philosophie de l'histoire was first published in 1765, but

[65] XI, 125, 126.   [66] *Letters of certain Jews,* I, 328, note.

Voltaire's impertinences on the prophets are found earlier in *Jean Meslier* and in the *Sermon des cinquante,* in 1762, in the *Dictionnaire philosophique* in 1764, and again in all his later attacks on the Jews and the Old Testament. Voltaire added many obscenities concerning Ezekiel of which he was very proud. In December, 1760, he sent a manuscript to Mme. du Deffand containing "une plaisante découverte que j'ai faite dans mon ami Ezéchiel," adding: "Je ne demande pas que ces rogatons vous divertissent autant que moi, mais je voudrais qu'ils vous amussent un quart d'heure."[67] A month later in a letter to the same address, he wrote: "Vous méprisez trop Ézéchiel, madame. . . . Je vous passe de ne point déjeuner comme lui. . . . Le *Pentateuque* et l'Arioste font aujourd'hui le charme de ma vie."[68] If the chapter from the *Philosophie de l'histoire* proves, as it seems to do, that Voltaire was drawing material from Tindal's *Christianity as Old as Creation,* the letters above seem no less to fix the date of Voltaire's annotations in that work.

Many other passages would have served equally well to show the resemblance in method and detail in Tindal and Voltaire, among them, Jacob's wrestling with the Lord, Saul and the Amelekites, Hagar and Ishmael, and especially the strange story of the tribe of Benjamin. The criticism of David's conduct, launched by Bayle, had yet to pass through the hands of another Englishman, Peter Annet.

Voltaire's usual grouping of ideas led him from the prophets of the Old Testament to a criticism of its successor, the New Testament, and from the historical background of the coming of the Messiah to Woolston's comments on the miracles, and to the difficulties connected with Christ's parables: Tindal is apparently the source for many of Voltaire's remarks on the parables, and often Voltaire even followed the steps of his transition.

Tindal turned immediately from the prophets to discuss the absurdity of trying to reconcile the Old and New Testaments. From examples of cruelty in the Old, he turns his attention to the spirit of the New, and then to the difficulty of understanding the parables of Christ in the light of reason. The holy fathers did

---

[67] XLI, 90, 91.   [68] *Ibid.,* pp. 151, 153.

not dare admit contradictions between the Testaments because they would thereby destroy the authority of both. The following paragraph is Tindal's introduction to the problem:

> Our saviour, by saying, He came not to destroy the lives of men, but to save them; condemns their taking away the lives of any, except in defence of their own, and of what is necessary for their support; and this he declares, upon a most remarkable occasion: Some of his disciples, upon his not being received into a Samaritain village, because his face was towards Jerusalem, strait cried, Wilt thou we command fire from Heaven, and consume them, as Elias did? He rebuked them, and said, ye know not what manner of spirit ye are of; for the son of man is not come to destroy the lives of men, but to save them. If any precedent might have been pleaded from the Old Testament, · it would, no doubt, have been Elias, the forerunner of our saviour; who came from Heaven (to which he went up by a whirlwind in a chariot of fire) to meet our saviour on a high mountain.[69]

Tindal's work is far from well ordered, and he goes on to discuss other instances of barbarous cruelty among the Jews. But to both Tindal and Voltaire, than Elias, "never was there a Jew more barbarous."[70]

To pass from the prophets to the New Testament is of course the natural and orderly procedure. But Voltaire has confined himself to the same prophets as Tindal, has treated them with the same spirit and the same method, and then proceeds like Tindal either from the cruelties of the Jews often illustrated by Elias, or more often from the last prophet treated, Hosea. Like Tindal, he often passes directly from the immorality of the Old Testament to the parables as expressing the immorality of the New.[71]

In the *Sermon des cinquante,* we find a typical transition:

> C'est Elie qui monte au ciel dans un char de feu; ce sont des enfants qui chantent dans une fournaise ardente. Je n'aurais jamais fini si je voulais entrer dans le détail de toutes les extravagances dont ce livre fourmille; jamais le sens commun ne fut attaqué avec tant d'indécence et de fureur.
>
> Tel est, d'un bout à l'autre, cet Ancien Testament, le père du Nouveau, père qui désavoue son fils, et qui le tient pour un enfant bâtard et rebelle: car les juifs, fidèles à la loi de Moïse, regardent avec exécration le chris-

[69] *Op. cit.,* pp. 241, 242.   [70] XXX, 220, n. 1.
[71] Confirmation of this influence is found in Voltaire's copy of Tindal's work at Leningrad, where the markers skip from the prophets, p. 229, to the parables, p. 302.

tianisme, élevé sur les ruines de cette loi. Mais les chrétiens, à force de sub-
tilités, ont voulu justifier le Nouveau Testament, par l'Ancien même.[72]

On the following page, having discussed the prophets and Ezekiel's breakfast, Voltaire continues:

> Après cet exemple, il est inutile d'en rapporter d'autres, de perdre notre
> temps à combattre toutes les rêveries dégoûtantes et abominables qui font
> le sujet des disputes entre les juifs et les chrétiens: contentons-nous de
> déplorer l'aveuglement le plus à plaindre qui ait jamais offusqué la raison
> humaine; espérons que cet aveuglement finira comme tant d'autres; et
> venons au Nouveau Testament, digne suite de ce que nous venons de
> dire.[73]

In the *Dîner du comte de Boulainvilliers,* Voltaire attacks the
New Testament immediately after Elias, "transporté aux régions
célestes orientales dans un chariot de feu, lequel Éliah, par paren-
thèse, n'a jamais existé."[74] Details change, but not the main trend
of thought. In the *Examen important de milord Bolingbroke,* the
chapter on the person of Jesus is immediately preceded by the
following rabid paragraph:

> Venons enfin de l'Ancien Testament au Nouveau. Venons à Jésus, et à
> l'établissement du christianisme; et, pour y arriver, passons par-dessus les
> assassinats de tant de rois, et par-dessus les enfants jetés au milieu des
> flammes dans la vallée de Tophet, ou écrasés dans les torrents sous des
> pierres. Glissons sur cette suite affreuse et non interrompue d'horreurs sacri-
> lèges. Misérables Juifs! c'est donc chez vous que naquit un homme de la lie
> du peuple qui portait le nom très-commun de Jésus? Voyons quel était ce
> Jésus.[75]

And a few pages farther on: "Tout ce qu'on conte de ce Jésus est
digne de l'Ancien Testament et de Bedlam." A similar transition
appears in his *Dieu et les hommes.*[76] Voltaire could pick an
entirely different set of maxims when he wanted to prove half
ironically, in the *Traité sur la tolérance,* that Jesus was only less
tolerant than the extremely tolerant Jews, but the effect is very
much the same; both Testaments are seen to be barbarous and
immoral.

[72] XXIV, 447.   [73] *Ibid.,* p. 448.
[74] XXVI, 542.   [75] *Ibid.,* pp. 219–220.
[76] XXVIII, 200–201.

Tindal found that the New Testament was full of parables, and that reason alone could instruct us as to whether a moral precept should be taken in a limited sense, an extended sense, or in a contrary sense in the case of obvious contradictions:

> Is not the new testament full of parables, nay, is it not said, that without a parable Jesus spake not to the multitude; and for this remarkable reason, that seeing they might see, and not perceive; and hearing they might hear, and not understand lest at any time they should be converted, and their sins be forgiven them?[77]

To prove the absurdity of the literal interpretation, Tindal gives the following words of Jesus:

> Whatever you shall ask in my name, that will I do. If two of you shall agree on earth, touching anything they shall ask, it shall be done for them of my father, which is in heaven. If you have faith as a grain of mustard seed, you shall move mountains, and nothing shall be impossible to you. And you may say to this sycamore tree, be thou plucked up by the roots, and be thou planted in the sea, and it shall obey you,[78] etc.

In the *Extraits de sentiments de Jean Meslier,* Voltaire writes in very similar fashion:

> Jésus-Christ dit qu'il n'y a qu'à demander et qu'on recevra, qu'à chercher et qu'on trouvera. Il assure que tout ce qu'on demandera en son nom on l'obtiendra; et que si l'on avait seulement la grosseur d'un grain de moutarde de foi, l'on ferait, par une seule parole, transporter des montagnes d'un endroit à un autre. . . . A l'égard du transport des montagnes, il dit positivement que quiconque dira à une montagne: Ote-toi de là, et te jette dans la mer, pourvu qu'il n'hésite pas en son cœur, mais qu'il croie, tout ce qu'il commandera sera fait. Ne sont-ce pas des promesses qui sont tout à fait générales, sans restriction de temps, de lieu, ni de personnes?[79]

Voltaire has sought other verses here to say the same thing, but the resemblance is none the less striking. As an introduction on parables, Tindal had noted that the moral treatises of Aristotle, Cicero, Grotius, and Puffendorf, etc., explain clearly the duties of man, with reasons and connection:

[77] *Op. cit.,* p. 301.   [78] *Op. cit.,* pp. 302, 303.
[79] XXIV, 326, 327.

but in the scripture, things, say they (the best authors), are not so generally treated, as that men may precisely know the nature and extent of their duty. Are they not, say they, for the most part, delivered in such general, undetermined, nay, sometimes parabolical and hyperbolical manner, as did we not consult our reason, and learn our duty from thence, the letter might lead us wrong; nay, the apostle himself says, the letter killeth.[80]

And on the subject of contradictions, Tindal writes:

What can be more surprising, than Christ's declaring in most express terms, he came to do that, which we must suppose he came to hinder: Think not, (says he) I am come to send peace, but a sword. For I come to set a man at variance with his father, etc. And, suppose ye, I am come to give peace on earth, I tell you, nay; but rather division. And again, I am come to send fire on earth, and what will I, if it be already kindled. And has not that fire burnt outrageously ever since, being blown up by those, whose business it was to have extinguished it?[81]

We have seen above how Voltaire applied the same material.

Tindal proceeds to show that the precepts of Jesus concerning wealth and property subvert the whole social and economic order of the Christian state. If we sold all we have to give to the poor, "there could be no buyers where all were to be sellers,"[82] and a community of goods, though in use among the Essenes and early Christians, is impracticable. Tindal quotes a great many texts for various purposes which are not found in Voltaire, and Voltaire has found many more for specific applications which are not found in Tindal. The criticisms are such as might naturally arise from their common deistic point of view in working over the same material. But that Voltaire was directly influenced by Tindal in his criticisms of the New Testament is certain, although he very carefully avoided textual borrowings, and often used him as a starting point for greater endeavors.

Tindal inaugurated another type of criticism of the Scriptures in pointing out the ignorance of the supposedly inspired authors in physics. The creation of the rainbow is explained in Genesis because people did not understand what caused it. More important still, Tindal attacks Christ's parable that a seed must die

---

[80] *Op. cit.*, pp. 300, 301.   [81] *Ibid.*, p. 305.
[82] *Ibid.*, p. 307.

before it could bring forth fruit. "There is scarce a countryman so ignorant," he says, "as not to know, that if the seed thrown into the earth is killed by drought, or dies by any other accident, it never rises."[83] This is the example picked out of many by Tindal to prove that we must depend on our reason in matters of religion, and it was the principal illustration chosen by Voltaire to prove that Jesus never claimed to teach us physics. Voltaire devotes a page of criticism to the parable of the seed in his *Histoire sommaire des quatre évangiles,* with text in Greek and in French, beginning thus: "Les critiques prétendent que Jésus et tous ses disciples ont toujours ignoré la manière dont toutes les semences germent dans la terre."[84] One is not surprised to find biblical cosmology attacked in both authors, but the emphasis placed by both on this New Testament parable and its isolated use again suggest influence. The attack on the physics of the Scriptures was used very early by Voltaire in his *Remarques sur les Pensées de Pascal,* but Tindal's contribution was not added until 1739.[85]

Tindal's works were not translated into French, and it was suggested by l'abbé Guénée that Voltaire thus thought to delude his critics. Voltaire replied that he did not dare enter into the dispute over the authorship of the Pentateuch:

Il y a des choses qu'on dit hardiment en Angleterre, et qu'il serait dangereux peut-être de dire à Paris. On peut y jouer avec un prodigieux succès toutes les pièces du divin Shakespeare; mais on ne peut y professer toutes les découvertes de Newton.

C'est par la même circonspection que je ne vous parlerai ni du magistrat Collins, ni du maître ès arts Woolston, ni du lord Shaftesbury, ni du lord Bolingbroke, ni du célèbre Gordon, ni de ce fameux membre du parlement Trenchard,[86] ni du doyen Swift ni de tant d'autres grands génies anglais.

Quid de cumque viro, et cui dicas: *Sæpe caveto.*

[83] *Christianity as Old as Creation,* pp. 185, 186.

[84] XXX, 309. Tindal noted on the page referred to above that Paul had continued the error. Cf. XXV, 365; XXX, 4, 18; XI, 136, where Voltaire attributes the error to Paul.

[85] Lanson, *Lettres philosophiques,* II, 212.

[86] Gordon and Trenchard, often mentioned vaguely by Voltaire, were popular in France for their anticlerical writings, some of which were translated by d'Holbach. Voltaire possessed *Cato's Letters* and the *Independent Whig.*

J'ajoute: "Caveto in Gallia et in Hispania plus quam in Italia." Il est vrai qu'actuellement toutes ces disputes théologales ne font plus aucun effet en Angleterre, ni en Hollande, ni en aucun pays du Nord: on est assez sage pour les mépriser; un homme qui voudrait aujourd'hui expliquer certaines choses contradictoires ne serait que ridicule.[87]

Voltaire here admits the antiquity of the deistic controversy in England, and bemoans the slowness of the southern countries in lopping from their religion theological doctrines which were so contradictory to the light of reason. Guénée made the mistake of charging to Tindal Voltaire's borrowings concerning David from Annet. Voltaire, in *Un chrétien contre six juifs* (1776), takes the occasion to deny his knowledge of Tindal:

Vous ajoutez que l'Anglais Tindal a prétendu que David avait dansé tout nu devant l'arche. Je n'ai point lu Tindal: je le condamne s'il l'a dit. . . . etc.

Unfortunately for Voltaire's veracity, both the internal evidence and Voltaire's marked copy of Tindal's work give him the lie.[88]

Tindal's *Christianity as Old as Creation* thus influenced Voltaire profoundly both in its constructive appeal to natural religion and the light of reason and in its destructive criticism of the Christian revelation. The English deist ends his work with the chapter already referred to, in which he defends the deists against Clarke, and applies Clarke's doctrines to the problem of original sin. We have suggested that this was a possible source for Voltaire's poor opinion of Clarke as a theologian, for Tindal has ably shown that Clarke's philosophy is contradictory to his theology. In supporting his thesis of the sufficiency of the light of nature in matters of reason, Tindal was the first English deist to attack the Scriptures in detail from the point of view of morality, and this was one of Voltaire's most favored methods. Striking similarities in details and associations of ideas in their respective treatments of the cruelties of the Jews and of the coarseness of the prophets suggest very strongly a direct influence from Tindal to Voltaire, an influence accompanied by a large amount of material. Finally, Tindal's comparisons between the Old and New Testa-

[87] XXIX, 513–514.   [88] *Ibid.*, p. 540.

ments, his method of transition from one to the other, and his strictures on the teachings of Jesus gave Voltaire at least the inspiration and the framework for much similar criticism. Voltaire's markers in the copy of Tindal's work now at Leningrad confirm these findings. He labored hard to conceal his sources, and textual borrowings are not to be expected; but the influence, general and evasive during the formative years, becomes apparent and marked in Voltaire's first overt attacks and continues through to his final productions.

CHAPTER VI

CHUBB AND BOLINGBROKE: MINOR INFLUENCES

THOMAS CHUBB, the humble artisan, and the haughty Lord Bolingbroke may be conveniently classed together as minor influences on Voltaire's deistic thought and works. Chubb was of great importance to the deistic movement as a constructive deist and a champion of the light of nature among the working classes. But as biblical critic, he wrote little of importance. A reading of his voluminous tracts alone convinces one that Voltaire never set for himself that task. In regard to Bolingbroke's works, Voltaire made the effort, but with little reward. By his own admission, confirmed by examination, he found little fruit in the midst of an abundance of leaves.

Voltaire possessed none of Chubb's works during the most productive period of his deistic activity at Ferney. Yet in the early period of metaphysical researches he read some few of Chubb's tracts in French translation. In 1736 he wrote to Thiériot:

Vous aurez incessamment, mon petit Mersenne, votre Descartes et votre Chubb. Il n'y a pas grand'chose à prendre ni dans l'un ni dans l'autre. Chubb dit longuement une petite partie des choses que sait tout honnête homme.[1]

It was probably due to a dictionary influence rather than to first-hand knowledge that Voltaire, thirty years later, classed Chubb among the critical deists.

Chubb began his career as a glover and later gained his livelihood as a tallow chandler. He received a debating society education, knowing no other language than English, and had a debating society mind. Even so, he could match his wits against Waterland and other divines, many of whom were too lazy to exercise their minds at all, and could protect themselves easily

[1] XXXIV, 141.

with the shield of authority. As a constructive deist, he probably had some influence on Tindal, while his later critical deism was a weak imitation of Toland, Tindal, Woolston, and Annet.

Chubb first came into prominence as the author of a tract entitled *The Supremacy of the Father asserted,* in 1715. Encouraged by the reception of this work, he published approximately two tracts a year until his death in 1747. He admitted that men of free inquiry were obliged to change their minds as the perception of the evidence changed.[2] His position, barring the usual exaggeration, has been neatly summed up by one of his opponents:

> He went from bad to Worse; from mistaking and perverting, to open abuse and burlesquing of Scripture; from a pretended regard to it, to an avowed Disregard of all. In short, he set out an Arian only, but ended a Deist, I had almost said, Atheist. You need but compare his first with some of his last Pieces, to be fully convinced of this. It will be easy to judge of the Intermediates by the Extreams. In his first he talks wickedly for God, and in his last as wickedly against Him.[3]

The last statement is true only in so far as Chubb could not finally reconcile the Jehovah of the Jews with the Supreme Being of the deists.

A few titles from the collected tracts of the first fifteen years[4] will illustrate the nature of Chubb's work and explain why Voltaire was little interested therein: *An Enquiry concerning Prayer,* in which it is argued that God was not arbitrary and would not change his immutable laws for individual bequests, but that prayer might have its good effects on the individual praying; *A Vindication of God's Moral Character, as to the Cause and Origin of Evil, both Natural and Moral; Human Nature vindicated,* in which it is shown that supernatural influences are unnecessary to salvation, and that the heathen might be saved; *The Glory of Christ,* where it is argued that the Christian salvation is the only proper expedient to take away divine displeasure; *Some short Reflexions on Virtue and Vice,* etc. Chubb considered himself profoundly grave and religious, and usually chose a text

---

[2] *Collection of Tracts* (London, 1730), in 4, preface.
[3] *Memoirs of Mr. T—C—* (London, 1747), p. 27.
[4] Collected in a *Collection of Tracts* (London, 1730).

or texts for his deistic sermons. He condemned the use of wit and levity against the Scriptures. The one tract which might be called antibiblical was *The Case of Abraham, with Regard to his Offering up Isaac in Sacrifice,* an anticlerical subject which interested him all his life, but did not take a truly critical form until much later. A French translation of several of these essays appeared in 1732, under the title, *Nouveaux Essais sur la Bonté de Dieu, la Liberté de l'homme et l'Origine du mal,* which Voltaire read in 1736[5] in preparation for his *Éléments de la philosophie de Newton.*

In 1739 Chubb published *The True Gospel of Jesus Christ asserted,* of which his enemies said that it sets us right on Christ and tells us what he ought to have done. In 1746 appeared four dissertations on Melchizedek, on Esau and Jacob, on Balaam, and on the expulsion of the Canaanites by Joshua; and in 1748, his *Posthumous Works,* containing remarks on the Scriptures, on Warburton's *Divine Legation,* and a farewell to his readers. In these works he has adopted the position of the more radical deists, with, however, more reverence and caution. His critical deism may be best studied directly in relation to Voltaire and the other deists.

Chubb's axioms with which he starts his debates were: that there is a natural and essential difference between good and evil which is evident to reason and the natural understanding of men; that man, as a moral agent, can choose between the good and evil thus made manifest; that God rewards or punishes men according to their free choice of good or evil. Here he not only differs from Collins but calls Collins' theory of determinism atheistic.[6] Voltaire followed Collins, but clung to the idea (as beneficial for others) of future reward and punishment. Although Chubb is the only deist who actively maintained this position, it cannot be said that Voltaire got such a common idea from him, rather than from Clarke. Yet this is the only point in Chubb's metaphysics which might have influenced him. Moreover, Chubb got into endless difficulties trying to square the essential goodness of God with man's God-given freedom to choose evil. The modern escape from the dilemma through "double-mindedness" had not yet been invented.

Chubb followed Toland in the belief that there was nothing mysterious in divine institutions, once the mysteries had been cleared by divine revelation, and that one could accept nothing on faith which was contrary to reason.[7] Voltaire was little interested in the details of this argument. Chubb finds many things in the Bible which are "incredible, and exceeding the bounds of belief,"[8] such as the history of the Amelekites, of Abraham, of Sodom and Gomorrah, of Jacob and Esau, of Rahab, of Joshua and the Canaanites, etc.[9] The influence of Tindal in the later works is evident. With Tindal, he finds that certain precepts of Jesus, such as "Love your enemies," cannot be carried out in society as then ordered.[10] Reason is the only guide to tell us which to take figuratively and which literally. But Chubb insists that such cruelties and immoralities should be granted to unbelievers as minor points which do not at all affect the general truth of Christianity.[11] He thus attempted to defend Christianity against Tindal, while Voltaire used Tindal as a starting point for further blasts. With Collins, Chubb refuses the miracles as proofs of the truth of Christianity.[12] But he defends religion against Collins and Tindal by stating that the God who showed his back parts to Moses could not have been the Supreme Being, but some delegated power.[13] At the close of his life, however, he was willing even to use the details of Woolston's miracles, often quoting Woolston's own words,[14] though he had condemned the use of wit and ridicule on questions of religion and on the Scriptures. The grave, ponderous Chubb had very little indeed in common with his French follower, who lumped him together with all the

[7] *Ibid.*, pp. 161 ff., 363.

[8] *Some Observations occasioned by the Opposition to Dr. Rundle's Election*, etc. (London, 1735), p. 22.

[9] See also, *Four Dissertations* (London, 1746), especially the *Enquiry* on Dr. Sherlock's *Thus far all is well*.

[10] *Posthumous Tracts* (London, 1748), pp. 294 ff.

[11] *Some Observations* (1735), p. 38; and the *True Gospel of Jesus Christ asserted* (1738), p. xii.

[12] *Collection of Tracts* (1730), p. 216, and *Discourse on Miracles* (London, 1741).

[13] "Farewell to his Readers," *Posthumous Tracts* (London, 1748), I, 198.

[14] *Ibid.*, II, 180 ff.

other deists as a brazen *incrédule.* Chubb's earnest desire was that unbelievers and skeptics should accept the Gospel in its primitive simplicity.[15] In the discussion of Toland, it was found that Voltaire was willing to admit no such distinction between primitive and latter-day Christianity.

When Chubb made original contributions to critical deism, he was not followed by Voltaire. Voltaire did not make use of his details concerning Abraham and the sacrifice of Isaac, Abraham and Melchizedec and the payment of tithes, or of the story of Jacob and Esau. Chubb was much abused by orthodox defenders, who realized his importance as advocate and vulgarizer of the pernicious doctrine of self-sufficiency,[16] inaugurated by Lord Herbert of Cherbury. For try as hard as he might, Chubb could finally leave no place for revelation, which was a mere republication of the religion of nature and moreover to be used with extreme care.[17] Nor could he see any excuse in reason for positive religious duties or for paying tithes to the Church for the sake of having the truth corrupted for gain. But Chubb was only incidentally a biblical critic. This was a field for scholars or for men with less reverence for the Scriptures.

We shall leave Chubb with Voltaire's second correct reference to him in his *Lettres . . . sur Rabelais, etc.* The article was very probably taken from a dictionary, with original comments from his early readings added. There is no reason to suspect, as Voltaire asserts, that Chubb wrote under a veil:

Thomas Chubb est un philosophe formé par la nature. La subtilité de son génie, dont il abusa, lui fit embrasser non-seulement le parti des sociniens, qui ne regardent Jésus-Christ que comme un homme, mais enfin celui des théistes rigides, qui reconnaissent un Dieu et n'admettent aucun mystère. Ses égarements sont méthodiques: il voudrait réunir tous les hommes dans une religion qu'il croit épurée parce qu'elle est simple. Le mot de christianisme est à chaque page dans ses divers ouvrages, mais la chose ne s'y trouve pas. Il ose penser que Jésus-Christ a été de la religion de Thomas Chubb; mais il n'est pas de la religion de Jésus-Christ. Un

---

[15] *Collection of Tracts* (1730), p. 408.
[16] See *Deism Revealed* (London, 1749), II, 368. The author asserts that Chubb borrowed so much from Tindal that some wondered which had written the *Posthumous Tracts;* II, 366.
[17] *Posthumous Tracts,* I, 292.

abus perpétuel des mots est le fondement de sa persuasion. Jésus-Christ a dit: Aimez Dieu et votre prochain, voilà toute la loi, voilà tout l'homme. Chubb s'en tient à ces paroles; il écarte tout le reste. Notre Sauveur lui paraît un philosophe comme Socrate, qui fut mis à mort comme lui pour avoir combattu les superstitions et les prêtres de son pays. D'ailleurs il a écrit avec retenue, il s'est couvert d'un voile. Les obscurités dans lesquelles il s'enveloppe lui ont donné plus de réputation que de lecteurs.[18]

Voltaire thus sums up with approximate accuracy Chubb's position and competence. In his long-winded debates, he had shown little originality and had written "what every true gentleman already knew." Voltaire could see no real excuse for writing thousands of dull pages on the law of nature which is engraved impartially in the hearts of all men. We may be sure that he read no more than Chubb's one volume which was early translated into French, and that he cared little for that.

No English deist has been more discussed in connection with Voltaire than Bolingbroke. For Bolingbroke was an important political figure, who had definite personal relations with Voltaire, and whose name appears with great frequency in Voltaire's works. Yet no other English deist was so falsely quoted by Voltaire, while Toland and Chubb alone, of the important figures in the movement, seem to have had less direct influence on the course of Voltaire's deistic criticism. Critics have spoken so long of Bolingbroke as master and of Voltaire as pupil that a tradition has been established, for which there seems to be little foundation in fact.[19]

The apparent necessity of accounting for this supposed influence has led, moreover, to exaggeration in the degree of intimacy existing between the two men. There are strong reasons to suspect that Bolingbroke, at first enthusiastic over Voltaire's genius as a poet, soon grew to dislike him personally and "kept him

[18] XXVI, 489.

[19] A portion of this chapter was previously published in the *Publications of the Modern Language Association* (September, 1927), XLII, 788–797, under the title "Bolingbroke and Voltaire—A Fictitious Influence." I have come to believe that "exaggerated" is the better adjective, although the exaggerations are largely based on fictions. Edouard Sonet, in the chapter on Bolingbroke in his *Voltaire et l'influence anglaise* (1926), has fallen into the traditional exaggerations, though with much commendable reserve and caution.

at a civil distance."[20] During Voltaire's brief visit at La Source, in December, 1722, his *Henriade* was warmly praised. He was inspired to write a flattering portrait of his host and even considered honoring him with the dedication of the poem. Bolingbroke would undoubtedly have been flattered, but was soon undeceived as to Voltaire's true intentions by Mme. de Ferriol, to whom he subsequently wrote: "Ce que vous me mandez de Voltaire et de ses projets est dans son caractère, et tout à fait probable; ce qu'il me mande y est tout à fait contraire. Je lui répondrai dans quelque temps d'ici, et je lui laisserai toute sa vie la satisfaction de croire qu'il me prend pour dupe avec un peu de verbiage."[21] This letter is dated December 28, 1725. It was during these three years that the intimacy between the two men appears at its height.[22] Pope, in a letter to Bolingbroke, in April, 1724, reviews Voltaire's epic poem which Bolingbroke had sent him, and judges Voltaire "worthy from his rational temper of that share of friendship and intimacy with which you honour him."[23] Voltaire was much impressed by Bolingbroke's erudition and by his discernment of the differing merits of French, English, and Italian poetry, an ideal which he endeavored to reach in his *Essay on Epick Poetry* and in his *Lettres philosophiques.* Lady Bolingbroke, too, tried to interest the Princess of Wales in Voltaire's behalf by sending her a copy of *Marianne.*[24]

By 1726, however, Bolingbroke appears to have lost interest in the young poet. Voltaire's first days in England have been the subject of much romancing, based largely on his own highly imaginative and untrustworthy account.[25] Until his return in August from his secret trip to Paris, "he had neither seen his English friends nor been to London."[26] Proceeding directly to London upon his return, he found himself bankrupt and Lord Bolingbroke away in the country, and expressed the evident

20 Walter Sichel, *Bolingbroke and his Times* (London, 1901), II, 167.

21 Desnoiresterres, *La jeunesse de Voltaire* (Paris, 1871), p. 369.

22 F. Baldensperger, "Voltaire anglophile avant son séjour d'Angleterre," *Revue de littérature comparée* (janvier–mars, 1929), pp. 46–51.

23 A. Ballantyne, *Voltaire's Visit to England* (London, 1893), p. 71.

24 Foulet, *Correspondance de Voltaire* (Paris, 1913), p. 30, n. 2.

25 *Œuvres* (éd. Moland), XXII, 18–22. Cf. Ballantyne, *op. cit.,* p. 35.

26 C. Chase, *The Young Voltaire* (New York, 1926), p. 94.

intention of retiring himself to the country to guard both his health and his pocketbook. Bolingbroke came to his aid neither then nor during the winter when he again complains of financial distress. Nevertheless, Voltaire blithely writes to Thiériot some two months later:

> I have seen often mylord and mylady Bolingbroke; I have found their affection still the same, even increased in proportion to my unhappiness; they offered me all, their money, their house; but I have refused all, because they are lords, and I have accepted all from Mr. Faulknear, because he is a single gentleman.[27]

Bolingbroke's biographer, Sichel, notes that Bolingbroke could never forget his royal blood. It was this spirit which had galled Voltaire so recently in France.

During the first winter, Voltaire spent the day occasionally in London and wrote letters from Bolingbroke's residence in Pall Mall, receiving his correspondence there as he was later to receive it also at Lord Peterborough's. He makes it plain, however, that this address was purely in the interest of security and expedition, and never intimates that he is established at Bolingbroke's house. It took him nearly two months to learn of Pope's accident, which occurred near Bolingbroke's country estate. There would seem to be little ground to postulate the intimate correspondence between Bolingbroke and Voltaire which M. Foulet assumes and of which he regrets the loss. Nor does it appear likely that the politic English lord, who refused to have his philosophical works published during his lifetime, found time to discuss freely his religious views with a young Frenchman whose integrity he had long before suspected and who had such influential friends in the opposing political party.

Sichel and Collins have charged that Voltaire was a paid spy in the service of the Whigs. M. Foulet has shown the lack of evidence connecting Voltaire with any of the collected documents. The unpleasant possibility still lingers, nor can it be banished by attempts to prove continued amicable relations between Voltaire and Bolingbroke's group. But Sichel's picture of Voltaire as a spy

---

[27] Foulet, *op. cit.*, p. 60. M. Foulet believes that "single gentleman" should read "simple gentleman."

at Bolingbroke's table at Dawley is one of pure, unfounded surmise.[28] If Voltaire had been admitted to the intimacy of this circle, it seems incredible that his letters would have passed by such an honor in silence. The evidence from the correspondence of Pope, Swift, and Bolingbroke is also conclusively negative. To prove Voltaire a spy at Dawley, it would seem necessary to prove first that he had ever been at Dawley.

If Voltaire saw Bolingbroke and Pope occasionally during his first winter in England, he appears to have seen them little or none after the incident of *The Occasional Letter* in the spring of 1727. The intense political antagonism in England, which he wrongly thought he could ignore, is enough in itself to explain the coldness that arose between him and Bolingbroke. His English notebook shows that his sympathies were with the Whigs, while his friendship with Hervey, who replied to *The Occasional Letter,* could not have pleased Bolingbroke. The following winter, we find him established at London, visiting Lord Peterborough, Walpole, Dodington, and many men of letters. He writes Swift in March, 1728, that he had not seen Pope all winter.[29] And Bolingbroke had given up his London residence.[30] Later in the year, he writes to Bolingbroke's secretary to inquire after Lady Bolingbroke's health.[31] It is true that Bolingbroke, with magnanimous aloofness, subscribed for twenty copies of the *Henriade.* M. Foulet has shown convincingly that Voltaire left England in the fall of 1728,[32] reducing his exile in England to slightly more than two years. In November, 1728, Lord Peterborough wrote: "It is as hard to account for our politics as for Mr. Voltaire's resolutions and conduct"; though he blames England and the English for Voltaire's sudden departure, thereby disproving one of the infamous tales that grew up concerning

---

[28] "But to the mind's eye another scene arises." *Op. cit.,* II, 216. Sichel's imagination leads him even to see Voltaire drinking to the point of indiscretion.

[29] Foulet, *op. cit.,* p. 124.   [30] *Ibid.,* p. 135.

[31] *Ibid.,* p. 165.

[32] *Ibid.,* Appendix VII. Late in life, Voltaire was fond of saying that he had lived three years in England with Lord and Lady Bolingbroke, though in the dedication of *Brutus,* he speaks of his two years of study of the English language in England. His word is not to be trusted. It is likewise more than doubtful that he had lived, as he said, three months with Swift at Lord Peterborough's. See S. Goulding, *Swift en France* (Paris, 1924), p. 45, and Ballantyne, *op. cit.,* pp. 52, 55.

his relations with the French poet.[33] In 1731 Bolingbroke was honored with the dedication of *Brutus*. Appearances had to be kept up, and Voltaire admired Bolingbroke's literary judgments, if not his political beliefs. In 1732 a manifestly unfair article appeared in the *London Journal* of May 6, which states that Voltaire, "having enrich'd himself with our contributions, behaved so ill that he was refused admittance into those Noblemen's and Gentlemen's Families in which he had been received with great marks of Favour and Distinction."[34] There must have been some foundation in fact for this and later tales, even if we adopt Lord Peterborough's judgment that the break was the fault of the noblemen, and not Voltaire's. Finally, Bolingbroke was in France from 1735 to 1742, and it is more than strange that the two men never met during those years, unless something serious had come between them. Whether justly or not, Bolingbroke acted as if he believed in Voltaire's duplicity. And as for Voltaire, if he had played up his friendship for his lordship for more than it was worth, he took beautiful revenge, some forty years later, in attributing to his English friend one of his most virulent attacks on Christianity, the *Examen important de milord Bolingbroke,* and in including him invariably in his lists of *incrédules.*

Voltaire very cleverly put critics off the scent by his gratuitous references to Bolingbroke. From Villemain to Aldington, one finds the practically unanimous opinion that Voltaire borrowed much from and gave little thanks to his English acquaintance. Churton Collins writes again, "Most probably Voltaire owed infinitely more to Bolingbroke than to all the other English deists put together";[35] and Sichel, that Bolingbroke's literary genius "left an undying imprint on Pope and Voltaire."[36] Luckily such was not the case in regard to Voltaire. In his thesis *Voltaire et Bolingbroke: étude comparative sur leurs idées philosophiques et religieuses,*[37] Hurn has shown, what he did not intend and what he did not adequately admit, even in his conclusion, that Voltaire

---

[33] Ballantyne, *op. cit.,* pp. 232–234.
[34] Lanson, *Lettres philosophiques,* II, 254, n. 5.
[35] *Voltaire, Montesquieu and Rousseau in England* (London, 1908), pp. 61–62.
[36] *Op. cit.,* I, 2.
[37] *Thèse pour le Doctorat d'Université,* Paris, 1915.

borrowed nothing textually from Bolingbroke's works and that a direct borrowing of ideas was extremely problematical. In fact, their ideas were generally so divergent that no attempt could satisfactorily bring them together. When Sherlock visited Voltaire at Ferney, the latter pointed to Bolingbroke's volumes on his shelves. "Were you personally acquainted with Bolingbroke?" asked Sherlock. "Yes," replied Voltaire, "his face was imposing and so was his voice; in his works there are many leaves, and little fruit; distorted expressions, and periods intolerably long."[38]

It has been often argued that Bolingbroke formed Voltaire the historian. Collins, in his early studies on the two men, has given definite instances of direct influence. Some of these are chronologically impossible, and all of them very improbable in the light of a study of Voltaire's more certain sources. At La Source, Voltaire had admired Bolingbroke's knowledge of ancient and modern history. But the *Letters on the Study of History,* translated by Barbeu Du Bourg with Bolingbroke's permission in 1741, were published only after the author's death, in 1752. Voltaire read them at Berlin that same year, and at Frederick's instigation wrote a *Défense de milord Bolingbroke,* using the controversy to state his own theories concerning the Pentateuch, and ironically emphasizing the necessity of a complete separation of faith and reason. Some influence here there undoubtedly was, though it would be folly to assert that Bolingbroke, in 1752 or even in 1722, upset Voltaire's faith in the Pentateuch. With the temporary liberty of speech afforded by Frederick's patronage, Voltaire was already working on *Abraham* and other articles for his *Dictionnaire philosophique,* which were to wait another decade before they could be safely published. Voltaire's own *Pyrrhonisme de l'histoire* shows no use of Bolingbroke's *Letters,* but points rather to Bayle, to La Mothe le Vayer's *Du peu de certitude qu'il y a dans l'histoire,* and to Fleury's *Discours sur l'histoire ecclésiastique,* which Voltaire judged far superior to Fleury's history itself. Considering the great influence of Bayle on all the English deists, it is not difficult to understand Collins' error. Moreover, there is

---

[38] Cf. Voltaire, *Œuvres,* XX, 90; XXXIX, 569; XL, 193, for adverse criticisms on Bolingbroke's works.

nothing in all Bolingbroke's pedantic works or thought that gives any intimation of the freshness and originality of Voltaire's *Histoire de Charles XII*. Chesterfield remarked: "Lord Bolingbroke has just taught me how history should be read; Voltaire shows me how it should be written."[39] The *Siècle de Louis XIV* was published before Bolingbroke's *Letters* saw the light of day.

Voltaire appears to have been jealous of the privilege of translation accorded to Du Bourg. The notes in his copy of the work, now at Leningrad, show also that he was infuriated by the attacks on his historical veracity in the translator's preface. Du Bourg objected that the Marquis de Villette, first husband of Lady Bolingbroke, was not the nephew of Mme. de Maintenon, and still less was his wife the niece, adding that Voltaire, having had "occasion to see" Lady Bolingbroke should have known better. Voltaire defends himself by means of marginal notes: "petit neveu, ainsi l'appelle sa nièce selon lui, ainsi que Mme. de Caylus;" and again, "occasion de voir! j'ai passé trois ans avec eux." Du Bourg attacks Voltaire's portrait of Mme. de Maintenon as written "dans un goût tout neuf," for which Voltaire has substituted in a note "tout vrai." Enraged by Du Bourg's doubts as to the truth of his remarks on Fénelon, he writes, "j'en ai la preuve, et je vous donnerai sur les doigts." But here Voltaire is attacking only the translator. That he was pleased with the *Lettres sur l'histoire*, or at least with the doubts expressed concerning the Pentateuch, is witnessed in a letter to d'Argental, in 1754:

> Ce qu'il y a de plus hardi dans ses *Lettres sur l'histoire* est ce qu'il y a de meilleur: aussi est-ce la seule chose qu'on ait critiquée. Les Anglais paraissent faits pour nous apprendre à penser.[40]

Bolingbroke's *Secret Memoirs,* translated in 1754, were purely historical, with no relation to deism. In that same year, Voltaire read them and cited from them and disliked them immensely, as is shown by his correspondence with d'Argental:[41]

> Que je suis mécontent des *Mémoires secrets de milord Bolingbroke!* Je voudrais qu'ils fussent si secrets que personne ne les eût jamais vus. Je ne

[39] Cited by R. Aldington, *Voltaire* (1925), p. 131.
[40] XXXVIII, 206.   [41] *Ibid.*, pp. 206, 211.

trouve qu'obscurités dans son style comme dans sa conduite. On a rendu un mauvais service à sa mémoire d'imprimer cette rapsodie; du moins c'est mon avis, et je le hasarde avec vous, parce que, si je m'abuse, vous me détromperez.

The English notebook speaks slightingly of Bolingbroke's character and personality;[42] here one finds the beginnings of Voltaire's disillusionment in the printed works of the object of his youthful admiration at La Source. Bolingbroke's influence in forming Voltaire, the historian, may be reduced almost entirely to that early hero worship, and its importance will be variously estimated.[43]

Voltaire's disillusionment was completed some years later, in 1758 and 1759, when he read Bolingbroke's *Philosophical Works*.[44] His remark that he found in Bolingbroke many leaves and little fruit was not a mere witticism, but the result of a patient reading of Bolingbroke's discursive, long-winded, pedantic, undigested *Essays*. In the volumes at Leningrad, Voltaire has left an abundance of markers and stickers which indicate his patient search, and which reveal, where other evidence is lacking, the reactions of his mind to Bolingbroke's printed word. The essays deal mainly with metaphysical problems, though much incidental support is given to the historical and moral argument against Christianity. It is strikingly evident that Voltaire ignored the metaphysics which was not at all to his taste, but gleefully welcomed the English lord into the band of *incrédules* who had helped to weaken the pernicious hold of the infamous established religion.

In the Mallet edition of the *Philosophical Works* used by Voltaire, the first four volumes and a half contain the *Letters* or *Essays* addressed to Pope, followed and continued by the *Fragments or Minutes of Essays*. The other works in the fifth volume are the *Substance of some Letters to M. de Pouilly* and a *Letter occasioned by one of Archbishop Tillotson's Sermons*. Voltaire possessed also the introductory letter to the *Essays* addressed to Pope, which was separately translated and published in France in

---

[42] "Voltaire's English Notebook," *Modern Philology*, XXVI (February, 1929), 318.
[43] Cf. F. Baldensperger, *op. cit.*, pp. 33–34.
[44] Mallet edition, London, 1754–55, 5 vols. in 8. Notes will refer to this edition unless otherwise stated.

1766. Voltaire has left but one marker in this copy indicating a quotation from Foster, "Où le mystère commence, la religion finit."[45] Bolingbroke's point of view is stated in the concluding lines of the letter:

> It remains, then, that we apply ourselves to the study of the first philosophy without any other guides than the works, and the word of God. In natural religion the clergy are unnecessary, in revealed they are dangerous, guides.[46]

The first long *Essay* to Pope concerns the nature, extent, and reality of human knowledge. Voltaire left no markers, showing that he was not at all interested in the main discussion nor in the incidental information. Twenty-five years had elapsed since his own *Lettres philosophiques* and *Traité de métaphysique*. That is why he seems to have passed rapidly over points that might otherwise have compelled his attention, such as Bolingbroke's recommendation of the learned ignorance of Newton rather than the ignorant learning of Descartes and Leibnitz, his praise of Bacon as the dispeller of the imaginative fictions of the scholastics, his explanation of the theist's demonstration of the existence of one supreme, infinite, all perfect being, and his confirmation of the ignorance of philosophers concerning matter and the soul. Bolingbroke might have borrowed here from Voltaire, but hardly Voltaire from Bolingbroke.

The second *Essay* concerns the folly and presumption of philosophers, the rise and progress of their boasted science, the propagation of error and superstition, and the attempts to reform the abuses of human reason. Bolingbroke follows Bacon in his attack on the philosophies of Plato and Aristotle. Two passages out of four marked in this essay by Voltaire are striking enough to warrant quotation:

> That arts and sciences travelled from the east to the west, from Chaldea to Egypt, and from Egypt to Greece, has been a received opinion.[47]

---

[45] *Lettre de Mylord Bolingbroke, servant d'introduction à ses Lettres philosophiques, à M. Pope* (s. l. 1766) pp. 74–75.

[46] Bolingbroke, *Works* (Philadelphia, 1841), III, 64. This letter did not appear in the Mallet edition.

[47] *Philosophical Works*, I, 290.

The second passage appears at first sight to mean much more than it actually says:

> In a word, can he be less mad, who boasts a revelation superadded to reason, to supply the defects of this, too, at the same time? This is madness, or there is no such thing incident to our nature: and into this kind of madness the greatest genii have been the most apt to fall: a St. Paul, profound in cabalistical learning; a St. Austin, deep read in Plato; a father Malbranche, and a bishop of Cloyne.[48]

The third *Essay* deals with the *Rise and Progress of Monotheism, that first and great principle of natural theology, or the first philosophy*. Bolingbroke attempts to prove that a belief in one supreme being was held by other peoples besides the Jews, and continuously attacks Locke's *Reasonableness of Christianity,* in which Locke blindly accepts Jewish history. Voltaire has left markers, often accompanied by stickers to indicate exact passages, showing his interest in monotheism among the Egyptians before the time of Abraham[49] and among the Chinese,[50] and in the ridiculous idea that Seth alone brought down the true God to Christ and the modern world.[51] When Voltaire has discussed similar ideas, his sources are always much wider, and a textual influence from Bolingbroke is never found. Considered in relation to the vast amount of his reading, the general influence must also have been slight. His library, for instance, contains many volumes with many annotations on Confucius and the Chinese. He chose to ignore almost entirely, however, the religious ideas of his "grand homme," Locke. His very brief comments were that the *Reasonableness of Christianity* was really a new religion,[52] that it was a bad book,[53] that in it Locke had degraded his understanding,[54] and that its lack of influence was proof of the incompatibility of Christianity and reason.[55] His copy of the work contains one marker only, while the *Essai sur l'entendement humain* is abundantly supplied.

The fourth *Essay* concerns authority in matters of religion.

---

[48] *Philosophical Works,* II, 140–141.
[49] *Ibid.,* II, 170, 179, 183.
[50] *Ibid.,* II, 188.
[51] *Ibid.,* II, 195.
[52] "Voltaire's English Notebook," *Modern Philology,* XXVI (February, 1929), 324.
[53] XXXII, 462.
[54] XX, 230.
[55] XXVI, 550–551.

Voltaire's markers show that he read this carefully. Bolingbroke's style seems once to have struck him:

> They who pretend to face, like so many intellectual eagles, the sun of eternal wisdom, and to see in that abyss of splendor, are so truly metaphysical madmen, that he who attends to them, and relies on them, must be mad likewise.[56]

Possibly Voltaire was thinking, when he read this passage, of the long distant past when he himself had followed Clarke into that same abyss.[57] Another marked passage deals with the unsociable, cruel, rebellious, persecuting nature of the Jews, who "thought themselves authorized by their religion to commit such barbarities as even they perhaps, if they had had no religion, would not have committed."[58] Other markers indicate passages on the corruption of Christianity by theology, on Cicero's ridicule of the fear of hell, on bishops who presumed to change the very nature of virtue and vice;[59] with many on the ceremonies of communion and baptism, and a marker on which is written a quotation from Athanasius, "conjungimur deitate."[60] After a marker indicating St. Paul's trifling and his corruption of pure Christianity,[61] we find a second note in Voltaire's hand; "women silent allow'd to pray."[62] The rest of the markers in the long essay refer chiefly to opinions and quotations from the Church fathers, none of which are found in Voltaire's works, save Irenæus' explanation of the four gospels from the four parts of the world and the four cardinal winds,[63] and on this subject Voltaire, who used Fabricius, had sources much more complete than Bolingbroke. Voltaire also marked passages which heaped ridicule upon the miracle of the Eucharist, and upon transubstantiation and consubstantiation. Nor did he fail to place a sticker beside the sentence: "They conjured their God into a wafer."[64] He had written down a naughty little story

---

[56] *Op. cit.*, II, 247–248. Voltaire refers to Locke as an intellectual eagle in a passage referred to above (XX, 230).

[57] "Clarke sautait dans l'abîme et j'osai l'y suivre." XXIII, 194.

[58] *Op. cit.*, II, 284.   [59] *Ibid.*, II, 284, 286, 300.

[60] *Ibid.*, II, 312, 313, 315.   [61] *Ibid.*, II, 346.

[62] *Ibid.*, II, 352–353.   [63] *Ibid.*, III, 37.

[64] *Ibid.*, III, 287.

on that point thirty years earlier in his English notebook.[65] He was interested also in the statement that the belief in the future state of rewards and punishments came from the Egyptians and not from Moses.[66] Collins and other deists had emphasized this point, and Warburton, in his *Divine Legation of Moses,* had developed it in such a peculiar and compromising way as to make him the butt of Voltaire's wit.

Voltaire's markers in the *Fragments or Minutes of Essays* are scarce and bunched, often skipping a hundred pages at a time. Bolingbroke abandons Locke, and attacks Clarke's *Evidences of natural and revealed Religion.* Voltaire again was wisely not interested in Bolingbroke's metaphysics, but continues to show an interest in incidental passages. A few which present similarities to Voltaire's thought may be quoted:

> One law of nature forbids murder, as well as one law of the decalogue [but] the whole system of the law of Moses . . . was founded on murder.[67]
>
> Agreeable sensations, the series whereof constitutes happiness, must arise from health of body, tranquillity of mind, and a competency of wealth.[68]

(Voltaire wrote later that he had seen this aristocratic, optimistic lord "rongé de chagrins.")

> He will have mercy on whom he will have mercy, and whom he wills, he hardens.[69]
>
> The most barbarous nations had the most barbarous deities generally, and the gods seem to have been civilized no faster than their adorers were. . . .[70]

The marked passages become, if possible, more and more irrelevant to Bolingbroke's main discussion, the thread of which Voltaire, if he had picked it up at all, had long since lost.

In the *Substance of some Letters to M. de Pouilly,* Bolingbroke argues that the world began, and in this simple way he overthrows the atheistic position. The argument is weak and puerile,

---

[65] "Voltaire's English Notebook," *Modern Philology,* XXVI (February, 1929), 315.
[66] *Op. cit.,* II, 377. Both marker and sticker.
[67] *Ibid.,* IV, 138.   [68] *Ibid.,* V, 9.
[69] *Ibid.,* V, 161.   [70] *Ibid.,* V, 171–172.

while Bolingbroke characteristically pities his antagonist for his blindness and obstinacy in not accepting it. Rarely has a more presumptuous writer attacked others so roundly for presumption. Voltaire was reasoning more ably on the existence of God long before Bolingbroke's works were published. His one marker in the work refers to an incident concerning Sommonocodom[71] for which he never found use in his own works.

If he had not had better sources elsewhere, Voltaire might have used much from Bolingbroke's brief *Letter occasioned by one of Archbishop Tillotson's Sermons*. His four markers do not even hit the passages which might be thought the most interesting for his purposes. The first marker and sticker shows his delight in Bolingbroke's strong language against divines:

> These orthodox bullies affect to triumph over men who employ but a part of their strength; tire them by unjust reflections, and, often, by the foulest language.[72]

The second marker appears to refer to the bare statement that Moses knew nothing of immortality, and that Solomon decides against it;[73] the third refers slightingly to Jacob's conditional engagement with God.[74] The final marker is found between two of the most antibiblical pages in Bolingbroke's works, in which he briefly discusses Moses, the creation of day and night before that of the sun and the moon, the unworthy notions entertained concerning the Supreme Being, and the ridiculous, trifling story of Eve and the serpent.[75]

It would be difficult to follow Voltaire through these volumes without agreeing with him emphatically that they contained many leaves and little fruit. From the comparative carefulness of his search, it is evident that he expected to find much more than he actually found. He gave Bolingbroke at least a fair chance to speak for himself, and cannot be blamed if he arrived at the con-

---

[71] *Philosophical Works,* V, 234.

[72] *Ibid.,* V, 335. Voltaire had written in English to Falkener in 1752: "I hope, my dear and worthy friend, my worthy Englishman, you have received mylord Bolingbroke's vindication against priests, whom I have hated, hate, and I shall hate 'till doomsday." (XXXVII, 527–528.)

[73] *Ibid.,* V, 356.   [74] *Ibid.,* V, 358.

[75] *Ibid.,* V, 370–371.

clusion that Voltaire could speak much more effectively for him. With Voltaire's other certain sources in mind, Bolingbroke's contribution is far from impressive.

Whether or not Bolingbroke's philosophy, or metaphysics, was worth borrowing from, Voltaire paid almost no attention to it. If both believed in one God, Bolingbroke accepted the methods of Descartes, in spite of his condemnation of them, for the proof of his existence, while Voltaire refers continually to Clarke and Newton. Bolingbroke believed firmly in the freedom of the will, and thought that determinism overturned the whole moral order. Voltaire, on the other hand, if he hesitated some years between Clarke and Collins, finally denied with the latter both free will and the danger of determinism. On the question of the goodness of God, Bolingbroke adopted the method of Malebranche to explain away evil, and decided that "l'ensemble de l'univers est le meilleur des mondes possibles," no matter how much the individual might suffer. Voltaire answered brilliantly the pedantic and frivolously optimistic arguments of Bolingbroke with his *Candide;* and as late as 1772, in his *Il faut prendre un parti,* he writes: "J'ai vu Bolingbroke rongé de chagrins et de rage . . . qu'on me donne du moins des heureux qui me disent: *Tout est bien.*"[76] Voltaire and not Bolingbroke followed through, with Collins, to their logical conclusions the remarks of Locke on the soul and on matter. Since their thought was at variance on such important philosophical questions as these, it matters little that both praised Locke and condemned Plato. In all Bolingbroke's philosophical works, Voltaire is never once mentioned, while, to fill his cup of bitterness to overflowing Maupertuis is treated at some length, and is called "a very ingenious man, a very good philosopher, and one with whom I have long been acquainted."[77] The "master and pupil" evidently despised each other as philosophers.

The greatest point of resemblance between Bolingbroke and Voltaire is their common use of the historical argument against the authority and divine inspiration of the Old Testament. Yet the similarities are general and are due often to the use of com-

[76] XXVIII, 535–536; cf. XVII, 584.   [77] *Op. cit.,* II, 250.

mon sources, such as the dissertations on Aristeas and on the Phenician Sanchoniathon by Van Dale, whom Voltaire praises, preferring him to Fontenelle, his superficial popularizer. Bolingbroke was usually willing to assume that Moses was the author of the Pentateuch, but stressed the lack of collateral evidence to support his authority. He pointed out that the documents concerning the creation and the flood were already ancient when Moses wrote his history, and had not therefore the value of a contemporary document. "Another condition of the authenticity of any human history . . . is," he wrote, "that it contain nothing repugnant to the experience of mankind."[78] But the Pentateuch and the Old Testament are founded on nothing but incredible anecdotes,

like the tales of our nurses. We may laugh at Don Quixote as long as we please, for reading romances till he believed them to be true histories, and for quoting archbishop Turpin with solemnity; but when we speak of the Pentateuch, as of authentic history, and quote Moses, as solemnly as he did Turpin, are we much less mad than he was?[79]

Writing on the same subject in his *Examen important,* Voltaire has kept the epigrammatic style, but he has not used the details nor in any way followed the steps of Bolingbroke's argument. The following passages present the closest approach:

Quelqu'un a dit que *l'Orlando furioso* et *Don Quichotte* sont des livres de géométrie en comparaison des livres hébreux. [And again,] Il est bien sûr que je ferais enfermer à Bedlam un homme qui écrirait aujourd'hui de pareilles extravagances.[80]

But Voltaire was generally much more ambitious, much more radical than Bolingbroke in these, his most daring remarks. Voltaire's customary procedure was first to question whether or not Moses actually existed, then to prove that if he did exist, he could not possibly have written the Pentateuch in the desert, and finally, as above, that if he did write such extravagances, he only proved himself a madman. Voltaire is much nearer in treatment

[78] *Philosophical Works,* V, 343.

[79] *Ibid.,* V, 343-344. It is surprising to find no markers left by Voltaire at these pages of the *Letter occasioned by one of Archbishop Tillotson's Sermons.*

[80] XXVI, 204, 208.

and in style to that most radical of English deists, Peter Annet, and the sources of his criticisms of the Pentateuch were far wider and much more definite than anything he could find in Bolingbroke.

Hurn has collected the common material on the Old Testament in his comparative study of the philosophical and religious ideas of Bolingbroke and Voltaire. After a study of the influence of another English deist, Matthew Tindal, Hurn's work only confirms the evidence that Voltaire found little fruit in Bolingbroke, and, moreover, his references are apt to be misleading. For example, he writes: "Ils trouvent ridicule l'histoire des aventures d'Abraham et sa femme," with references to the works of both men.[81] But Bolingbroke merely writes: "The whole history, from Noah to Abraham, and from Abraham to the Exode, is a series of tales that would appear fit to amuse children alone,"[82] with no mention of Sarah. Hurn again refers to both writers a comparison between Joshua and Pizarro, but the words this time are Bolingbroke's, and Voltaire does not mention Pizarro; whereas, both Voltaire and Tindal were fond of comparing Aod and Ravaillac, Hebrew and French regicides. Moreover, Hurn has found no textual borrowings and proved no direct influence. Bolingbroke did not discuss the morals of the prophets, on which subject Tindal had an obvious influence on Voltaire.[83] To Voltaire's criticism of the Old Testament, Bolingbroke's only contributions may have been a stimulus to the search for collateral authority, and doubts merely expressed as to Moses' authorship of the Pentateuch, on both of which questions Voltaire had to find elsewhere the elaborate details of his arguments. On the New Testament, Bolingbroke was much more cautious. He thought that the remarks of cavillers should have little weight.[84] Voltaire's writing the *Examen important* under his name was therefore nothing short of preposterous. Bolingbroke believed indeed that Christianity would have fared better without the Gospel according to

[81] *Op. cit.*, p. 96 and n. 3.   [82] *Op. cit.*, V, 374.

[83] Voltaire's most frequent references to Bolingbroke's criticisms are nevertheless on this head. Cf. *table de matières*, Moland edition. His certain source was Tindal's *Christianity as Old as Creation*.

[84] *Op. cit.*, III, 18.

John and the later additions of the Church, and criticized Paul severely, but this was far from Voltaire's scathing criticism of the person of Christ, of the immorality of his teachings, of the absurdities of his miracles, and of the madness of his apostles. Bolingbroke accepted the New Testament miracles and even some of the Old. In view of Voltaire's use of Woolston, Collins, Tindal, Fabricius, Middleton, and Annet, there is no room here for Bolingbroke, except as he opened the way for Annet's much more radical criticism of Paul. The very *Examen important* contains a discussion of the miracles from Woolston and Middleton, the criticisms of Annet against Paul, the immoralities of the prophets from Tindal, and even Greek quoted from the *Codex Apocryphus* of Fabricius. It was reprinted in 1817 in Carlile's *Deist* as "attributed to Bolingbroke, but written by M. de Voltaire," and the Abbé Guénée early suspected that Bolingbroke had little or nothing to do with it.

Beuchot has pointed out occasionally in his notes that many of Voltaire's later references to Bolingbroke are rather to the supposed Bolingbroke of the *Examen important*. An even more flagrant instance of Voltaire's disregard for the truth is found in his article on Bolingbroke in the *Lettres . . . sur Rabelais, etc.* (1767), published some months later. Voltaire's purpose was plainly to throw the odium of his writings on English authorities, whether he used them or not. Of Bolingbroke he writes:

> On a publié après la mort du lord Bolingbroke quelques-uns de ses ouvrages plus violents encore que son *Recueil philosophique;* il y déploie une éloquence funeste. Personne n'a jamais écrit rien de plus fort: on voit qu'il avait la religion chrétienne en horreur. Il est triste qu'un si sublime génie ait voulu couper par la racine un arbre qu'il pouvait rendre très-utile en élarguant les branches, et en nettoyant sa mousse.[85]

It is even more regrettable that a Houdon did not catch the expression of Voltaire's countenance as he penned these lines, or that an Abbé Guénée did not explain his mental reservations as he thus exchanged rôles with his former English "friend."

It is to this Bolingbroke turned Voltaire that the crafty French philosopher refers constantly in his *Dieu et les hommes* and espe-

[85] XXVI, 488.

cially in his later works such as *La Bible enfin expliquée*. And although critics are agreed that the *Examen important* is at least a very distorted picture of Bolingbroke's thought, yet they still continue to be fooled by the very number of these false references, and form false conclusions on the esteem in which Voltaire held Bolingbroke, even to the point of refusing to take seriously the unpleasant incidents that occurred between the men and the not at all flattering estimate that Voltaire gave repeatedly of Bolingbroke's works, once that distinguished author was safely in his grave. When, in his *Histoire de l'établissement du christianisme*, Voltaire calls Bolingbroke "le théiste le plus déclaré,"[86] he is hardly thinking of Lord Bolingbroke, the English Tory, but rather of Voltaire, the author of the *Examen important*, whose style was so much superior. It required no little audacity to attribute this work to such a well-known man, whose complete philosophical works had been published posthumously and were causing no little stir in England. No one can maintain, however, that the ruse was not eminently successful.

Under cover of the name of Bolingbroke, Voltaire felt free to attack the established religion more rabidly than he had before dared. Some of his boldest criticisms occur in the *Examen important*. This liberty was much more important to him than the faithful quoting of Bolingbroke's milder criticisms. He had an efficacious means of covering his tracks, namely, a veritable smoke screen of English atmosphere. His only concession to Bolingbroke seems to have been a few sentences in the *avant-propos*, which begin:

> Je ne suis point de l'avis du "Whig indépendant," qui semble vouloir abolir tout sacerdoce, etc.[87]

Thereafter follows the atmosphere:

> Notre grand Newton, notre enchanteur Merlin, lady Blackacre . . . dans la salle de *common plays*, Bedlam, la maison des fous à Londres, nos écrivains de Grub-street, notre apothécaire Moore, qui met dans nos gazettes: *"Prenez mes pillules, gardez-vous des contrefaites,"* un *sir rever-*

---

[86] XXXI, 113.   [87] XXVI, 199.

end, en anglais, est un étron, les disciples de Fox contre les disciples de Brown, ces *contes du Tonneau,* etc.[88]

The same procedure is maintained in *Dieu et les hommes,* and many minor works attributed to Englishmen. Leslie Stephen thinks that Voltaire got from Bolingbroke a thousand epigrams. Yet such expressions were typical of English polemical works of the period. Many came directly from Woolston's *Discourses,* and Voltaire may well have gleaned some from the *Independent Whig,* or from Bolingbroke's *Craftsman,* which followed him to France. They have a journalistic flavor.

It would seem that the intimacy, both personal and intellectual, between Voltaire and Bolingbroke, has been greatly exaggerated. They were far apart on essential points of metaphysics. The similarity in their historical criticisms of the Old Testament is general and elusive. Voltaire certainly found his details elsewhere. On the New Testament and on the miracles, they again widely differed. Voltaire attributed much to Bolingbroke and never to anyone more falsely. Along with Toland, Collins, Woolston, Tindal, and Annet, Bolingbroke became confused in Voltaire's mind as the personification of a typified English *incrédule,* which, more often than not, was actually Voltaire himself. But Bolingbroke was a lord. His great gift to Voltaire, both in his lifetime and after his death, was his name.

[88] *Ibid.,* pp. 202, 204, 208, 217, 218, 227, 238, etc.

CHAPTER VII

CONYERS MIDDLETON AND THE CONTINUA-TION OF THE HISTORICAL ARGUMENT

CONYERS MIDDLETON took up the historical argument where Toland had left it. Leslie Stephen considers him one of the acutest writers of the time. Born in Yorkshire in 1683, he entered Trinity College, Cambridge, and became a fellow of that institution in 1706. In 1717 he received the degree of doctor of divinity from the hands of King George, and was later appointed principal librarian of the University of Cambridge. A large part of his life and writings was given over to polemics against Bentley and Waterland, and it was largely due to him that Bentley was deprived of his Cambridge degrees. He entered the deist controversy in 1731 with an answer to Waterland's abusive treatment of Tindal's *Christianity as old as Creation*, having published, two years before, his *Letter from Rome*. In 1740 he finished his *Life of Cicero*, which was translated into French by the Abbé Prévost and much praised by Voltaire.[1] In 1748 appeared his *Free Inquiry into the Miraculous Powers of the Christian Church*, in which he attempted to show there was no sufficient evidence to believe that such powers were continued after the days of the Apostles. In 1750, the year of his death, he published an attack on Bishop Sherlock's *Use and Intent of Prophecy*, which had been written in turn against Collins. Many of his most critical essays, such as his remarks on the biblical story of the creation, were left to be published posthumously with his collected works in 1752. A second edition of these *Miscellaneous Works* was published three years later, and Voltaire, in his article for the *Gazette littéraire*, May, 1764, speaks of the project of a third edition which never was carried out.[2]

1 VI, 210; XXV, 177; XXXVI, 292, etc.
2 XXV, 176.

Middleton [says Stephen] closes the deist controversy, for he explicitly challenges the assumption which characterizes, as we have seen, the whole school of apologists and their assailants—namely, the breach of continuity between sacred and prophane history—and he challenges it in such a way that evasion is impossible.[8]

Although constructive deism now found little credit in England, critical deism secured its philosophical victory with Middleton and Hume. Middleton's arguments remained unanswered because, it is assumed, they were unanswerable. Hume admitted that Middleton's work on the miracles was superior to his own essay on miracles which appeared the same year.[4] Middleton's inquiry had the direct effect of turning Gibbon to Catholicism, and later had a great influence on him in a contrary sense. The critical works of Middleton, says Stephen, were "amongst the most powerful agents in the intellectual development of the time."[5]

Like Toland, Middleton was careful not to attack the miracles of Christ and the Apostles, yet his enemies were not slow in inferring that he had left them rather flimsy support. Although he kept his ecclesiastical preferment to the end of his life, there has been some question of his sincerity in upholding Christianity. Even if the Christian religion were an imposture, he says, it is only reasonable to keep it as a tradition religion, which no state can do without.[6] In defending Cicero against Warburton's charges of inconsistency, he thinks it very natural and proper that Cicero should ridicule the auguries as a philosopher, and should recommend them as a politician.[7]

There seems little reason to suspect Middleton of insincerity. He was evidently firmly convinced that the salvation of the Church against the deists depended on its willingness to give over the dogma of the perpetual inspiration and infallibility of the sacred authors. It was chiefly against this assumption that the arguments of the critical deists were, and continue to be, valid. Unlike the other deists, Middleton had what he believed to be a

---

[8] *English Thought in the Eighteenth Century*, I, 269–270.
[4] *Ibid.*, I, 264. [5] *Ibid.*, I, 254.
[6] *Miscellaneous Works*, 2d ed. (London, 1755), 5 vols. in 8; III, 56.
[7] *Ibid.*, I, 56.

sensible solution to offer that would leave the victory in the camp of the Church.

That Voltaire read Middleton carefully is attested by the markers and stickers and occasional marginal notes which he left in his Middleton volumes. By means of these indications, we can also trace other borrowings which might otherwise be difficult to find, but which definitely establish Middleton as the source, sometimes complete, sometimes to be elaborated, of many of Voltaire's pages on the miracles, on the martyrs, on the Church fathers, on the lack of originality of Jewish customs, and on the general weakness of the authority of the Scriptures. Many of the marginal notes in English prove Voltaire's ability to think in English and reveal some of his interesting reactions on questions of religion.

Voltaire's chief article on Middleton was a brief review of his works which appeared in the *Gazette littéraire*,[8] May 9, 1764. The tone of the article is moderate and scholarly, showing how well Voltaire could adapt himself to his literary medium. He calls Middleton one of the most learned and one of the best writers in England, and devotes a paragraph each to his important works, the *Letter from Rome,* the *Free Inquiry into the Miraculous Powers of the Christian Church,* and the *Life of Cicero.* Of the first work he writes in part:

> Il a fait une dissertation pour prouver que plusieurs des cérémonies augustes de l'Eglise romaine avaient été pratiquées par les païens; Jurieu et plusieurs autres protestants s'étaient déjà exercés sur cet objet; mais que prouve-t-elle, sinon que l'Eglise a sanctifié des pratiques communes à beaucoup de religions? Toutes les cérémonies sont indifférentes par elles-mêmes; c'est l'objet et le motif qui les rendent saintes ou impies.

Voltaire declares here the same indifference, belied in other works, to the fact that most of the ceremonies and laws of the Hebrews were taken over from the Egyptians. Turning to the famous treatise on miracles, Voltaire states Middleton's belief that miracles had begun to wane as early as the second century, as they were becoming less and less necessary. He notes also Middleton's doubts of the visit of Peter to Rome, and his allegorical

[8] XXV, 176–178.

interpretation of the first chapter of Genesis, questions to which he will soon devote articles in his *Dictionnaire philosophique*. But Middleton writes with praiseworthy candor and moderation, virtues to be praised if not always to be imitated:

> Quoique par sa naissance, par sa profession, et par les serments qu'il avait prêtés à l'Etat et à l'université de Cambridge, dont il était membre, il fût ennemi de l'Eglise romaine, il n'en parle jamais ni avec dérision ni avec aigreur. Il examine les monuments de Rome ancienne et moderne, non-seulement en antiquaire, mais encore en philosophe qui sait combien les usages tiennent aux opinions et aux mœurs.[9]

The review continues on the same moderate and scholarly note to discuss the reception accorded to Middleton's *Life of Cicero*. But we must look elsewhere for Voltaire's many borrowings from Middleton, although his name will henceforth be rarely connected with his contributions.

Middleton's *Letter from Rome*[10] claimed to show, indeed, *the exact Conformity between Popery and Paganism, or the Religion of the Present Romans, derived from that of their Heathen Ancestors*. Voltaire read the French translation by Prévost,[11] and the prefatory discourse in the English original as it was reprinted in the *Miscellaneous Works*. Many interesting passages attracted Voltaire's attention, several of which were later incorporated in his own works. In the prefatory discourse, one of two markers indicates the Jesuit miracles in India,[12] the other Middleton's statement that judging from the nature and end of the popish miracles "they were all without exception, either wrought by wicked spirits, or forged by wicked men."[13] On a marker in the French translation,[14] he has written, "à Rome eau bénite aux chevaux," a reference to a superstition which Middleton reports to have witnessed. Again when Middleton discusses the error in reading an inscription through which a mountain, Soracte, became St. Oreste, Voltaire has written on a marker[15] the two

---

[9] *Ibid.*, p. 177. [10] London, 1729.
[11] Amsterdam, 1744.
[12] *Miscellaneous Works* (London, 1755), 5 vols. in 8; V, 68–69.
[13] *Ibid.*, V, 72–73.
[14] *Lettre écrite de Rome*, pp. 156–157. [15] *Ibid.*, pp. 196–197.

words, "Soracte, St. Oreste." Still another marked passage[16] refers to the similarity between the begging priests mentioned by Cicero and the modern begging friars. Finally, a marker[17] on which is written, "Cicéron de natura deo. vesca deo," refers to a quotation from Cicero concerning the heathen: "hommes stupides qui croient qu'ils mangent leur Dieu." Voltaire's use of this remark in his dictionary article, "Eucharistie," is interesting and enlightening:

> Vingt nations, dans cette partie du monde, ont en horreur le système de la transsubstantiation catholique. Elles crient que ce dogme est le dernier effort de la folie humaine. Elles attestent ce fameux passage de Cicéron, qui dit que les hommes ayant épuisé toutes les épouvantables démences dont ils sont capables, ne se sont point encore avisés de manger le dieu qu'ils adorent.[18]

Voltaire has carelessly added in a footnote: "Voyez la *Divination* de Cicéron," in spite of the correct reference which he himself wrote on the marker. But more remarkable than this, Middleton has now become "vingt nations." Voltaire used the quotation, but more modestly, in his *Philosophie de l'histoire,*[19] and again in his *Pyrrhonisme de l'histoire.*[20] Bayle had used it skilfully before him in a note in his article "Averroès,"[21] but this is again an example of Bayle's influence on Voltaire through the English deists.

A marker in the English edition leads us to another much-used source of Voltaire's criticism. Middleton discusses the cessation of the miraculous power of the gift of tongues in modern times:

> Yet St. Xaverius himself, the Apostle of the Indies, and one of their great Saints and workers of miracles, laments, in several of his letters, the insuperable difficulties, which he had to struggle with in his Mission, and his incapacity of doing any good in those countries, for the want of this gift. And in Japan particularly, "God grant," says he, "that I may soon learn their language, so as to be able to explane things divine, and do some service at last to the Christian cause. For at present, indeed, I am nothing better than a statue among them. . . ."[22]

[16] *Lettre écrite de Rome,* pp. 268–269. [17] *Ibid.,* pp. 210–211.
[18] XIX, 37. [19] XI, 67.
[20] XXVII, 244. [21] See Voltaire, *Œuvres,* XI, 67, n. 1.
[22] *Op. cit.,* V, 69.

Voltaire translated this passage literally, with some omissions, in his article "Miracles" in 1764,[23] the year of his review of Middleton's works. Rather than give a reference to Middleton, Voltaire, as usual, gives the original reference, but garbles it, changing "Hospinian de Origin. Jesuitar. p. 230" to "Ospiniam, page 230." The passage occurs in the first section of the article, of which the last three pages are taken directly from Middleton, as will appear presently. However, Voltaire did not borrow servilely, but added ironical touches to his story of Xavier that were distinctly and delightfully his own:

> Cependant les jésuites ont écrit qu'il avait ressuscité huit morts: c'est beaucoup; mais il faut considérer qu'il les ressuscitait à six mille lieues d'ici. Il s'est trouvé depuis des gens qui ont prétendu que l'abolissement des jésuites en France est un beaucoup plus grand miracle que ceux de Xavier et d'Ignace.[24]

Voltaire's early doubts concerning Peter's visit to Rome were likewise confirmed by Middleton's *Letter from Rome*. In his review of Middleton's works, he writes: "Il embrasse et fortifie autant qu'il peut l'opinion de Scaliger, que saint Pierre n'est jamais venu à Rome."[25] Middleton indeed admits that many learned men have doubted this story, with references to Scaliger and Spanhemius, and shows further that there are no authentic monuments of the visit which a historian could accept.[26] Voltaire himself pushed the inquiry much further, and devoted a dictionary article to Peter's supposed visit.[27] Middleton's remark was his inspiration, but Scaliger and Spanhemius were among his sources.[28] The article above quoted gives the first mention chronologically of his often expressed doubts on this point.

The most important part of Middleton's *Miscellaneous Works* was the *Free Inquiry into the Miraculous Powers of the Early Christian Church*, "by which it is shewn that we have no sufficient reason to believe, upon the authority of the primitive Fathers, that any such powers were continued to the Church, after the

23 XX, 81.
24 *Ibid.*
25 XXV, 177.
26 *Op. cit.*, V, 86–88.
27 XX, 593–596. Much of this article was taken from the Codex of Fabricius and from the works of the Church Fathers.
28 See *ibid.*, p. 595 and note.

days of the apostles." Middleton was striving to weaken the authority of the early Fathers and to support his argument for the necessity of continuity between sacred and profane history. Attempts had been made by Dodwell and others to fix the cessation of miraculous powers in the fourth century of our era.[29] Whiston had stated "that these miraculous powers were totally withdrawn when the *Athanasian Heresy,* as he calls it, was established, and that as soon as the Church became *Athanasian, Antichristian,* and *Popish,* they ceased immediately and the devil lent it his own cheating and fatal powers in their stead."[30] Middleton would go back at least to the time of the Apostles, and suggests that Paul himself, instead of curing Timothy of his ailment, advised him to drink wine instead of water for his stomach's sake.[31] Voltaire, of course, was all-inclusive in his ridicule of miracles from the creation to his own day. He was nevertheless delighted to find this respectable English theologian attacking the Church Fathers on account of their fabulous stories of miracles and martyrdom. He did not abandon Middleton's work after his brief review in the *Gazette littéraire.* Six months later, in November, 1764, he wrote enthusiastically to d'Argental:

Croyez que Middleton, ce même Middleton qui a fait cette belle *Vie de Cicéron,* a fait un excellent ouvrage sur les miracles, qu'il nie tous, excepté ceux de notre Seigneur Jésus-Christ. C'est de cet illustre Middleton qu'on a traduit le conte du miracle de Gervais et de Protais, et celui du savetier de la ville d'Hippone. Remerciez Dieu de ce qu'il s'est trouvé à la fois tant de savants personnages qui tous ont contribué à démolir le trône de l'erreur, et à rendre les hommes plus raisonnables et plus gens de bien.[32]

And it was in his article "Miracles" of the same year that Voltaire himself transcribed these miracles, along with the miraculous death of Polycarp and many others, nearly three pages in the Moland edition, and, as usual, no credit is given to his source. Of the four sections of the completed article, the first which is largely from Middleton and the fourth which is preponderantly from Woolston are much the longer sections, and thus these Eng-

---

[29] Middleton, *op. cit.,* I, xlii–xliii, 302.
[30] Cited by Middleton, *ibid.,* I, xliii; Voltaire has marked this passage with a sticker.
[31] *Ibid.,* II, 294, n. 2.   [32] XLIII, 375–376.

lish deists appear to be responsible for the salient features of Voltaire's criticism on the important subject of miracles.

Voltaire's admission in his letter to d'Argental of his findings in Middleton, and the coincidence of his markers, often widely separated, with the material used, make it unnecessary to prove by parallel passages his borrowings in the article "Miracles." Of greater importance is the manner and spirit of his borrowing. The first miracle related at length, reported by "un homme simple auquel on a donné le nom de grand,"[33] concerns a monk who suspended a falling workman in mid-air until he could get authority from his superior to use his miraculous powers to save the workman's life. The story itself is not found in Middleton, but references occur in abundance to the works of Gregory the Great, who "gave more attention to fables, than he ought to have done, as all, who judge equitably and without prejudice, will easily allow."[34] Voltaire, as has been seen, paid considerable attention to footnotes, and looked up original works when he was able. We are not surprised therefore to find him reproaching Thiériot in 1762 and again early the following year for delay in sending him Gregory's *Dialogues* on the miracles of the Italian monks, and adding: "Je les avais autrefois; c'est un livre admirable en son espèce; la bêtise ne peut aller plus loin."[35] Middleton gave him the inspiration and the reason to review the book. His second miracle concerns the finding of the relics of the martyrs Gervasius and Protasius, as reported by Augustine, "immense populo teste res gesta est."[36] This is taken directly from Middleton, together with the Latin quotation and the reference in the footnote.[37] Voltaire concludes his paragraph with a quotation from Lucian, also found and marked in Middleton's *Free Inquiry*:[38] "Quand un joueur de gobelets adroit se fait chrétien, il est sûr de faire fortune." "Mais comme Lucien est un auteur profane," he adds ironically, "il ne doit avoir aucune autorité parmi nous." This same quotation appears again in the *Examen important de milord Bolingbroke*,[39] in which the chapter on mira-

---

[33] XX, 79.
[35] XLII, 296, 387.
[37] *Op. cit.*, I, xlix.
[39] XXVI, 271.

[34] *Op. cit.*, I, lxix.
[36] *Loc. cit.*
[38] *Ibid.*, I, 144.

cles is discovered to be merely a reworking of this same section
of the dictionary article devoted to the material from Middleton,
in spite of Voltaire's references to Fleury and Carré de Mont-
geron. Next follow the miracles attending the death of Polycarp,
with details all found in Middleton on pages marked in Voltaire's own copy.[40] Voltaire then quotes from Chrysostom and
Augustine, who imply the cessation of miracles in their time
because the Church no longer had need of them; both quotations
are from Middleton, the second copied from the original Latin
in a footnote.[41] From Augustine again Voltaire relates the story
of the old cobbler of Hippo,[42] with direct translations of quotations found in Middleton.[43] The latter is likewise the source for
Voltaire's questioning the miraculous powers of Paul the Her-
mit,[44] of Symeon Stylites,[45] and, as previously shown, of Xavier,
the Jesuit missionary. After these very considerable borrowings,
Voltaire grants with Middleton that all Christians of course
believe in the miracles of Jesus Christ and the Apostles, but that
more recent miracles may be doubted if they rest on uncertain
authority. He then gives the conditions under which miracles
should be operated:

> On souhaiterait, par exemple, pour qu'un miracle fût bien constaté,
> qu'il fût fait en présence de l'Académie des sciences de Paris, ou de la
> Faculté de médecine, assistées d'un détachement du régiment des gardes,
> pour contenir la foule du peuple, qui pourrait, par son indiscrétion, empê-
> cher l'opération du miracle.[46]

Middleton mentions the Jansenist miracles at the tomb of the
Abbé Pâris, and the epigram:

> De par le Roy. Défense à Dieu
> De faire miracles en ce lieu.

Voltaire had shown unusual interest in these miracles long before
he knew of Middleton's works. Yet his marker at the page of the
epigram,[47] its use in connection with other Middleton material,

---

[40] *Op. cit.*, I, 352–353; cf. I, 251–252.
[41] *Ibid.*, I, 257; 265, n. 3.   [42] XX, 80; also XXVI, 271.
[43] *Op. cit.*, I, 268–269. On the marker is written "Savetier de St. Augustin."
[44] *Ibid.*, I, 280.   [45] *Ibid.*, I, 294 ff.
[46] XX, 81.   [47] *Op. cit.*, I, 357–358.

and a careful comparison of the texts, show that Middleton was one of the principal sources for this material in his dictionary article "Convulsions,"[48] also of 1764, when the influence appears the greatest.

The article "Miracles" is the longest continuous section of Voltaire's direct borrowings from Middleton, yet it represents but a small part of the total influence. It is more difficult to establish exactly Middleton's rôle in Voltaire's treatment of the martyrs. It is possible that Voltaire knew Dodwell's *De paucitate martyrorum* chiefly through Middleton, and that from Middleton's frequent references came Voltaire's inspiration to attack Dom Ruinart's *Véritables actes des martyrs*[49] in his dictionary article "Martyrs" and in many minor critical treatises.[50] Voltaire refers to Middleton among others as sources for his criticisms:

Le savant Dodwell, l'habile Middleton, le judicieux Blondel, l'exact Tillemont, le scrutateur Launoy, et beaucoup d'autres, tous zélés pour la gloire des vrais martyrs, ont rayé de leur catalogue une multitude d'inconnus à qui l'on prodiguait ce grand nom.[51]

And again in another section of the same article "Martyrs," Voltaire writes that those who repeat these fables "ne connaissent ni Middleton, ni Dodwel, ni Brucker, ni Dumoulin, ni Fabricius, ni Grabe, ni même Dupin, ni aucun de ceux qui ont porté depuis peu la lumière dans les ténèbres."[52] The stories related in the article are chiefly from Ruinart, as Voltaire's markers in that work attest. On them he has written for easy reference "Le martyre de saint Rogatien et de saint Donatien," "aparition," "Théodate," "saint Théodore incendiaire," "saint Cassien fessé par ses écoliers," etc. His criticism, however, is often Middleton's, with many gibes of his own, for example: "On nous berne de martyres à faire pouffer de rire."[53] The story of Polycarp is again the translation of his marked passage in Middleton's essay.

In Voltaire's many and varied disparaging remarks concerning the Church Fathers, the influence of Middleton is definitely

---

[48] XVIII, 268.
[49] Trad. du latin en français, par Drouet de Maupertuy (Paris, 1708), 2 vols. in 8.
[50] See *table des matières* (éd. Moland) under *Ruinart.*
[51] XX, 37.   [52] *Ibid.*, p. 47.   [53] *Ibid.*

marked. The voluminous notes to the *Traité sur la tolérance,* much more hostile to religion than the text itself, contain several direct borrowings. On one of Voltaire's markers in Middleton's works is written in his own hand "Vigilantius du temps de Jérôme écrit contre reliques et célibat."[54] Voltaire's note contains a quotation from Vigilantius which is a brief summary of Middleton's more accurate quotations:

> Est-il nécessaire que vous respectiez ou même que vous adoriez une vile poussière? Les âmes des martyrs aiment-elles encore leurs cendres? Les coutumes des idolâtres se sont introduites dans l'Eglise: on commence à allumer des flambeaux en plein midi. Nous pouvons pendant notre vie prier les uns pour les uns; mais après la mort, à quoi servent les prières?[55]

Voltaire continues to note, as did Middleton, the quarrel between Vigilantius and Jerome. On Justin Martyr, the borrowings are almost endless. In his dictionary article "Allégories," Voltaire wrote:

> Saint Justin dit, dans son *Apologétique* (apolog., i, no. 55), que le signe de la croix est marqué sur les membres de l'homme; que quand il étend les bras, c'est une croix parfaite, et que le nez forme une croix sur le visage.[56]

Voltaire marked this passage in Middleton with a sticker,[57] but gives in his text a number rather than the page reference given by Middleton, showing that he verified Middleton's quotation. The evidence is almost conclusive enough to prove that Voltaire was using Middleton in 1761, when his article first appeared.[58] A sticker also marks Middleton's quotation from Cave that "Justin was wholly ignorant of the Hebrew tongue."[59] These and the following pages were much used by Voltaire. In his article "Christianisme," he notes the reproaches made to Justin for preaching the enjoyment of sensual pleasures in the new Jerusalem and for his extravagant notion of the origin of demons:

> On a reproché à saint Justin, l'un des premiers Pères, d'avoir dit, dans son *Commentaire sur Isaïe,* que les saints jouiraient, dans un règne de

---

[54] *Op. cit.,* I, cxii.   [55] XXV, 29, n. 1.
[56] XVII, 118.   [57] *Op. cit.,* I, 149.
[58] *Mélanges,* tome V, 1761; note by Beuchot (XVII, 117).
[59] *Op. cit.,* I, 152.

mille ans sur la terre, de tous les biens sensuels. On lui a fait un crime d'avoir dit, dans son *Apologie du Christianisme,* que Dieu ayant fait la terre, en laissa le soin aux anges, lesquels étant devenus amoureux des femmes, leur firent des enfants qui sont les démons.[60]

Voltaire's failure to check this reference gives definite proof of his borrowing directly from Middleton. Justin's first statement above appears in his *Dialogues,* as noted by Middleton, but Voltaire carelessly took the reference in Middleton's second note to Jerome's *Commentaire sur Isaïe.*[61] When he used the material again in his *Philosophie de l'histoire,* which contains many other gleanings from Middleton, he gives the correct reference: "C'est ce qu'atteste précisément saint Justin, dans la seconde partie de ses Dialogues."[62] This return to Middleton is interesting in the light of Wagnière's statement regarding Voltaire's methods:

> La mémoire de Voltaire était prodigieuse. Il m'a dit cent fois: *Voyez dans tel ouvrage, dans tel volume, à peu près à telle page, s'il n'y a pas telle chose?* et il arrivait rarement qu'il se trompât, quoiqu'il n'eût pas ouvert le livre depuis douze ou quinze ans.[63]

In the same article, "Christianisme," Voltaire continues to follow paragraph by paragraph his markers in Middleton's *Essay.* After dealing with Justin, Middleton relates the reproaches made to Lactantius and other Fathers for having forged the Sibylline books. He gives in a note the Greek verses cited from the *Sibyl* by Lactantius, together with an English translation.[64] Voltaire probably turned the English rather than the Greek into French:

> On a condamné Lactance et d'autres Pères, pour avoir supposé des oracles de sibylles. Il prétendait que la sibylle Erythrée avait fait ces quatre vers grecs, dont voici l'explication littérale:
>
> "Avec cinq pains et deux poissons
> Il nourrira cinq mille hommes au désert;
> Et, en ramassant les morceaux qui resteront,
> Il en remplira douze paniers."[65]

[60] XVIII, 169.   [61] *Op. cit.,* I, 153, and nn. 1, 2.
[62] XI, 216.
[63] Longchamp et Wagnière, *Mémoires sur Voltaire* (Paris, 1826), I, 53.
[64] *Op. cit.,* I, 158–159.   [65] XVIII, 169.

Both authors proceed immediately to charge the early Christians with the forgery of an acrostic from the Erythæan Sibyl.[66] But Voltaire, now launched on his favorite subject of forgeries, here leaves Middleton for Fabricius, and gives much of the material which he will print later in full in his *Collection d'anciens évangiles*. He used this same Middleton material, however, in *De la paix perpétuelle* (1769),[67] for several paragraphs in his *Philosophie de l'histoire* (1765),[68] in the *Examen important* (1767),[69] in *l'Épître aux Romains* (1768),[70] and in the dictionary article "Apocryphes."[71] The verse is repeated three times in his published works and a fourth time in a letter to M. le Marquis d'Argence de Dirac[72] on the first of February, 1764, five months before his review of Middleton appeared in the *Gazette littéraire*.

Voltaire's next interest in Middleton was the story, due to a gross blunder on the part of Justin, of the fabulous statue of Simon the magician. Voltaire wrote "Simon magicien"[73] on his marker to facilitate the finding of the reference, and used the story in his works several times,[74] very often in connection with other Middleton material. In his dictionary article, "Adorer,"[75] Voltaire follows closely and in order Middleton's notes. But it was from Van Dale that Middleton in turn got his material and to him that he often refers. Voltaire went to Van Dale for additional details in his own account, and when he repeated it again in his article "Éclipse," he has used also a work on inscriptions by Gruter. In fact his next marker in Middleton bears the words "Gruter inscriptions."[76] This was all scholarly labor and Voltaire here worked the references he found in footnotes, as we find him doing in his careful study of Fabricius. In the article "Oracles," which first appeared in 1774, where Simon the magician is also mentioned, the material is taken from Van Dale, and accompanied by a eulogy of that learned enemy of the devil and of ancient superstitions.[77] Through Middleton to Gruter again, with "Escu-

---

[66] XVIII, 169.
[68] XI, 89–91 (232), (281).
[70] XXVII, 97.
[72] XLIII, 113–114.
[74] See *table de matières*, LII, 417.
[76] *Op. cit.*, I, 202–203.

[67] *Ibid.*, p. 116.
[69] XXVI, 238.
[71] XVII, 313–314.
[73] *Op. cit.*, I, 190–191.
[75] XVII, 63.
[77] XX, 138–139.

lape—miracles" on the marker,[78] Voltaire seeks Tertullian's remarks concerning the curing of diseases by that demon. It is certain, however, that in spite of the many marked pages in Middleton referring to Tertullian he read, too, the latter's *Apologie pour la religion chrétienne* for his chapter in the *Examen important de milord Bolingbroke* and for other references to Æsculapius.[79] On another marker,[80] Voltaire wrote: "diables chassez avec l'anneau de Salomon," and referred to this fabulous story from Josephus in his article "Église," "du Pouvoir de chasser les diables donné à l'église."[81] Middleton is here nearly lost in a profusion of other sources.

Thus the influence on Voltaire of Middleton's *Inquiry into the Miraculous Powers of the Early Christian Church* runs down the scale from definite extensive borrowings to the use of a lonely note in the midst of other material gleaned from the vast number of learned books that Voltaire had ready at hand in his private library. It is certain that he welcomed the confirmation that the learned English divine gave him in his own studies of early Church history; certain, too, that he was inspired by Middleton to seek new sources or to renew his acquaintance with such well-known works as Van Dale's treatises and dissertations. Often he used Middleton's arguments against such works as Ruinart's *Acta principorum martyrum sincera et selecta,* using the text and detail from Ruinart but putting the odium of the criticism on Middleton and other learned men and philosophers.

We find Voltaire again borrowing directly and extensively from Middleton's *Reflections on the Dispute between the Apostles Peter and Paul,* concerning the attitude and the dissemblances of the one and the other in regard to Jewish ceremonies. Middleton relates that Chrysostom, to save appearances, took great pains to prove the quarrel itself to be wholly feigned and dissembled; and that Jerome was of much the same opinion.[82] Voltaire gave this as Jerome's opinion, but again used the wrong footnote for his reference, in such a way that Jerome is made to state his case in

---

[78] *Op. cit.,* I, 202–203.　　　　　[79] XXVI, 253 ff.; XXVIII, 110.
[80] *Op. cit.,* I, 210–211.　　　　　[81] XVIII, 485.
[82] *Op. cit.,* II, 276.

one of Chrysostom's works.[83] The position of the note made it very easy to make this error, but it is conclusive evidence again of Voltaire's direct borrowing. The Middleton material is used for about a page in his dictionary article "Église."[84] Here Voltaire quotes from Augustine's epistle to Jerome: "Je suis fâché qu'un aussi grand homme se rende le patron du mensonge, *patronum mendacii.*" Middleton had quoted in a footnote this passage beginning "Patrocinium mendacii susceptum esse."[85] Voltaire's little inaccuracy is here not important. He used the same material for two paragraphs in his article "Conciles," and much more briefly in "Tolérance" and "Viande."[86]

In the *Examination of Sherlock's Discourses on the Use and Intent of Prophecy,* Middleton condemned the bishop's treatment of creation, original sin, and the fall of man. Sherlock claimed the story was "historical, but clothed in parables and similitudes, and in some part metaphorical."[87] Middleton, unwilling to let such a statement pass unchallenged, claimed it was "one of those instructive and moral fictions, to which we may give the name *Apologue,* or *fable,* or *allegory,* or of any thing rather, than of a *Historical narration,* with which it is utterly incompatible.[88] Voltaire had many sources for his criticisms of the book of Genesis, yet he did not fail to mark this page nor to state, in his review of Middleton's works in the *Gazette littéraire:*

> Il avance ailleurs que le premier chapitre de la *Genèse* est purement allégorique. Nous n'avons garde d'adopter ou de justifier ces paradoxes, et il ne nous appartient pas de les discuter; mais nous rendons justice à l'érudition, à la candeur, et surtout à la modération du théologien anglais.[89]

The *Gazette littéraire* was at least not a convenient medium for such discussion.

Voltaire's markers in Middleton's *Reflections on the Variations found in the four Evangelist*s are far from numerous, though he treated these variations at length in many of his works, and espe-

[83] XVIII, 483. "Il dit dans sa première Homélie, tome III," etc.
[84] *Ibid.,* pp. 482–483.
[85] *Op. cit.,* II, 278.
[86] XVIII, 206; XX, 521, 575.
[87] *Op. cit.,* V, 272.
[88] *Ibid.,* V, 278.
[89] XXV, 177.

cially in his dictionary article "Contradictions." In this article he draws much from the anonymous *Analyse de la religion chrétienne,* and writes at length of the contradictions that so shocked the "deplorable" Meslier.[90] It seems probable that he was too well documented on this subject to need Middleton, and it is moreover impossible to determine to what extent he used the latter's *Reflections.* He referred of course again and again to the impious ancestors of Jesus of Nazareth and to the differing genealogies in Matthew and Luke, but did not use references and quotations from Erasmus and Grotius which he had marked in Middleton's treatise.[91] He marked also pages bearing on the contradiction in Mark and John concerning the hour of the crucifixion, but uses it as from Meslier.[92] Finally he appears to have noted for future reference Middleton's own hardy conclusion:

> The belief then of the Inspiration and absolute infallibility of the Evangelists, seems to be more absurd, than even of Transubstantiation itself: for this, tho' repugnant to sense, is supported by the express words of Scripture; whereas the other, not less contrary to sense, is contrary at the same time to the declarations of the Evangelists themselves.[93]

In Middleton's *Essay on the Gift of Tongues,* there appears but one marker, pointing evidently to Paul's very meager knowledge of Greek, in spite of the fact that he was "indued also with the gift of tongues more eminently than any man."[94] All that can be proved is that Voltaire read the *Essay.* Strangely enough, he read, too, and borrowed several paragraphs in his article "Médecins" from Middleton's Latin work, *De medicorum apud veteres Romanos degentium conditione Dissertatio.* Two markers, autographed "médecins esclaves valeur 60 louis,"[95] and again "médecins esclaves,"[96] indicate the source for his statement that

> le célèbre Musa, médecin d'Auguste, était esclave; il fut affranchi et fait chevalier romain, et alors les médecins devinrent des personnages considérables.[97]

[90] XVIII, 264.
[92] XVIII, 266.
[94] *Ibid.,* II, 404.
[96] *Ibid.,* IV, 95.

[91] *Op. cit.,* II, 306–307; cf. II, 302.
[93] *Op. cit.,* II, 348.
[95] *Ibid.,* IV, 87, n. *a.*
[97] XX, 57.

A work which greatly interested Voltaire and which drew from him several interesting marginal comments was Middleton's *Letter to Dr. Waterland; containing some Remarks on his* VINDICATION OF SCRIPTURE: *in answer to a book, intitled,* CHRISTIANITY AS OLD AS THE CREATION, *together with the sketch or plan of another answer to the said book.* Middleton felt that Waterland, in attacking Tindal, was exposing the Scripture to fresh ridicule and contempt. Since his own plan to answer Tindal rather gave the case away, Middleton's sincerity might be open to question. Voltaire, however, appears to take Middleton seriously, and rises to the defense of Tindal. The work deals especially with Tindal's charges of the unoriginality and the barbarity of ancient Jewish customs. Voltaire was later to have the same sort of polemical discussion with the Abbé Guénée, in whose *Lettres de quelques juifs* Tindal, as we have seen, also figured prominently. On the question of circumcision, Voltaire has marked pages on which proof is given that this custom came from the Egyptians, on the authority of Herodotus, Diodorus Siculus,[98] Strabo, and the learned Marsham.[99] In his review in the *Gazette littéraire,* Voltaire guardedly wrote:

> Que la plupart des cérémonies et des lois des Hébreux aient été prises des Egyptiens, comme le prétend le savant Marsham, l'économie mosaïque n'en sera pas moins d'institution divine.[100]

Middleton here gave Voltaire a new authority to cite in his attacks on Jewish ceremonies.[101]

In his *Philosophie de l'histoire* he is sure at least that circumcision did not originate with the Jews:

> La circoncision vient-elle des Egyptiens, des Arabes, ou des Ethiopiens? Je n'en sais rien. Que ceux qui le savent le disent.[102]

The discussion which precedes and follows this remark bears very evident traces of Middleton's influence. Voltaire's markers follow the discussion of the dangers of circumcision, of whether

---

[98] *Op. cit.,* III, 27.   [99] *Ibid.,* III, 28.
[100] XXV, 177.
[101] Cf. also XI, 115, where Marsham and Middleton are given together as authorities.
[102] XI, 68.

the rite was ordered by God, and if so, whether God repented having given man a foreskin.[103] His article "Circoncision," in 1764, is a summary of these pages in Middleton, but with quotations at length from Herodotus, and with several paragraphs from other sources, of which one is a passage from his English notebook.[104] Briefer mention is of course to be found in many of his other works.

Voltaire skips now to Middleton's "rough Draught" of a suitable answer to Tindal. His argument is the universal conviction that reason has never been and never can be a sufficient guide to life, and that this insufficiency of reason has ever been the cause of the invention and the establishment of religion: that "the authority of the latter might restrain those whom the former had found too weak to keep in order."[105] "In consequence of which," continues Middleton, "we find in fact, from the records of all History, that there never was a nation in the world, whose public Religion was formed upon the plan of Nature, and instituted on the principles of meer Reason."[106] Voltaire, hanging on to one of his fondest illusions, would not give in; "the relligion of Chinese government," he wrote on the margin. Middleton continues that by reason it can be proved immoral to subvert the established religion;[107] Voltaire comments in the margin: "Not at all, but natural relligion for the magistrates, and damn'd stuff for the mob." There can be no question here of Voltaire's ability to follow an argument in English or to express himself succinctly in that language. His point of view differs considerably from Middleton's or Cicero's. He himself was not writing for the mob, yet he could not agree that intelligent people should defend the prevailing infamous superstitions. Middleton attempts again to show against Tindal and Voltaire that " 'tis not the Believers of Religion, but Infidels and Atheists, who in every country have always been the severest persecutors, and cruellest oppressors of all Civil as well as Religious Liberty."[108] Voltaire marked the page, but

---

[103] *Op. cit.,* III, 36–38.
[104] On phallic symbolism among the Egyptians; cf. XVIII, 193.
[105] *Op. cit.,* III, 50. Quotation from Cicero's *De natura deorum.*
[106] *Ibid.,* III, 50–51.   [107] *Ibid.,* III, 52.
[108] *Ibid.,* III, 55.

did not comment. It is not doubtful what he would have said, but we wish that he could have said it here once in English. Middleton, using the *ad hominem* argument against Tindal's remark that "if God's Works shew infinite Wisdom, there's no reason to imagine but that his Laws do the same," restates and changes Tindal's argument, which he says should read thus: "God forbid, that in the whole frame of God's laws, there should not be the same proof of his Wisdom as in the whole frame of his Works."[109] Voltaire's marginal note at this point shows a keen penetration of the argument: "Well [bien], if we are as certain the laws are of God as we are sure the works are of God." Middleton was after all something of a disappointment to Voltaire, another compromiser, who, after collecting priceless weapons against infamous religion, refused to be a party in the final crushing of her superstitions. For Middleton, in a later passage marked by Voltaire, wished to make established religion amiable, plain, rational, intelligible to common understandings.[110] He saw no harm in a fair examination, but even if it were proved to be an imposture, it should be kept as a political necessity. Middleton is here treading on dangerous ground and making dangerous admissions. His works were quite as well calculated to "unhinge religion" as Tindal's own. Voltaire understood this, and he saw also, as history has since proved, that the dusty work of scholars is not enough without active propaganda in literary form. This service he rendered to Middleton. For who, even today, except a few scholars and theological students, and the readers of Voltaire, know the truths elaborated and propounded by the English deists?

As late as 1776, in his *Histoire de l'établissement du christianisme,* Voltaire still remembers Middleton's work as a deadly weapon to be used against the frauds of the early Church. Rather than bore the reader mortally with the repetition of these numberless acts of shame, he writes: "Je renvoie à notre Middleton, qui a prouvé, quoique avec trop de retenue, la fausseté des miracles."[111] He is still writing as an Englishman, hence "our Middleton." It cannot be said that he failed to give any credit to

109 *Op. cit.,* III, 60.　　110 *Ibid.,* III, 270.　　111 XXXI, 78.

Middleton, but he at least neglected to use the name in connection with his most extensive borrowings. As usual, too, there are in his works many unjustifiable references. He confuses Middleton, author of the *Life of Cicero,* with the poet Lyttelton, when he quotes and translates the latter's poem on the spirit of the French nation.[112] In the *Examen important,* he cites Middleton without warrant as the discoverer of an ancient Alexandrian chronicle in which is stated the violent protest of a considerable body of bishops and priests against the canonical books accepted by the Council of Nicæa.[113] In the *Philosophie de l'histoire,* he again cites Middleton without cause as supporting the view that Moses was not the author of the Pentateuch.[114] In the *Questions sur les miracles,* Middleton's name appears in a long list of men who did not believe that the Son of God performed miracles in Galilee.[115] Again, in the late *Histoire de l'établissement du christianisme,* Voltaire, in maintaining his argument that God's promises to the Jews were terrestrial and temporal, quotes Arnauld, and adds: "Notre sage Middleton a rendu cette vérité sensible." Voltaire undoubtedly meant Warburton, whose *Divine Legation of Moses* he had often commented upon; for Middleton, in his *Letters to Mr. Warburton,* had tried as kindly but as firmly as possible to point out the dangers of the latter's extraordinary hypothesis.[116] Voltaire had read the letters, for he left markers, on one of which was written "quinze premiers évêques de Jérusalem circoncis."[117] It is not easy to determine how many of these false references were wilful or how many were careless. It should be borne in mind, however, that Voltaire's exaggerations and errors are always in connection with his attributions and references, and not in the essential facts of his documentation. He appears to have used honestly the best sources he could find in his studies of the history of the primitive Church.

In conclusion, it would seem necessary to establish Middleton as the most important English source of Voltaire's documentation against the historical argument of the truth of Christianity, a place which has formerly been given to Bolingbroke almost by

[112] XXVI, 159 ff.

[114] XI, 115.

[116] *Op. cit.,* I, 382–383.

[113] *Ibid.,* p. 281.

[115] XXV, 361.

[117] *Ibid.,* I, 395.

common consent, but with no adequate proof. Voltaire read carefully the works of both men. He consistently praised the work of Middleton and almost consistently scorned Bolingbroke's offerings. More convincing evidence of the relative influence of the two men is obtained by searching out the use he made of passages marked in their volumes. The indications in Bolingbroke's works lead almost nowhere. On the contrary, nearly every marker in the Middleton volumes leads us directly to passages used in Voltaire's own works, and some of them prove conclusively that Voltaire got much material directly from Middleton on such important questions as the miracles, the martyrs, the credulity, frauds, and contradictions of the Church Fathers, the unoriginality of Jewish customs, and the weakness of the authority of the Scriptures. Middleton also inspired Voltaire to renew his acquaintance with many learned works, and to read much more extensively than he had previously done into the history of the early Church and the works of the primitive Fathers. Judging both from the dates of the use of Voltaire's findings and from definite indications in his correspondence, we find that Voltaire was reading Middleton probably in 1761, surely in 1762, and that the greatest influence is apparent in 1764, in the *Dictionnaire philosophique,* and in the *Philosophie de l'histoire* in 1765, but that Middleton was remembered as late as 1776, when Voltaire was preparing his *Histoire de l'établissement du christianisme.*

Middleton's contribution to Voltaire was largely documentary, though Voltaire gladly welcomed the surprisingly audacious ideas of this orthodox entry into the field of biblical criticism. Yet in spite of several forced references to Middleton as an unbeliever, Voltaire could not persuade even himself that the English divine was an irreconcilable enemy to established religion. He praised the latter's learning and moderation through the medium of the *Gazette littéraire,* but his frank and final decision was that Middleton attacked the miracles with too much reserve. Voltaire's method, then, was to use the details of Middleton's attack and to supply all the additional animus, irony, and literary form that was needed to attract the attention of the intelligent readers of his generation.

CHAPTER VIII

VOLTAIRE AND ANNET: RADICAL DEISM

IF Middleton had the last word and settled the deist controversy with a compromise, there were naturally many bitter-enders on both sides who were not satisfied. Among these was the radical Peter Annet, the last and the most thorough of deists, whose writings were a connecting link between the deism of the early part of the eighteenth century and the more aggressive and outspoken deism of Paine and the revolutionary period.[1] In this later period, Annet's works were singled out among English deistic writings to be reprinted along with Voltaire's and d'Holbach's.[2] Annet was writing his attacks as late as 1761, and had both a direct and an immediate influence on Voltaire.

There is very little trustworthy information concerning Annet's life.[3] He is said to have been born in Liverpool in 1693, a year before the birth of the great French philosopher. His first publication was *Judging for Ourselves*, printed in 1739, and signed "P. A., minister of the gospel." There is at least no evidence to disprove that he was an apostate of the Woolston-Meslier type who later became a schoolmaster from economic necessity. Even this position he is said to have lost in 1744 on account of his wholesale skepticism concerning the resurrection and his attacks on Sherlock's *Tryal of the Witnesses*. He was many years a member of the Robin Hood debating society, to which Oliver Goldsmith also belonged. Though all his critical works were published anonymously, his opinions must have been well known. Because his first work was composed of lectures delivered at Plaisterer's Hall, Robertson concludes that while all the English and French deists had written for the upper and middle classes, Annet was practically the first who sought to reach the multitude.[4] In truth,

[1] Leslie Stephen, *English Thought in the Eighteenth Century*, I, 247.
[2] Robertson, *Short History of Freethought*, II, 327.
[3] See L. Stephen's article in the *Dictionary of National Biography*.
[4] *Op. cit.*, II, 327.

his style is much more popular than Chubb's and even coarser than Woolston's. His *Free Enquirer,* a weekly begun in 1761, was stopped by legal procedure after nine numbers, and he was severely condemned for blasphemy. At the age of seventy he was obliged to stand twice in the pillory, was imprisoned for a month with an additional year of hard labor, and released only on parole. The few remaining years of his life were spent in adversity, but his spirit remained undaunted. He became a schoolmaster again, and invented a system of shorthand. But his *Lectures,* corrected and revised just before his death, show the restraining influence of persecution.

All of Annet's works except his first manifesto in defense of reason and his *Lectures* were published anonymously, and with varying degrees of success in shielding their author from the arm of authority. Many of his most important tracts have become extremely rare, and his history of *David, the Man after God's own Heart* has been attributed to other writers. Toland had objected to all additions to the simple Gospel, Collins was essentially unreligious; but Annet's attitude toward Christianity was one of revolutionary antipathy. In his *Judging for Ourselves,*[5] he suggests that men's reasons should look backward as well as forward; for the traditional errors in which they are brought up mislead their judgment and cause them to swerve from moral rectitude.[6] To Annet, the Christian was not only deceived but immoral. His criterion of the worth of historical evidence, which he applies to sacred history as rigorously as to profane, has been noted by Stephen: "If a man says he has crossed Westminster Bridge, his story may be true and deserves examination, though the bridge is not quite finished (1747); but if he says he jumped the river, I know the story to be a lie, and trouble myself no more about it." "Apply this simple criterion to the Bible," adds Stephen, "and it is easy to see what becomes of it."[7]

[5] The first of a *Collection of the Tracts of a certain Free Enquirer, noted by his sufferings for his opinions.* In the copy belonging to the Harvard-Andover Theological Library, from which references will be taken, there is written in on the title-page, "By Peter Annet, London ?, 1766?" The pagination is continuous, and corresponds, as far as it goes, to the collection used by Leslie Stephen.

[6] *Coll. of Tracts,* pp. 18, 22.   [7] *Op. cit.,* I, 252.

Annet's first application of this simple criterion to the Bible was in his *Resurrection of Jesus Considered,* in 1744, in answer to Sherlock's *Tryal of the Witnesses,* which in turn had been written in answer to Woolston's sixth discourse, on the resurrection. Woolston had argued from the literal word, and Sherlock had answered in kind. But Annet thought that Woolston had admitted too much, and seeks in a thorough manner to discredit the whole story.[8] His argument was continued into the following year by his *Resurrection Reconsidered* and *The Resurrection Defenders stript of all Defence.*[9] The canonical gospels are not worthy of credence, says Annet, because they are full of interpolations and forgeries, were fixed in a very uncertain time and manner, were rejected by large bodies of early Christians, even by Paul who charged the Galatians to receive no Gospel but his, though it should come from heaven, and, moreover, they were kept secret so long that we have not the benefit of contemporary refutation. To prove the book by the book was therefore no proof at all. Again, practically nothing is known of the writers of the New Testament except Paul, and he was an impostor and a proven liar. As for the others,

might not the writers, whoever they were, who could report prophecies which were never delivered by the prophets, report others which were never uttered by Christ? And write what they pleased of him, long after his departure; and much more easily and boldly, if their own words were to be the only proof of it?[10]

For example, the report of Christ's comparing his coming entombment and resurrection to Jonas' three days in the belly of the whale not only resembles a fraud, but was a clumsy fraud, for only people who could stretch one into three could stretch the two nights and one day of entombment into three full days and nights.[11] Woolston had based his case against the literal word on the establishment of the watch at the tomb, but Annet thinks that the whole story of the watch sounds like a futile attempt to give credence to an idle tale.[12]

[8] *Ibid.,* I, 247.
[10] *Resurrection of Jesus Considered,* p. 14.
[11] *Ibid.,* pp. 19, 20.

[9] London, 1744 and 1745.

[12] *Ibid.,* pp. 24 ff.

Annet affirms that the miracles wrought at the crucifixion, as well as those said to be done afterward to prove it "do all want equal proof as the resurrection itself." The real miracle is that those for whom they were effected were unaffected by them:

> And yet the nature of the Jews remained the same; their hearts were not rent, tho' the rocks rent; nor quaked, tho' the earth quaked; and tho' the graves opened, their understandings appear not to be opened! What a strange thing is infidelity, that no miracle can work upon it.[13]

On Christ's appearances, not publicly but to his disciples only, after his death, the evangelists disagree hopelessly. The so-called eyewitnesses must have been deceived. Their sincerity cannot be proved by their miserable lives and deaths for the sake of the truth, as argued by Annet's opponents, for they probably made a better thing at preaching than they had at fishing.[14] Paul was probably "in his visions" when he asserted that five hundred saw Christ after his resurrection, and the proof "depends but upon his single testimony, or of some other in his name, or of the greatest lyar in the world, the Church of Rome."[15] As a final triumphant card, Annet reprinted the various and varying accounts of the resurrection as they appear in the New Testament, so that the reader could the more easily check up the endless contradictions he finds.[16]

Voltaire refused to enter into the detail of this English controversy. In his main attacks, he usually passes over the resurrection with a few sentences. Yet he is fully as skeptical as Annet in considering the scriptural accounts of it absurd and the authors untrustworthy. He is concerned in refuting the miracles and prodigies that are reported to have accompanied the resurrection, and especially the orthodox argument of an eclipse of the sun, which Kepler and Halley had proved false.[17] This was to him scientific demonstration of the unreliability of the account. After a wretched life spent in performing ridiculous miracles and in insulting the Pharisees, he writes, Jesus was finally hanged between two thieves;

---

[13] *Resurrection Defenders* (1745), p. 21.
[14] *Resurrection Considered*, p. 68.
[15] *Ibid.*, p. 67.
[16] *Ibid.*, pp. 85–92.
[17] XVIII, 339.

et ses historiens ont le front de nous dire qu'à sa mort la terre a été couverte d'épaisses ténèbres en plein midi, et en pleine lune: comme si tous les écrivains de ce temps-là n'auraient pas parlé d'un si étrange miracle. Après cela il ne coûte rien de se dire ressuscité, et de prédire la fin du monde, qui n'est pourtant pas arrivée.[18]

Although Voltaire regards the Scripture story in much the same light as Annet, it appears unlikely that he had any first-hand acquaintance with Annet's three tracts on the resurrection. There is more evidence that he found much more to his purpose in Annet's next attack, this time on the person and authority of Paul.

Annet's *History and Character of St. Paul* grew out of the previous controversy and, though undated, was published after 1747, as a comment on a letter from Lyttelton to West which appeared in that year. Annet considers that Paul's epistles, like the other books of the New Testament, were "picked up from Stories and flying Reports, by I know not what Set of half Jews," who laid their errors and lies to the Apostles by writing under their names.[19] He refers to Toland's *Amyntor* as a fine catalogue of pious frauds. But since his enemies had stifled this main point, he is willing to suppose the epistles genuine, and demolish them on internal evidence.[20] He attempts to prove that Paul was an enthusiast, an impostor, and a liar. His treatment of Paul as an enthusiast is in line with the modern theory of Paul's epilepsy. This book was translated and published by d'Holbach in 1770, but manuscript extracts, such as those of Meslier and of Woolston, were undoubtedly circulating among the *philosophes* before the translation. There is no trace of the work in Voltaire's library today.

The argument begins with the story of Paul in the apocryphal Acts accepted by the Ebionites to the effect that

Paul was originally a Heathen, that he came to Jerusalem, staid there for some Time, and had a Mind to marry the High Priest's Daughter, on the Account of which he became a Proselyte, and was circumcised; but that afterwards, not obtaining the young Woman he was angry, and wrote against Circumcision, against the Sabbath, and against keeping the Law.[21]

[18] XXIV, 451.
[20] *Ibid.*, pp. 39, 42.

[19] *Coll. of Tracts*, p. 36.
[21] *Ibid.*, p. 35.

Voltaire found the same material in the *Codex* of Fabricius, from which he quotes the Latin version in his article "Apôtres," and which he uses in most of his numerous attacks on Paul.[22] Fabricius is also his source for the picture of Paul given by Lucian, for Clement's affirmation that Paul was married, for the dispute concerning his origin, and for his pretended correspondence with Seneca. And Voltaire went to Grabe's *Spicilegium* for his *Actes de Thècle* which he used in the introduction to his apocryphal lists and translations.[23] In his *Dialogue du douteur et de l'adorateur,* he vents his spleen on Paul:

> Que pensez-vous de Paul, meurtrier d'Etienne, persécuteur des premiers galiléens, depuis galiléen lui-même et persécuté? Pourquoi rompit-il avec Gamaliel, son maître? Est-ce, comme le disent quelques Juifs, parce que Gamaliel lui refusa sa fille en mariage parce qu'il avait les jambes torses, la tête chauve et les sourcils joints, ainsi qu'il est rapporté dans les *Actes de Thècle,* sa favorite? A-t-il écrit enfin les épîtres qu'on a mises sous son nom?[24]

Voltaire had a more thorough historical critic in Fabricius than Annet could find in England, and his historical arguments are more ample. For the argument from internal evidence, however, no better could be found than Woolston, Tindal, and Annet.

Annet's treatment of Paul is as radical as the later works for which he was pilloried. Woolston had claimed to be the modern Origen risen to combat the infidel school of Celsus. "I doubt not but undeniably to prove," writes Annet, "as the wise Celsus did, that the Christian Traditions destroy their own Authority."[25] The main outline of his attack presents striking similarities with Voltaire's, but there is often a divergence in detail between the two accounts. It was Voltaire's habit, once he received an inspiration from a work, to seek added information and to verify the sources.

Annet assures us that Saul was not disinterested in becoming a Jew under Gamaliel. He had the spirit of a high priest and wanted to become a priest. This lowly tentmaker was stung by

[22] Cf. XVII, 328, 329; and *Cod. Apoc. N. T.,* II, 764.
[23] XXVII, 445, and n. 10. Voltaire's copy is abundantly marked.
[24] XXV, 132.   [25] *Coll. of Tracts,* p. 42.

Gamaliel's disdain, and decided to be high priest of a new religion, hence his pretended vision on the road to Damascus.[26] Voltaire treats Saul as Gamaliel's valet, who studied at his feet and kept the clothing of Stephen whom he had had stoned.[27] Like Annet, he refers to Paul as a "demi-juif" and a "faiseur de tentes." Annet adds also that Saul was probably scared out of his job as informer against the Christians by the savage cutting off of Malchus' ear and the terrible revenge wreaked on Judas[28] (though he notes that the two accounts of the death of Judas are flatly contradictory). Annet's excuse for his unusual criticisms is that he has as much right to guess his way through the labyrinth as the orthodox commentators.

A brief account of Annet's chief findings in the labyrinth will illustrate his method and style, and make possible a comparison with Voltaire. Paul decided that, considering the credulousness of the Christians, "a miracle was the best door to get in at." A vision was the simplest way, for no one can detect the falsehood of it. But the absurdities of the accounts of his visions destroy their own authority: "A bad Relation of a dark Relator; on this is built a blind faith."[29] Saul alone heard the voice on the road to Damascus and could therefore report the words differently on different occasions. Contradictions and absurdities abound. The men with Saul stood still and at the same time fell down. What was become of the Holy Ghost in letting two different accounts slip in? Paul couldn't see what the others did anyway, for he was blinded, and for the plausible reason that he might open the eyes of others. Annet humbles the pride of those who had set their hero on horseback. He was plainly walking, and "I don't think the Business would pay Horse-hire." What did the expositors mean by accounting for the rumbling as "low Thunder?" These visions "made our poor Brother Paul's Head weak." They "knocked his stomach" and he was "subject to Paroxisms of a Fever, or a spiritual Fever, all his Life after."[30] The whole story was probably imagined in a delirium, and Annet thinks it best to deny it flatly

[26] *Ibid.,* pp. 53, 54.
[28] *Coll. of Tracts,* p. 53.
[30] *Ibid.,* pp. 63–66.

[27] XXVI, 231.
[29] *Ibid.,* pp. 54, 61.

than to account for it in the manner of the expositors. "If angels never blush at what they say, I think this Saint should at what he said."[31]

Annet now convicts Paul of perjury. After the vision, he swears that he came to Jerusalem to see Peter, and James, the Lord's brother, that he saw no other, and that before God he lies not. The last phrase half convicts him already. But other accounts in the same Acts contradict his account. One sends him into Arabia, and another says, "But Barnabas took him and brought him to the Apostles." And Annet writes, "Now though he swears that he does not lye, I believe before God that he swears to a lye, and that there is no Dependance for Truth in these sacred Stories."[32]

Voltaire wrote of Paul in very similar fashion under the name of Bolingbroke:

> Il dit qu'il était citoyen romain; j'ose affirmer qu'il ment impudemment. . . . Dédaigné par Gamaliel et par sa fille, comme il méritait de l'être, il se joignit à la secte naissante de Céphas, de Jacques, de Matthieu, de Barnabé, pour mettre le trouble chez les Juifs.
>
> Pour peu qu'on ait une étincelle de raison, on jugera que cette cause de l'apostasie de ce malheureux Juif est plus naturelle que celle qu'on lui attribue. Comment se persuadera-t-on qu'une lumière céleste l'ait fait tomber de cheval en plein midi, qu'une voix céleste se soit fait entendre à lui, que Dieu lui ait dit: "Saul, Saul, pourquoi me persécutes-tu?" Ne rougit-on pas d'une telle sottise? . . . à quoi bon ce ridicule miracle? Je prends le ciel et la terre à témoins (s'il est permis de se servir de ces mots impropres, le ciel et la terre) qu'il n'y a jamais eu de légende plus folle, plus fanatique, plus dégoûtante, plus digne d'horreur et de mépris.[33]

The radical, uncompromising attitude is the same in the two accounts. Voltaire, who was the more scholarly, found some of his facts in Fabricius and Grabe, but the interpretations and certain expressions, such as Saul's blushing at his own report of his vision and the charge of untruthfulness, seem to have been inspired by Annet.

Annet explains that Paul's love for power and authority as seen in his letters to the Corinthians shows him to have been an enthusiast and an impostor. "Superiority and Love of Power was no small ingredient in the Composition of Paul's Temper; he

[31] *Coll. of Tracts*, p. 44.   [32] *Ibid.*, p. 68.   [33] XXVI, 231, 232.

affects Humility to raise himself, and boasts of his sufferings to exalt himself."[34] He calls himself less than the least of the saints: "There is many a true Word spoke in Jest," writes Annet. Imagining that he was already "clothed with the Purple and the Mitre," he writes to the Corinthians: "If I come again, I will not spare you," not even those who had not sinned.[35] To support his authority, he writes of a man (himself) who was "caught up to the third heaven . . . and heard unspeakable words, which it is not lawful for a man to utter." Whitefield or Wesley would certainly be called impostors if they reported such a tale. And was this a "Law made on Earth to cut off news from Heaven?"[36] His reported vision of Christ was a like imposture, often aped by Paul's enthusiastic followers.[37] Mahomet was at first considered an impostor, but custom and time put truth and falsehood on a level. "No art was ever better calculated to deceive than Inspiration. The Religion founded on Nature don't require it; but all others do."[38]

There is striking similarity in treatment in Voltaire's *Dialogue du douteur et de l'adorateur*:

Le voyage d'Astolphe dans la lune est plus vraisemblable, puisque le chemin est plus court. Mais pourquoi veut-il faire accroire aux imbéciles auxquels il écrit qu'il a été ravi au troisième ciel? C'est pour établir son autorité parmi eux; c'est pour satisfaire son ambition d'être chef de parti; c'est pour donner du poids à ces paroles insolentes et tyranniques. Si je viens encore une fois vers vous, je ne pardonnerai ni à ceux qui auront péché ni à tous les autres. . . . Hélas! c'est ainsi que la plupart des sectes populaires commencent: un imposteur harangue la lie du peuple dans un grenier, et les imposteurs qui lui succèdent habitent bientôt des palais.[39]

On the question of circumcision, Annet convicts Paul of double dealing. To please the Jews, he persuaded Timothy, whose father was known to have been a Greek, to undergo circumcision, "even if Christ should profit Timothy nothing."[40] Voltaire has often noted the same detail:

[34] *Coll. of Tracts*, p. 57.
[36] *Ibid.*, p. 44.
[38] *Ibid.*, p. 62.
[40] *Coll. of Tracts*, pp. 58, 76.

[35] *Ibid.*, p. 59.
[37] *Ibid.*, pp. 61, 68.
[39] XXV, 133.

Paul fit-il bien de circoncire son disciple Timothée, après avoir écrit aux Galates: "Si vous vous faites circoncire, Jésus ne vous servira de rien"?[41]

Paul confesses, says Annet, that "he is all things to Man, that by all Means he might gain some"; so he is hazy on circumcision, on grace, on salvation by works or by the efficacy of the Law, which is now "void," now "made good"; "an enthusiast cannot reason well."[42] Voltaire follows Annet here very closely in the *Examen important*:

Quel galimatias quand il écrit à la société des chrétiens qui se formait à Rome dans la fange juive! La circoncision vous est profitable si vous observez la loi; mais si vous êtes prévaricateurs de la loi, votre circoncision devient prépuce, etc. . . . . Détruisons-nous donc la loi par la foi? à Dieu ne plaise! mais nous établissons la foi. . . . Si Abraham a été justifié par ses ouvrages, il a de quoi se glorifier, mais non devant Dieu! Ce Paul, en s'exprimant ainsi, parlait évidemment en juif, et non en chrétien; mais il parlait encore plus en énergumène insensé qui ne peut pas mettre deux idées cohérentes à côté l'une de l'autre.[43]

It is apparent that Voltaire got many of his ideas and biblical references from this tract of Peter Annet, which far surpassed Bolingbroke's milder dislike for the "cabalistical St. Paul" and for the unintelligibility of his intricate and dark system of religion,[44] and which was evidently circulating in France, some years before the latter's works appeared in print.

Annet wrote again:

This Saint had too much Heat to reason cooly; . . . he cries: "thou Fool, that which thou sowest is not quickened except it die." But this is answering like a fool.[45]

Tindal had laid this error principally to the charge of Jesus; Annet, to Paul. Voltaire varies between the two according to the subject in hand. In 1770, however, Voltaire charges d'Holbach, who noted this passage, with abusing the Scriptures in unwarranted fashion, and attempts to prove that the error was justifiable as being the accepted opinion of the time.[46] Considering his

[41] XX, 187; cf. XXVI, 230.   [42] *Coll. of Tracts*, pp. 49, 50.
[43] XXVI, 229.
[44] See especially his *Works* (Philadelphia, 1841), III, 426–430.
[45] *Op. cit.*, p. 51.   [46] XVII, 81.

own use of this argument from the *Remarques sur les pensées de Pascal* to the *Bible enfin expliquée,* he is as little sincere here as in his defense of the "bitter attacks" of Bolingbroke, and his tone is plainly ironical.

Annet treats Paul much more thoroughly than Voltaire. Both point out the various contradictions of his doctrines. But Annet puts more emphasis on Paul's turbulent temper and madness. It was not for his moral teachings, he says, that Paul was persecuted and driven from Antioch by "the devout and honourable Women and the chief Men of the City."[47] It was on account of "the blessed Zeal of his cursing Spirit." "His doctrine and Practice were like his Temper; he was 'all things to all men.'" To the same Corinthian converts he wrote, "I caught you with guile." Annet considers Paul a very dangerous example to both high priests and Methodists. He ridicules especially his distinction between the spirit and the body:

Certainly St. Paul, if we are to believe the Writings which are received for his, and the History of him, was as strange and heterogeneous a Mixture of Stuff, as odd a compound of Flesh and Spirit, as e'er was jumbled together in human Chaos. There were two men, in this one Man Paul . . . he had two Bodies, a natural Body and a spiritual Body . . . the spiritual Person danced him up to the third Heaven, the carnal and sensual Person brought him down to the Devil, who buffeted him, and pricked him with a Thorn. Never was a poor Wretch so tossed in a Blanket as this poor Saint was between these two.[48]

Paul could make cripples dance, but could not save himself from persecution. "Dancing after this Apostle has almost tired me," adds Annet.[49] It is noteworthy that Voltaire appears to have made no use of this modernistic criticism of Paul's doctrine.

Paul seems to Annet to be one of the first to introduce the Holy Ghost, in the miracle of Pentecost.

The Holy Ghost [he writes] is pretended to as a cover to all holy Lies to usher them into the World, and defend them afterwards. . . . For my own Part, I don't know if there be any Holy Ghost, or what is meant by it, and imagine now I never had it, though once I thought I had been

47 *Coll. of Tracts,* p. 74. 48 *Ibid.,* pp. 48, 49.
49 *Ibid.,* p. 87.

plunged in it, and not merely sprinkled; if ever I was baptized with this holy Water, it has been long ago all dried up; but if I ever drank it, I have it still, because I never thirst after it; for it is said, he that drinketh of this Water shall never thirst.

The Holy Ghost, he finds, is never considered as a God in all the Scriptures. The first suggestion of it is "when the angel Gabriel came a courting of Mary by Proxy for the Holy Ghost." It is "a kind of Divine Mercury, the Parent of Faith."[50]

Luckily for Annet, England was not yet in a mood for persecution. The later rationalists received much harsher treatment than the earlier deists. But Voltaire is not a whit less "blasphemous." Summing up the Jewish legends of Christ, he prefers their story to that of "any one of fifty gospels" of the Christians, and continues:

Il est plus vraisemblable que Joseph Panther avait fait un enfant à Mirja qu'il ne l'est qu'un ange soit venu par les airs faire un compliment de la part de Dieu à la femme d'un charpentier, comme Jupiter envoya Mercure auprès d'Alcmène. . . . On fait venir je ne sais quel *agion pneuma*, un saint souffle, un Saint-Esprit dont on n'avait jamais entendu parler, et dont on a fait depuis la tierce partie de Dieu, Dieu lui-même, Dieu le créateur du monde; il engrosse Marie . . . , etc.[51]

The details following are obscene rather than blasphemous, and from a different source.[52] The similarity of Voltaire's treatment and of his phraseology again strongly indicates a direct influence from Annet.

Annet accompanied his treatment of Paul with an undated tract entitled *Supernaturals examined,* in which he attacks again the evidence of the resurrection, shows the impossibility of the miracles and the falsity of the prophecies, and attacks the peculiar institutions of the Christian Church. On the subject of miracles, he says that his work was in the hands of the printer long before Chubb's similar work appeared, in 1748.[53] The subjects are too general to prove any direct influence on Voltaire, and none is

[50] *Coll. of Tracts*, pp. 82, 83.
[51] XXVI, 223. (Attributed to Bolingbroke.)
[52] From Sanchez: *De sancto matrimonio* (Lugd. 1739). Passages in the copy in Voltaire's library are marked.
[53] *Coll. of Tracts*, p. 102.

apparent. Annet is as forceful as Middleton or Hume, whose discussions of the miracles appeared the same year, but his work is much less known. In 1749 he published also a tract on *Social Bliss,* a defense of divorce, for which his chief sources of inspiration seem to have been Milton and Mandeville. It contains Franklin's curious *Plea for bastards,* attributed to a Miss Polly Baker, of Connecticut.[54] In 1761 appeared Annet's two important publications, *David, the History of the Man after God's own Heart,* and the fateful *Free Enquirer.*

This *Life of David* was very evidently Annet's, though it has been attributed to Archibald Campbell, the younger, and to Peter Noorthouck. The external evidence in favor of the other men is very weak, while internal evidence reveals the work to be the very essence of Annet's deism. Noorthouck is advanced on the evidence of a bibliophile who had seen a manuscript of his, in which there appear comments on his history of David, the man after God's own heart.[55] But this was a common title, and Noorthouck's *Lives of the Most Eminent Persons in Every Age* appeared only some sixteen years after Annet's tract, and are written in a very different spirit. His claim to authorship is evidently no longer seriously considered. But Halket and Laing attribute the work to Campbell on the authority of a writer in *Notes and Queries* who "does not wish to be known, but you may rely on the accuracy of his information." He considers the elder Campbell none too orthodox for a divine, and says the son wrote "some other light, or rather very immoral productions."[56] We must follow Annet's critical methods and not accept the story "on his single authority." Campbell was the author of *Lexiphanes,* directed against Samuel Johnson and his abuse of the English language. He is not known to have entered into biblical criticism on one side or the other.[57]

Our *Life of David* is written with exactly the same attitude and

[54] *Coll. of Tracts,* p. 255.

[55] *Notes and Queries,* 1st series, XII, 204.

[56] *Ibid.,* p. 255; cf. 5th series, VIII, 98.

[57] The reprints of the *Life of David* differ widely, and may have later passed through several hands, possibly through Campbell's.

in the same style as Annet's attacks on Paul and Moses. "Mrs. Abigail" is a counterpart to "Mrs. Adam."[58] Moreover, it may be proved from Annet's *Supernaturals examined* that he was already at work on the subject. Much of the identical material appears there in a shorter discussion on the prophecies, written in the same style. David killed all of Saul's offspring except the cripple Mephibosheth, and he treated shamefully Michal, Saul's daughter. But after Saul's death, *"the Lord had, by good Luck, now gotten a Man after his own heart."*[59] The *Life of David,* too, is headed with the same motto as the *Free Enquirer* published in the same year: "Omnia probatis," and was later reprinted with Annet's name. Leland did not know who wrote it, but later scholars have generally attributed the work to Annet.[60] The unsubstantiated testimony of an anonymous writer nearly one hundred years after the book was published cannot be allowed to rob Annet of the credit of his laborious and successful undertaking.

Leslie Stephen writes that the *History of the Man after God's own Heart* is interesting only as the original pamphlet—which is really well written—seems to have supplied the hint for one of Voltaire's keenest satires, the drama of *Saul.*[61] Besides being well written, however, the pamphlet is one of the keenest bits of English deistic criticism, and well deserved Voltaire's attention. And it gave him much more than the hint. A drama could hardly be adapted from a narrative and yet follow more closely the original. Voltaire was only half lying when he said his play was "traduit de l'anglais de M. Hut."[62] Moreover, Annet's narrative has many of the qualities of a drama, and lent itself readily to Voltaire's facile pen and biting sarcasm.

Voltaire had Annet's story in hand in October of the year of its publication, in 1761.[63] On the tenth of that month, in a letter to M. Bret, he writes:

---

[58] Annet thus modernized the names of the wives of Nabal and Adam.

[59] *Coll. of Tracts,* pp. 160–162; Annet's two later works are clearly presaged.

[60] The work is given as Annet's in the catalogue of books in the library of Frederick II of Prussia.

[61] *Op. cit.,* I, 247, n. 1.   [62] V, 569.

[63] Notes will refer to the reprint of the 1766 edition in R. Carlile's *Tracts,* Vol. I: *The Life of David; or the History of the Man after God's own Heart* (London, 1820).

Je suis très-fâché que votre Bayle ne soit pas encore imprimé. On craint peut-être que ce livre, autrefois si recherché, ne le soit moins aujourd'hui: ce qui paraissait hardi ne l'est plus. On avait crié, par exemple, contre l'article *David*, et cet article est infiniment modéré en comparaison de ce qu'on vient d'écrire en Angleterre. Un ministre a prétendu prouver qu'il n'y a pas une seule action de David qui ne soit d'un scélérat digne du dernier supplice; qu'il n'a point fait les Psaumes, et que d'ailleurs ces odes hébraïques, qui ne respirent que le sang et le carnage, ne devraient faire naître que des sentiments d'horreur dans ceux qui croient y trouver de l'édification.[64]

Two years later, the year of the publication of his own drama, he has invented a name for his English author:

M. Hut, qui a fait imprimer à Londres *l'Histoire de David*, l'appelle sans façon le Néron de la Palestine.[65] Personne ne l'a trouvé mauvais: voilà un bien abominable peuple! Tendresse aux frères. *Ecr. l'inf.*[66]

These passages explain clearly why Voltaire preferred Annet to Bayle, and show that he had Annet's material in hand before his first frontal attack on Christianity, the *Sermon des cinquante*. It was in 1762 that he was beginning to use also other important English deistic material, Tindal's *Christianity as Old as Creation*, Woolston's *Discourses on the Miracles of our Saviour*, and Middleton's *Works*.

Voltaire's private library at Leningrad contains the original 1761 edition of Annet's work, published by "R. Freeman" of "Pater-Noster-row." There is also a manuscript of Voltaire's adaptation entitled *"Saül et David*, tragédie d'après l'anglais, intitulé *The man after god's own heart*, imprimé chez Robert Freeman, in pater noster Row, 1760."[67] This manuscript is a copy by Wagnière and Bigex, and contains many variants, with notes and references in less corrupted form than those published. For example, the original text contained the words "Housah, housah," for which Voltaire wrote a note: "C'est le cri de la populace anglaise;

[64] XLI, 472; cf. *Life of David*, pp. 62–64. Four months later, Voltaire wrote to George Keate asking who the author was. It is probable that Keate could not tell him (XLII, 41).
[65] *Ibid.*, p. 64. Beuchot checked this reference in d'Holbach's translation of 1768.
[66] XLII, 560.
[67] Cf. F. Caussy, *Inventaire des manuscrits de la bibliothèque de Voltaire* (Paris, 1913), p. 6.

les hébreux criaient *Alleh luh yah,* et par contraction *yah.*"[68] This was merely gratuitous atmosphere, and does not appear in Annet's work. There is also an early printing of the work with Voltaire's own corrections. The title is now *Saül,* the false date MDCCLV[69] is crossed out, and Voltaire has added this foreword which he later changed:

> Un prédicateur à Londres ayant comparé le roi George II à David dans une de ses déclamations, M. Hute, gentilhomme anglais, indigné d'une comparaison si déplacée, fit imprimer son livre intitulé *the man after God's own heart* chez Robert Freeman in Pater-Noster Row, 1761. M. Hute en digne anglais a le courage de condamner dans David ce qu'il jugerait digne des plus grands châtiments dans tout autre homme. Il croit que ce serait insulter le genre humain et la divinité de n'oser dire qu'un juif est un scélérat quand il est scélérat. La conduite perfide et féroce de David, ses cruautés et ses débauches sont mises dans tout leur jour. Les faits sont si palpables et l'écriture est si fidèlement citée qu'aucun prêtre n'a osé entreprendre de la réfuter. C'est d'après ce livre qu'on fit la tragédie dont nous donnons la traduction. Tout ce qui est tiré du livre des rois est cité avec exactitude.

And below this foreword, the inveterate prevaricator has written: "On manque trop de respect dans cette pièce à ce qu'on doit respecter." The only excuse for this line, in view of Voltaire's use of the play, is the excuse which must be offered for most of his lying, that of self-protection.

Turning now to the content of Annet's criticism of David, several noteworthy passages must be given to show how Voltaire borrowed from and often improved upon Annet, especially in his drama *Saül.* Aside from many passages directly translated, the influence here is most remarkable in character study and general tone. Tindal noted the brutal injustice of Samuel's slaying of Agag. Leslie Stephen has shown how Waterland's serious reply reads much like Voltaire in one of his scoffing moods.[70] Waterland insisted that Samuel was justified in obeying a command from God. Annet could hardly accept this justification. He writes without comment:

[68] Cf. V, 594, n. 2.
[69] Beuchot reports an edition dated 1758 (V, 571). Dates meant little to Voltaire.
[70] *Op. cit.,* I, 258 ff.

We are not to imagine that the sparing Agag, king of the Amalekites, was the only cause of this rupture between him and Samuel. For we may gather from other parts of his story, that Saul was not over-well affected towards his patrons the Levites; in subjection to whom he had too much spirit to continue. Samuel quickly perceived he had mistaken his man, he haughtily avowed his intention of deposing him; and ordering Agag to be brought into his presence, he hewed him to pieces—"before the Lord."[71]

In his drama Voltaire has preserved this relationship between Samuel and Saul. Saul is introduced, in the first act, in mortal terror of Samuel, yet nobly pardoning Agag. Samuel enters "de la part de Dieu," and announces that God has repented making Saul king, because he had spared Agag:

> *Agag.* Comment! la plus belle des vertus serait regardée chez vous comme un crime?
> *Samuel* (à Agag). Tais-toi, ne blasphème point. (A Saül.) Saül, ci-devant roi des Juifs, Dieu ne vous avait-il pas ordonné par ma bouche d'égorger tous les Amalécites, sans épargner ni les femmes, ni les filles, ni les enfants à la mamelle?

Agag is then cut up on the very stage, contrary to all the rules and regulations not only of morality but of the French stage. Samuel says:

> Donnez-moi cette hache, au nom du Seigneur; et tandis que je couperai un bras, coupez une jambe, et ainsi de suite, morceau par morceau.

Voltaire has added in a footnote: "Le texte de la pièce anglaise porte: Heu, [*sic*] him into pieces before the Lord."[72]

Voltaire's second act likewise follows closely Annet's account of David's treachery and cruelty and of his love affairs with Michal and Abigail. Saul had demanded of David one hundred foreskins as the price of the hand of his daughter Michal. David produced double the number. Annet describes his triumphant return with his booty, and adds:

> If Miss Michal was present, how must her pretty little heart exult when the required number being told off, as many more were gallantly presented at her feet![73]

David's boast to Michal of this feat forms the introduction to Voltaire's second act. Annet shows here the characteristic incapacity of the deists to view the customs and morals of other times with other than the eyes of eighteenth-century decorum. The flippancy and lack of historical perspective which marks Voltaire's biblical criticism and in a measure condemns it, defines even more clearly than his use of details his debt to the English deistic school. It was left for the Germans and for Renan to collect what was valuable for the purposes of serious exegesis.

If Annet's humor is often imaginative, Voltaire's sarcasm is more biting. David continues thus his boast to Michal:

> Akis m'a traité comme son fils, il a eu en moi une entière confiance; mais je n'ai jamais oublié que je suis juif; et ayant des commissions du roi Akis pour aller ravager vos terres, j'ai très-souvent ravagé les siennes . . . je tuais tout sans miséricorde, . . . afin d'être pur devant le Seigneur . . . je faisais scier en deux, par le milieu du corps, ces insolents rebelles, ou je les écrasais sous les dents de leur herse, ou je les faisais rôtir dans des fours à brique. Voyez si c'est aimer sa patrie, si c'est être bon Israélite.[74]

Voltaire, with an eye to unity and the exigencies of the drama, has here combined two instances of David's cruelty. Later, in his *Bible enfin expliquée*,[75] he translated Annet's account word for word, but in the transposition above he brings out the horror implied in Annet's words, "how shall a man, not steeled to a very Jew, find expressions suited to the occasion?"

Annet treated Abigail as a flirt who helped David get rid of her husband and then married him. Voltaire has Abigail enter with dramatic effect to disturb Michal's tranquillity. David's account of the winning of Abigail is almost a direct translation of Annet's account, somewhat softened. Annet wrote at the end of the story:

> David loses no time, but returned God thanks for the old fellow's death, and then Mrs. Abigail was promoted to the honour of being one of the Captain's ladies.[76]

Voltaire's ending is pithier:

> David. . . . au bout de huit jours le brutal mourut! . . .
> Michal. Je m'en doutais bien.
> David. Et j'épousai la veuve.[77]

[74] V, 583. Cf. *Life of David*, pp. 35, 49.
[75] XXX, 193, n. 1. Cf. *Life of David*, p. 50.
[76] *Life of David*, p. 33.   [77] V, 584, 585.

Eighteen wives, he adds, are not too many "pour un brave homme."

Rather than follow Annet's remarks on Saul prophesying naked, Voltaire introduces a "Pythonisse, arrivant avec un balai entre les jambes." This is one of his few departures from Annet's text. He returns to his English original for his entire third and fourth acts, in which Bathsheba, wife of the deceived and slaughtered Uriah, is prominent. His climax is the last scene of the fourth act, in which he has transferred to Bathsheba, Michal's reproaches on David's dancing before the Lord, and shows David composing his Psalms in the midst of revelry. Annet's interpretation of David's dancing is original and indelicate: Michal sneered at David's dancing in "such a frantic indecent manner." But David had answered that he would be more vile, "and of the maidservants which thou hast spoken of, of them shall I be had in honour."

> Some staunch zealots have very prudently spiritualized this part of David's answer and given the mystical sense of it; the prophane, who are content with the evident signification of words, having construed it no otherwise than into an insinuation that he had no cause to be ashamed of what he exposed. Fie on them.[78]

Voltaire's transposition is merely indelicate:

> *Bethsabée.* Je m'en vais, si vous continuez à chanter ainsi, et à sauter comme un ivrogne. Vous montrez tout ce que vous portez: fi! quelles manières!
> *David.* Je danserai, oui, je danserai; je serai encore plus méprisable, je danserai devant les servantes, je montrerai tout ce que je porte, et ce me sera gloire devant les filles.[79]

Voltaire had found in Annet a man truly after his own heart, a Bayle untrammeled.

Voltaire's versification of the Psalm which David had been singing, and which Bathsheba had characterized as "airs de corps de garde," began thus:

[78] *Life of David*, p. 44.   [79] V, 603.

> Chers Hébreux, par le ciel envoyés,
> Dans le sang vous baignerez vos pieds;
> Et vos chiens s'engraisseront
> De ce sang qu'ils lècheront.[80]

This is a translation of the version given by Annet:

> And make them dip their feet in blood
> Of those that hate thy name;
> The tongues of dogs they shall be red
> With licking of the same.

"Very pious ejaculations," adds Annet, "for the whole congregation to *sing to the praise and glory of God.*"[81] Voltaire did not use this sarcasm directly, but it is significant that the only marker in his copy of Annet's work refers to this passage.

Both men treat similarly the treachery of David on his deathbed.[82] Voltaire seems to have borrowed from Bayle the jealousy of David's sons over the Shunammite maid who kept David warm in his old age, but the other details of David's last acts and death are from Annet. Annet approaches the end of his treatise with an apostrophe most typical of the attitude of English deism adopted by Voltaire:

> These, Christians! are the outlines of the life of a Jew, whom you are not ashamed to continue extolling as a man after God's own heart! This, Britons! is the king to whom your late excellent monarch has been compared! What an impiety to the Majesty of Heaven! What an affront to the memory of an honest prince! It is with great joy the writer of these memoirs takes leave of a story, with which, by this time, he is sufficiently disgusted.[83]

With much the same expression of weariness, Annet had left his account of Paul.[84] Apart from any consideration of detail, all that was most radical in Voltaire's attitude and method in dealing with the Christian tradition can be found in Peter Annet.

Voltaire continued to use Annet's material whenever he had occasion to mention David. His dictionary article on David, in 1767, a year before d'Holbach's translation of Annet's work, is a

---

[80] V, 603.
[81] *Life of David*, p. 63.
[82] *Ibid.*, pp. 64, 65; V, 610, 611.
[83] *Life of David*, p. 67.
[84] This is added internal evidence of Annet's authorship of the *Life of David*.

several-page summary of the latter's material. M. H. has now become "membre du parlement d'Angleterre." His twenty-five-page account of Saul and David in his *Bible enfin expliquée,* published the year before his death, follows Annet's account even more closely than his drama. Many direct borrowings and several translations are here attributed directly to "M. Huet," and the material appears on practically every page, with Dom Calmet often employed to set it off. On the incest of Amnon and Tamar, Voltaire comments as follows:

M. Hut s'exprime violemment sur cet inceste d'Amnon, et sur tous les crimes qui en résultèrent. "On ne sort, dit-il, d'une horreur que pour en rencontrer une autre dans cette famille de David."[85]

It is here also that he translates Annet's treatment of the inconceivable barbarities which David perpetrated upon the citizens of Rabbah. He preferred in every case his own free translations to d'Holbach's, which had appeared in 1768.

It is evident that Voltaire favored and used Annet rather than Bayle in his criticisms of David. Yet Bayle, who wrote very few antibiblical articles, was especially daring on the subject of David.[86] However, Bayle was as certainly used by Annet, who attributes to him some of the difficulties he found in the scriptural account of the life of David.[87] By the latter half of the century, authority was relaxing and the Jesuits were fast falling into discredit. Voltaire complains as early as 1752 that "Bayle n'est pas encore assez sceptique,"[88] and he would cut Bayle's dictionary down to a thin volume, which would nevertheless contain the article on David. Bayle was very thorough in his criticism, and Voltaire could have found there much of his material. But he preferred Annet because the latter was more brutally outspoken.

Annet's *Free Enquirer,* for which he was condemned in 1763, appeared in nine weekly instalments from October 17 to December 12, 1761. It was directed chiefly against Moses. In an early number, Annet clearly defined his deistic position:

---

[85] XXX, 193, n. 2; cf. *Life of David,* p. 50. Champion's "Doutes sur l'authenticité de l'ouvrage de Voltaire: *La Bible enfin expliquée"* (*Révol. Fr.* 1905) are decidedly unfounded.
[86] G. Lanson in *Revue des Cours et Conférences* (June 18, 1908).
[87] *Life of David,* pp. 33, 34.   [88] XIV, 38; *Siècle de Louis XIV.*

The intention of the following remarks on Moses and his writings, is not to subvert Christianity . . . but to shew that the body of it does not stand on the legs of Judaism, or on any false bottom which may fail the building . . . that it is erected *on a rock;* on the rock of Nature; that it was before Judaism, and is independent of it: in short, that true Christianity, is as old as the Creation.[89]

The attack is hardly more rabid than his previous works on Paul and David, but the author was better known and trying to reach a larger audience. He ridicules especially Moses' idea of God, concluding that "by the description and character Moses gives us of God, the character of Moses himself may be known."[90] It may be imagined that neither the one nor the other was particularly flattered. In his comment on the verse: "And it came to pass by the way in the inn, that the Lord met him, and sought to kill him," Annet writes, "Perhaps the Lord is put for Moses by mistake, for they were so like in word and deed, and so often together, that it is no wonder if one is sometimes mistaken for the other."[91] Now like Paul, Moses is proved to have been a liar; it might have been this that led to the charge of blasphemy. Annet was busy ridiculing the miracles of Moses and Aaron, performed before Pharaoh and his magicians, when his publication was discontinued. One example of Annet's popular style will suffice:

But in the next miracle, which is a lousy one, Moses out did them. . . . Pharoah's magicians try to make lice, but they cannot: therefore they told the king that this lousy miracle was done by the finger of God: but the king, without intreating him to kill them with his thumb, scratched himself again, though it makes one itch to think of it. This singular wonder, however, had no wonderful effect, more than the others. But this seems a less miracle than any of the rest; for what miracle could it be for the lousy Israelites to infect the Egyptians with lice.[92]

Annet's last words to the public before his condemnation were as follows:

We plead for no enormities, no immoralities, but expose them to shew our detestation of them, and declare against impious sanctified plots, dark

---

[89] Carlile's reprint, London, 1826, p. 20.   [90] *Ibid.,* p. 21.
[91] *Ibid.,* p. 47.   [92] *Ibid.,* pp. 80, 81.

insurrection, religious rebellion, and VILLANY *consecrated with the name of* THE MOST HIGH.[93]

It appears that Voltaire devoted much more research to Moses than to any other biblical character. His sources were many and varied, but never does he seem to have used or known Annet's *Free Enquirer*. His supplier of English books must have thought the weekly publications unworthy of notice. Voltaire did not connect "M. Huet, de Londres," with Peter Annet, whom he never mentions by name. Nor did he know that Annet was severely punished by the English people, whom he had ironically called "abominable" because they did not object to *The History of the Man after God's own Heart*.[94]

From the study of the influence of Annet on Voltaire, some interesting facts are revealed in regard to the attitude and methods of the French author in the handling of his sources. In 1761, the date of Voltaire's unreserved entry into the field of biblical criticism, English books were being sent to him with extraordinary dispatch. With the *Life of David* in hand, he immediately digested thoroughly the English original, and transformed the subject matter into his drama *Saül,* one of the most sarcastic and witty that he ever wrote. If his direct English sources were few, he nevertheless wasted nothing that he had once mastered, and continued to use them, with variations and adaptations, to the very end of his life. He appears eager to seize upon the most radical works that English deism produced, and was easily influenced by their tone and style. But his borrowings were never servile. He fitted Annet's *Life of David* into many moulds. For his own drama he took the best that Annet had to offer, and transformed the latter's heavier British humor into that brilliant, light and racy wit which set an indelible mark of originality upon so much of his work. Lanson, who studied Voltaire's relations to the earlier deists, believed that his method of dealing with critical material was his chief debt to the English school. It is true that the historical argument against the foundations of Christianity, which forms the bulk of Voltaire's critical work, was derived less from the English controversy than

[93] *Free Enquirer,* p. 96. [94] XLII, 560.

from common scholarly sources. It was the so-called moral argument represented by Woolston, Tindal, and especially by Annet, which had an important influence upon Voltaire's work; from them, Voltaire borrowed directly both detail and method.

CHAPTER IX

CONCLUSIONS

THIS comparative study of the English critical deists and Voltaire permits us to draw interesting and fairly definite conclusions. Voltaire's early philosophical deism was strengthened and modified by the deistic disciples of Locke. And in his later attack against the Christian religion he adopted every method that was used by his English predecessors. He had his favorites, however, and borrowed chiefly from the English extremists who had brought the searchlight of common sense and common morality to bear upon the Scriptures. In this field his faults and failures were their faults and failures, and his successes their successes. It was only in ethically-minded England that this method of attack could readily increase and multiply, and it was naturally from England that Voltaire, with his command of the English language and his admiration for English thought, borrowed his material. The historical argument, on the other hand, was cosmopolitan; and though many noteworthy contributions of the English deists in this field affected Voltaire directly or indirectly, the English influence is here nearly lost among the wealth of scholarly sources.

The importance of Toland in England has been apparent throughout the whole study of the English deists. His catalogue of apocryphal works inaugurated a new era of documentary criticism. We have seen, however, that Voltaire borrowed very extensively from the apocryphal codes of the learned Fabricius, and thereby drew upon himself a greater reputation for learning than he might have secured in following Toland's more popular work. The apocryphal codices of Fabricius were probably Voltaire's most used single source. Yet without Fabricius, much of Toland's thought and spirit would have been passed on to Voltaire through Peter Annet, who saw most clearly and developed with the least hesitation the implications of Toland's researches.

And it was in the spirit of Annet that Voltaire handled the material he found in Fabricius. Toland's other contributions to the historical argument were for the most part either lost upon Voltaire or derived from common sources, among whom Van Dale stands out as the most important. Greatly influenced by the labors of the Dutch scholars, Toland firmly laid the foundations of the English deistic controversy. The effect of his thought on Voltaire was therefore through the general movement, more often than by direct contact.

The study of Collins has served to emphasize two distinct periods of pronounced English influence on Voltaire: First, the Mme. du Châtelet period of metaphysical research; and secondly, the late period of borrowings of method and material for the antibiblical attacks of the last fifteen years of his life. In the first period, Collins and Chubb were read in conjunction with Newton, Locke, and Clarke. On the important questions of determinism and of the nature of the soul, Collins' opinions finally emerged victorious. As early as 1734 he had entirely accepted Collins' proofs that not a single prophecy of the Old Testament could be honestly considered as referring to Jesus or as being fulfilled by him. In the second period he read with some care not only d'Holbach's adaptation, but the original English of Collins' *Grounds and Reasons of the Christian Religion* and *Scheme of Literal Prophecy considered*. Voltaire's use of these works was fairly limited, for he wisely judged that he was writing to a different audience upon whom Tindal's remarks on the immorality of the prophets could be much more effectively stressed than the details of Collins' attack. Moreover, Collins' masterly defense of freethinking and his critical works on the prophecies again exerted a marked influence on Woolston and Annet, and hence indirectly on Voltaire.

Although Tindal was chiefly concerned in establishing the efficacy and sufficiency of the light of reason in matters of religion, his modest endeavors to show the inferiority of the revealed Scriptures by noting the barbarities and cruelties of the Jews, the questionable conduct of the prophets, and the contradictions and immoralities of Christ's teaching, were greedily received and magnified by Voltaire. Tindal's *Christianity as Old as Creation* was thus a very important source of Voltaire's deism. His adaptations of Tindal's material, however, depart from the usual moderation of the original to favor the more active animosity of Woolston and Annet.

Woolston's attack on the miracles was diabolical and purely destructive. To the opponents of the English deists he was a thorn in the flesh. Voltaire used his facile criticisms of the literal word in every critical work that came from his pen. Except in his major works on miracles, he reduced Woolston's ridicule of the letter to short and witty sarcasms, and abandoned those that could not be so reduced. His borrowings from Woolston thus modified, added a note of wit and levity to the fundamental seriousness of his attacks. He very wisely neglected Woolston's purposefully absurd typical interpretations, directed against the English clergy, but, in mocking this type of commentary, could be equally absurd himself when the occasion offered. He thought that Woolston, in his hatred for the clergy, had gone much too far in arousing the anger of bigots. But he adopted all that he dared of Woolston's intransigent spirit.

Chubb and Bolingbroke had relatively little effect on the critical deism of Voltaire. Chubb entered into the current of Voltaire's thought in the earlier metaphysical period, but the influence is negligible. Voltaire read Bolingbroke's philosophical works carefully during the later period but chose for some reason not to use them. It is difficult, moreover, to see what material contributions Bolingbroke could have made to Voltaire's wealth of sources. Annet developed all there was in Bolingbroke that would have suited Voltaire's purposes, and in much more convenient form. In revenge, Voltaire used Bolingbroke's name to cover his most virulent criticisms, and on so many occasions that the Bolingbroke influence has become a legend, while of his many supposed quotations from Bolingbroke's posthumous works, probably not one is justifiable. Bolingbroke has been charged with being a god unto himself; and Voltaire took his name in vain.

On the other hand, Conyers Middleton looms up rather unexpectedly as an important source of Voltaire's attacks on the historical foundations of the Church. Middleton did for the latter-day miracles what Van Dale had done for the heathen oracles. His criticisms were mild and his attitude compromising. Voltaire carefully read and reviewed his works, admired them, and used extensively many passages marked for reference, especially in his *Dictionnaire philosophique,* which he was preparing when the Middleton volumes came into his hands.

Annet, the "last of the deists," took the most valid arguments of Toland, Collins, Tindal, and Bolingbroke, and transfused them with the spirit of Woolston for Voltaire's use. He was the most complete of critical deists, and at the same time the most intransigent. Voltaire appropriated and adapted his *Life of David* immediately after its publication, and was influenced by his *History of Saint Paul* through d'Holbach, if not directly. Annet is responsible for much that is extreme in Voltaire's criticism, yet there is an underlying validity in his work that Woolston lacked. He realized fully that he was compromising in meeting his ortho-dox opponents on their own ground. Voltaire's use of Annet's *Life of David* shows with what rapidity he was receiving tracts from England in 1761, and how thorough was his reading knowledge of the English language. His drama *Saül,* based on this work, illustrates also the transforming power of his facile wit. His constant use of Annet for this subject on which Bayle could have been of great service to him, adds to the evidence of Bayle's relative unimportance in the inspiration of his antibibli-cal efforts, and at the same time illustrates the importance of Bayle's influence on the English deists.

There remains the danger that from the influence above indi-cated, there may still be some disagreement concerning the size of the debt that Voltaire owed the English deists. It is not enough to say that it was great or small; some distinctions must be made. In the development of his philosophical skepticism, Locke played a more fundamental rôle than any of the deists; yet Toland and especially Collins modified Locke's ideas to a considerable extent as they were gaining acceptance in Voltaire's mind. Again, the milder deism of Dryden, Pope, and the *Independent Whig* which interested him during his exile in England, was soon abandoned for the more pronounced deism of Tindal's *Christianity as Old as Creation*. In his later years, Voltaire plainly adopted the entire spirit and method of the extremists in the English controversy. He praised English philosophers, gave long lists of English deists as authorities, wrote very often under an assumed English name, and to give an English atmosphere to his works he adopted even their figures of speech and curt epigrams. "A Robinson Crusoe romance," "tales from Don Quixote," etc., were favorite expressions found in Annet's criticisms of the Scriptures, and many more were culled from Woolston's discourses on the miracles. In regard to the direct borrowing of material, it must be borne in mind that the great bulk of Voltaire's deistic criticism was historical, and that here the English movement, though it had much to offer, can account for only a small fraction of the total. Once imbued with the English critical spirit, Voltaire had only to draw his own conclusions from the learned works of Van Dale, Grabe, Fabricius, Fleury, and countless others, or from the commentaries of Dom Calmet. But next to the historical argument, it was the moral argument that Voltaire stressed the most, and here he was inspired by Woolston, Tindal, and Annet, and turned to their works again and again for his important material. Finally considering this time the more general influences of the critical spirit, there seems to be no question but that the contributions of the French *précurseurs*, Bayle, Fontenelle, and Perrault, were not felt directly to any great extent by the later French school, but first crossed the Channel, only to return, greatly augmented by Toland, Collins, and their followers, to the welcoming arms of Voltaire and d'Holbach.

No generalizations can be formed concerning Voltaire's honesty in referring to the English deists as authorities. When he has grouped them in lists he is usually, to use the Abbé Guénée's expression, throwing dust in the eyes of his readers. Bolingbroke he mentions the most often, and with the least justification. Toland and Collins were accorded an almost even break between true and false attributions. Tindal is never mentioned in connection with the particular details which Voltaire borrowed from his work, even after Guénée had charged Voltaire with copying from him. On the other hand, Woolston is almost always correctly referred to, and although the name of Annet does not appear in all of Voltaire's work, the pseudonym "M. Hut" or "Huet" which Voltaire chose for him is properly used in almost every case. Yet the *Dialogues entre A, B, C.; traduit de l'anglais de M. Huet* concern Annet not at all. The balance swings in favor of mystification rather than justification, and the crying example will always be the *Examen important de milord Bolingbroke.*

The English deistic attack was as complete and thorough as was possible without the advantages of modern researches in science, history, and archaeology, a field which Toland was approaching timidly and with some ideas far in advance of his age. His idea of evolution in the development of ideas and beliefs would have excused much in the conduct of the early patriarchs and prophets. But the later deists and Voltaire were too fond of their favorite argument that the "common ideas of morality" of the eighteenth century had been revealed by nature from the beginning, and were as old as creation. Their arguments were valid, therefore, only against their opponents who refused to consider the Scriptures as an historical document like any other, and are valid today only to that extent, considerable though it may be.

Voltaire had the methods and materials of this controversy well in hand from the very beginning of his openly critical attack. His later works are largely repetitions, enlargements, and modifications of his *Sermon des cinquante* and *Extrait des sentiments de Jean Meslier,* both published in 1762. In the latter work appears the following significant paragraph:

Quelles seront donc les vaines ressources des christicoles? Leur morale? elle est la même au fond que dans toutes les religions; mais des dogmes cruels en sont nés, et ont enseigné la persécution et le trouble. Leurs miracles? mais quel peuple n'a pas les siens, et quels sages ne méprisent pas ces fables? Leurs prophéties? n'en a-t-on pas démontré la fausseté? Leurs mœurs? ne sont-elles pas souvent infâmes? L'établissement de leur religion? mais le fanatisme n'a-t-il pas commencé, l'intrigue n'a-t-elle pas élevé, la force n'a-t-elle pas soutenu visiblement cet édifice? La doctrine? mais n'est-elle pas le comble de l'absurdité?[1]

[1] XXIV, 335–336.

No more concise summary could be made of the main points of the English controversy. The foregoing study has revealed some of the sources of this *Extrait* of Jean Meslier. It would be interesting to know to what extent the deep note of sincerity and the passionate and uncompromising hatred for Christianity were due to the influence of this early French revolutionary. Even when this study is made, one must remember that Voltaire had at this time also read Tindal, Woolston, and Peter Annet.

In spite of the constant repetition of material, Voltaire avoids tediousness by the constant change of angle from which he directed his attacks. One of his most interesting adaptations is the famous *Traité sur la tolérance,* in which, in a mock effort to prove the tolerance of Moses and Jesus, he has nevertheless succeeded in heaping the customary ridicule upon them. It has been noted how, in that work, the ridicule of Woolston's treatment of the miracles of Cana and of the Samaritan woman was used to prove the innocence and tolerance of Christ's character. Here is indeed evident the diabolical spirit of Woolston. Tindal's criticisms of the prophets could only be used in one way, and on this subject, indeed, Voltaire is sometimes boresome through repetition. But no two works could be more opposite in nature than his *Saül* and his *Bible enfin expliquée,* in both of which Annet's *Life of David* figures prominently.

One final question arises: Did Voltaire anonymously publish his attacks against Christianity under the name or upon the authority of the English deists and at the same time withhold his personal sanction? The evidence is entirely in the negative. It has been argued that he had a sincere respect for the Pentateuch on the strength of his admission: "Le *Pentateuque* et l'Arioste font aujourd'hui le charme de ma vie."[2] This is merely an indication that Voltaire had a taste for extravaganza from no matter what source. It is as if Woolston had written that Swift and the Church Fathers were the charm of *his* life. One must look beneath the veil. In his volume upon volume of attacks upon the entire Old

---

[2] E. Champion, *Voltaire: études critiques* (Paris, 1893), p. 234; cf. Voltaire, *Œuvres,* XLI, 90, 153. Voltaire's letter contains an impertinence concerning Ezekiel which well illustrates his "respect" for the Pentateuch.

Testament, Voltaire is ready to admit in its favor only a lyric beauty, of a crude sort to be sure, in the Song of Solomon. Passages have been taken from the *Traité sur la tolérance* and the *Dictionnaire philosophique* either to show that Voltaire had an underlying respect for the person of Christ, or to prove him inconsistent. The study of Woolston again warns us to look with great suspicion upon either statement. There is likewise little evidence that in employing the phrase *Écrasez l'infâme,* Voltaire made any mental reservation in favor of Christianity as distinguished from superstition. One must turn way back to Toland for any sincere trust in this distinction. Voltaire's only reservations were due to his attitude of intellectual snobbery, a fear of the results of his efforts on the unthinking multitude. Following the extremists of the English school, he appears to have sincerely and consistently attempted, during the final fifteen years of his life, to demolish Christianity from top to bottom.

In conclusion, the English deistic controversy was a primary factor both in Voltaire's philosophical deism and in his attacks on the established religion. It renewed and fortified his convictions that the Christian religion, like other revealed religions, was founded on fraud and imposture and that the history of the Church was fundamentally unreliable. It convinced him that no comfort could be found for the orthodox in the arguments drawn from the miracles and the prophecies. It furnished him with many facts, but above all, it gave him the methods, the atmosphere, and the authorities for his own attack. The so-called moral argument of the English deists, represented by Woolston, Tindal, and Annet, had the most important direct influence upon Voltaire's work. While the more scholarly works of Middleton against the latter-day miracles, and of Collins against the prophecies, were by no means neglected, it was especially the tracts of their more facile and witty successors that found strength and increase in their continental transplantation.

BIBLIOGRAPHY

THE general bibliography will be preceded by two chronological tables which were found indispensable for the comparative study of the English deists and Voltaire. The first table includes the important works of the deists, with an indication of corresponding French translations and their dates. The English books may be assumed to have been printed in London and in octavo unless otherwise indicated. An asterisk marks editions in Voltaire's library at Leningrad. The second table contains the principal works of Voltaire in which there appear traces of critical deism up to 1761 and definitely deistic criticism after that date. Volume and page references are from the Moland edition, though the dates are sometimes taken from Bengesco's bibliography of Voltaire's works and from the results of later research. The lists in Robertson's *Short History of Freethought* were especially helpful for this section, though they are not accurate in every respect.

For the selected alphabetical bibliography which follows, besides the well-known general works of Lanson and Quérard, the *Catalogue des livres de feu M. le Baron d'Holbach,* Paris, 1789, has been found especially helpful. This catalogue is rich in books of English origin which found their way into French or France. No attempt has been made to give an inclusive list of the vast number of books that appeared against the deists nor of the numerous critics who have written of Voltaire's philosophy. Lists of books that appeared during the English controversy may be found in works indicated by Leslie Stephen, Thorschmid, and Fabricius, as well as under the names of the deists in the British Museum Catalogue. The splendid manuscript catalogue of Voltaire's library at Leningrad has, of course, been of great service. The general bibliography contains only works which have been consulted, referred to, or quoted from, in the foregoing study.

CHRONOLOGICAL BIBLIOGRAPHY
OF ENGLISH CRITICAL DEISM (*1696–1761*).

1696 Toland, Christianity not Mysterious.
1698 ———— The Life of Milton. Amyntor.
1700 ———— Clito, a Poem on the Force of Eloquence.
1702 ———— Vindicius Liberius.
1704 ———— Letters to Serena. Trans. by d'Holbach: *Lettres philoso-phiques,* Londres (Amsterdam), 1768.
1705 Woolston, *The Old Apology . . . reviv'd.

1707 Collins, An Essay concerning the Use of Reason.

———Four letters . . . on the natural immortality of the Soul. (Printed in Clarke's Collected Works.)

1708 Shaftesbury, A Letter concerning Enthusiasm. Trans. by Samson, La Haye, 1708, in-18, and by Lacombe, Londres, 1762.

1709 Collins, Priestcraft in Perfection.

Toland, Adeisidæmon. Origines Judaicae.

Tindal, The Rights of the Christian Church asserted.

1710 Shaftesbury, Essai sur l'usage de la raillerie, etc. Trans. by P. Coste, 1710, and by Van Effen, La Haye, 1710, in-12.

1711 ———*Characteristicks, 3 vols. Trans. by Diderot, Principes de la philosophie morale, Amsterdam, 1745.

1713 Collins, Discourse on Freethinking. Trans. by H. Scheurléer and J. Rousset: Discours sur la liberté de penser, Londres, 1714, 1717; and by *de Crouzas, Londres, 1766.

1714 Mandeville, *The Fable of the Bees, or, Private Vices, Publick Benefits. Trans. by J. Bertrand, Londres, 1740 and 1750. MS translation by Mme. du Châtelet in Voltaire's library at Leningrad.

1715 Chubb, The Supremacy of the Father asserted.

1717 Collins, A Philosophical Inquiry concerning human liberty. Translation published by Desmaizeaux: *Recueil de diverses pièces, 1720, 2 vols. Also trans. by Lefèvre de Beauvray in Paradoxes métaphysiques, etc., 1754 and 1756.

1718 Toland, Nazarenus, or Jewish, Gentile, and Mahometan Christianity. *Trans., Londres, 1777.

1720 ——— Pantheisticon (an eighteenth-century MS translation was published by A. Lantoine in 1927).

——— Tetradymus (Hypatia republished separately in 1753).

Mandeville, Free Thoughts on Religion, the Church, and National Happiness. Trans. by Van Effen, Amsterdam, 1723, *1738, 2 vols. in-8.

1722 Gordon and Trenchard, the Spirit of the Ecclesiasticks. Trans. by d'Holbach, Londres, 1767.

1723 Woolston, Four Free-Gifts to the Clergy.

1724 ——— The Ministry of the Letter vindicated.

Collins, A Discourse on the Grounds and Reasons of the Christian Religion. *Reprinted 1737. *Trans. by d'Holbach (Examen des prophéties), Londres (Amsterdam), 1768.

——— Historical and Critical Essay on the thirty-nine Articles.

Woolston, The Moderator between an Infidel and an Apostate. Two supplements to the same.

1725 Collins, *A Scheme of Literal Prophecy considered. The Hague (London eds., 1726, *1727). Cf. d'Holbach, l'Esprit du judaïsme, Londres (Amsterdam), 1770.

1726 Woolston, A Defence of the Miracle of the Thundering Legion.
Toland, Posthumous works, published in "A Collection of Several
Pieces of Mr. John Toland," 2 vols. Reprinted as The Miscella-
neous Works in 1747. Vols. I, *II.

1727–1729 Woolston, *Six Discourses on the Miracles of our Saviour.
*Trans. by d'Holbach before 1778. *MS abridgment.

1729 Middleton, A Letter from Rome. *Trans. by Abbé Prévost. Amsterdam, 1744, in-12.
Collins, A Discourse concerning Ridicule and Irony in Writing.

1729–1730 Woolston, *Two Defences of his Discourses on the Miracles of
our Saviour.

1730 Chubb, A Collection of Tracts, 1715–1730, in-4. Several of these
tracts were translated under the title: *Nouveaux essais sur la
bonté de Dieu, la liberté de l'homme et l'origine du mal, Amster-
dam, 1732, in-12. Also Mémoires concernant la théologie et la
morale (Chubb and Abauzit), published by Saint-Hyacinthe,
Amsterdam, 1732.
———— The Comparative Excellence and Obligation of Moral and
Positive Duties.
Tindal, *Christianity as Old as Creation. D'Holbach gave an Extrait
d'un livre de Tindal for the Recueil philosophique, Londres
(Amsterdam), 1770.
Middleton, Answer to Waterland.

1732 Gordon and Trenchard, *The Independent Whig, 2 vols. in-8.
Chubb, Tracts, 1732–1738, 2 vols. The True Gospel of Jesus asserted.
———— The Sufficiency of Reason in Matters of Religion.

1733 Gordon and Trenchard, *Cato's Letters, 4 vols. in-12.

1739 Annet, Judging for Ourselves.

1741 Morgan, Physico-Theology.

1744 Annet, The Resurrection of Jesus Considered.

1745 ———— The Resurrection Reconsidered. The Resurrection Defenders
stript of all Defence.

1747 Chubb, Tracts, 1739–1747.

1748 ———— Posthumous Tracts, 2 vols. Farewell to his Readers, etc.
Annet, Supernaturals Examined. (Date approximate.)
———— The History and Character of St. Paul. (Date approximate.)
Trans. by d'Holbach, Londres (Amsterdam), 1770.
Middleton, Free Enquiry into the Miraculous Powers of the Chris-
tian Church.

1750 ———— An Examination of Sherlock's Discourses on Prophecy.

1752 ———— Miscellaneous Works, 4 vols. in-4. *Second ed. 1755, 5 vols.
in-8.
Bolingbroke, Letters on the study and use of history, 2 vols. in-8.
*Translation (Berlin, 1752) by Barbeu du Bourg, 2 vols. in-8.

1754 Bolingbroke, *Philosophical Works, 4 vols. Partial translations: Pensées . . . by Prault, 1771. *Lettre de milord Bolingbroke, servant d'introduction à ses lettres philosophiques à M. Pope, 1766.

1761 Annet, *The Life of David, the History of the Man after God's own Heart. Trans. by d'Holbach in 1768.
———— The Free Enquirer.

PRINCIPAL WORKS OF VOLTAIRE CITED

1722 Le Pour et le contre. Œuvres (Moland ed.), IX, 358 ff.

1733 Lettres philosophiques, XXII, 75–187.

1734 Remarques sur les Pensées de Pascal, XXII, 25–61.
Traité de métaphysique, XXII, 188–230.

1736 Le Mondain, X, 83 ff.

1737 Discours en vers sur l'homme, IX, 401 ff.

1738 Eléments de la philosophie de Newton, XXII, 393–582.

1752 La Loi naturelle, IX, 441–460.
Défense de milord Bolingbroke, XXIII, 547–554.
Siècle de Louis quatorze, XIV–XV.

1756 Poème sur le désastre de Lisbonne, IX, 465–478.

1759 Candide, XXI, 137–218.
Précis de l'Ecclésiaste, IX, 485–493.
Le Cantique des cantiques, IX, 501–506.

1761 Lettre de M. Eratou à M. Clocpitre, IX, 497–500.
Sermon du rabbin Akib, XXIV, 277–284.

1762 Extrait des sentiments de Jean Meslier, XXIV, 293–336.
Sermon des cinquante, XXIV, 438–454.

1763 Catéchisme de l'honnête homme, XXIV, 523–541.
Instruction pastorale, XXV, 1–4.
Saül, V, 569–611.
Lettre d'un quaker, XXV, 5–12.
Traité sur la tolérance, XXV, 13–118.
Dialogue du douteur et de l'adorateur, XXV, 129–135.

1764 Articles extraits de la Gazette littéraire, XXV, 151–227.
Le Dictionnaire philosophique, XVII–XX.

1765 Questions sur les miracles, XXV, 357–450.
La Philosophie de l'histoire (Essai sur les mœurs), XI, 1–164.

1766 Le Philosophe ignorant, XXVI, 47–95.
Idées de La Mothe le Vayer, XXIII, 489–491.
André Destouches à Siam, XXVI, 97–102.

1767 Les Questions de Zapata, XXVI, 173–190.
Examen important de milord Bolingbroke, XXVI, 195–300.
Homélies prononcées à Londres, XXVI, 315–354.
La Défense de mon oncle, XXVI, 367–433.

Lettres . . . sur Rabelais et sur d'autres auteurs accusés d'avoir mal
    parlé de la religion chrétienne, XXVI, 469–526.
Le Dîner du comte de Boulainvilliers, XXVI, 531–560.
1768 Relation du banissement des jésuites de la Chine, XXVII, 1–16.
    Conseils raisonnables à M. Bergier, XXVII, 35–53.
    Profession de foi des théistes, XXVII, 55–74.
    L'Epître aux romains, XXVII, 83–106.
    Des Singularités de la Nature, XXVII, 125–191.
    Le Pyrrhonisme de l'histoire, XXVII, 235–299.
    Instruction à frère Pédiculoso, XXVII, 301–309.
1769 L'A, B, C, XXVII, 311–400.
    Collection d'anciens évangiles, XXVII, 439–556.
    Discours de l'empereur Julien, XXVIII, 1–67.
    De la Paix perpétuelle, XXVIII, 103–128.
    Dieu et les hommes, XXVIII, 129–248.
    Les Lettres d'Amabed, XXI, 435–478.
1770–1772 Questions sur l'encyclopédie, XVII–XX.
1771 Lettres de Memmius à Cicéron, XXVIII, 437–463.
    Les Lois de Minos, VII, 163.
1772 Il faut prendre un parti, XXVIII, 517–551.
1774 De l'âme, XXIX, 329–342.
    Le Taureau blanc, XXI, 483–512.
1775 Histoire de Jenni, XXI, 523–576.
1776 Un chrétien contre six juifs, XXIX, 499–582.
    La Bible enfin expliquée, XXX, 1–316.
    Dialogues d'Evhémère, XXX, 465–531.
1777 Histoire de l'établissement du christianisme, XXXI, 43–116.

GENERAL BIBLIOGRAPHY

Abbadie, J., La Vérité de la religion chrétienne. La Haye, 1750, 2 vols. in-8.
Abravanel, Isaac, Liber de Capite Fidei, Amsterdam, 1638. (Fr. trans. Avignon, 1884.)
Addison, Spectator (Nos. 292, 516, 432—Locke and Toland on tolerance).
Aldington, R., Voltaire. 1925.
Ascoli, G., "Voltaire," R. C. C. (1923–1924).
Astruc, Jean, Conjectures sur les mémoires originaux dont il paraît que Moïse s'est servi pour composer le Livre de la Genèse. Bruxelles, 1753.
Atkinson, Geoffrey, Les Relations de voyages du XVIIe siècle. Paris, 1925.
Baldensperger, F., "Voltaire anglophile avant son séjour d'Angleterre," Revue de littérature comparée (janvier-mars, 1929), pp. 25–61.
——— "La Chronologie du séjour de Voltaire en Angleterre et les Lettres philosophiques," Archiv. H. (1913).

Ballantyne, A., Voltaire's visit to England (1726–1729). London, 1893.

Barbeyrac, Jean, Traité de la morale des pères de l'Eglise. Amsterdam, 1728, in-4.

Barral, Dictionnaire historique, littéraire et critique. Avignon, 1758–1759, 6 vols.

Basnage, Jacques, L'histoire et la religion des Juifs. Rotterdam, 1706–1707, 6 vols. in-12.

—— Histoire de l'église. Rotterdam, 1699, 2 vols. in-fol.

Bastide, Ch., John Locke, ses théories politiques et leur influence en Angleterre. Paris, 1907.

Bayle, Pierre, Dictionnaire historique et critique. Rotterdam, 1697, 4 vols. in-fol. English trans., London, 1710, 4 vols. in-fol.

—— Œuvres diverses, nouvelle édition. La Haye, 1737, 4 vols. in-fol.

—— Pensées diverses sur la comète. Rotterdam, 1683, 2 vols. in-12.

Bee, The, No. 25 (Tindal).

Beljame, A., Le public et les hommes de lettres en Angleterre au XVIIIe siècle. Paris, 1897.

Bengesco, G., Voltaire, bibliographie de ses œuvres. Paris, 1882–1890, 4 vols.

Benoît, Elie, Remarques sur les deux dissertations de M. Toland, intitulées, l'une, l'Homme sans superstition, et l'autre, les Origines judaïques. Delf, 1712.

Bentley, Richard, Phileleutherus Lipsiensis. 1713.

—— Remarks upon a late Discourse of Freethinking. London, 1713.

Betz, Louis P., La littérature comparée. Essai bibliographique, Strassburg, 1904.

Blount, Charles, The Oracles of Reason. London, 1693.

Bolingbroke, Henry St. John, Mémoires secrets sur les affaires d'Angleterre depuis 1710 jusqu'en 1716, etc. Londres, 1754, 2 vols. in-8.

—— Works. Philadelphia, 1841, 4 vols. in-8.

Boulainvilliers, Doutes sur la religion (Traité de Spinoza). Londres, 1767.

—— L'Athéisme renversé, ou Réfutation des erreurs de Spinoza. Bruxelles (Amsterdam), 1731, in-12.

Boulanger (or d'Holbach), L'Antiquité dévoilée par ses usages. Amsterdam, 1760, in-4.

Burigny (or Fréret), Examen critique des apologistes de la religion chrétienne (s.l.), 1766.

Calmet, Dom Augustin, Commentaire littéral . . . sur les Testaments. Paris, 1720, 28 vols. in-4.

—— Dictionnaire de la bible. Paris, 1730, 4 vols. in-fol.

Carlile, R., The Deist. London, 1820, 2 vols.

Carroll, William, Spinoza revived (Tindal). London, 1709.

Champion, E., "Doutes sur l'authenticité de l'ouvrage de Voltaire: La Bible enfin expliquée." Révol. Fr. 1905.

—— Voltaire: études critiques. Paris, 1893.

Chandler, Samuel, Vindication of Christian Religion. London, 1725.

Charles, Rudolf, Testament de Jean Meslier. 1861, 3 vols. in-8.

Chase, C., The Young Voltaire. 1926.

Chaudon, L. M., Nouveau dictionnaire historique et portatif. Amsterdam, 1766, 4 vols. in-8.

Chubb, T., Memoirs of M. T-C-. London, 1747.

Clarke, Samuel, Collected Works. London, 1738, 4 vols. in-fol.

——— Traité de l'existence de Dieu et de ses attributs, etc. Traduit par M. Ricotier. Amsterdam, 1727–1728, 3 vols. in-8.

Collini, C.-A., Mon séjour auprès de Voltaire. Paris, 1807.

Collins, Anthony, Some Familiar Letters between Mr. Locke and several of his friends. London, 1708.

Collins, J. Churton, Voltaire, Montesquieu and Rousseau in England. London, 1908.

Daillé, Jean, De usu patrum. Genevae, 1656.

Delvolvé, Jean, Religion, critique, et philosophie positive chez Pierre Bayle. Paris, 1906.

Deslandes, A. F. Boureau-, De la certitude des connaissances humaines (Locke, Chubb, Toland, Collins). London, 1741.

Desmaizeaux, Pierre, An Historical account of the Life and Writings of John Toland. London, 1722.

——— Recueil de diverses pièces (Clarke, Leibnitz, Newton, Collins, etc.). London, 1720, 2 vols. in-12.

Desnoiresterres, G., Voltaire et la société française au XVIIIe siècle. Paris, 1867–1876, 8 vols. in-8.

Diderot (D'Alembert, etc.), La grande encyclopédie, 1751–1772.

Disraeli, Isaac, Curiosities of Literature. London, 1840.

Dodwell, Henry, An Epistolary Discourse (on the natural immortality of the soul). London, 1706.

——— De paucitate martyrum (see Ruinart).

Dodwell, William, A free Answer to Dr. Middleton's Free Inquiry. London, 1749.

Droysen, H., and R. Koser, Briefwechsel Friedrichs des Grossen mit Voltaire. Leipzig, 1908.

Dupin, L. Ellies, Dissertations historiques, etc., sur la Bible. Paris, 1711.

——— Histoire de l'église. Paris, 1714, 4 vols. in-12.

Duvernet, T. J., Vie de Voltaire. Genève, 1786.

Epiphanius, Commentarium in Canticum Canticorum. Paris, 1750, in-4.

——— L'histoire et la vie de Saint Epiphane. Paris, 1738, in-4.

Fabricius, Jo. Albertus, Bibliotheca Graeca. Hamburg, 1705–1707, in-4.

——— Codex Apocryphus Novi Testamenti. Hamburg, 1719, 3 vols. in-12. (1st ed., 2 vols., 1703.)

——— Codex Pseudepigraphus Veteris Testamenti. Hamburgi et Lipziae, 1713–1733, 3 vols. in-12.

—— Delectus Argumentorum, etc. (bibliog. of writers against deists, etc.). Hamburg, 1725, in-4.

—— (Gaulmin, G., ed.) De vita et morte Mosis. Hamburg, 1714.

Fleury, Abbé Claude, Discours sur l'histoire ecclésiastique. Paris, 1720.

—— Histoire ecclésiastique. Paris, 1729–1743, 36 vols. in-12.

Fontenelle, Bernard de, Entretiens sur la pluralité des mondes. Paris, 1686, in-12.

—— Histoire des oracles. Paris, 1685, in-12.

Foulet, L., Correspondance de Voltaire (1726–1729). Paris, 1913.

—— "Le Voyage de Voltaire en Angleterre," R. H. L., 1906.

Gagnier, Jean, Vie de Mahomet. Amsterdam, 1732, 2 vols. in-12.

Grabe, J. E., Spicilegium SS. Patrum. Oxoniae, 1700, 2 vols. in-8.

Guénée, Antoine, Lettres de quelques Juifs portugais, etc. Lisbonne (Paris), 1769 (Eng. trans. by the Rev. Philip Lefanu, Dublin, 1777, 2 vols.).

Hahn, Joseph, Voltaires Stellung zur Frage der menschlichen Freiheit in ihren Verhältnis zu Locke und Collins. Borna-Leipzig, 1905.

Havens, G. R., and N. L. Torrey, "The Private Library of Voltaire at Leningrad," PMLA, XLIII (December, 1928), pp. 990–1009.

—— "Voltaire's Books: a Selected List," Mod. Phil., XXVII (August, 1929), 1–22.

Herbert, Edward (of Cherbury), De causis errorum. 1656, in-12.

—— De religione gentilium. Amsterdam, 1663, in-4.

—— De Veritate. London, 1633, in-4. (French trans. (?), 1639, in-4.)

Holbach, P. H. D., Baron d', Catalogue des livres de feu M. le Baron d'Holbach. Paris, 1789 (Bibl.).

—— Histoire critique de Jésus-Christ (s.l.n.d.), 1770 (?).

—— Le Christianisme dévoilé. Londres, 1756.

—— (Trad. Lehmann, J.-G.) L'Essai d'une histoire naturelle des couches de la terre. 1759.

—— Ed. Orobio de Castro (Isaac Balthazar). Israël vengé, ou Exposition naturelle des prophéties hébraïques que les chrétiens appliquent à Jésus, leur prétendu Messie (traduit par Henriquez). Londres, 1770.

—— Le Bon-Sens. Londres, 1772.

Huet, Pierre Daniel, Demonstratio evangelica, Parisiis, 1690, in-fol.

Hume, David, Essays. London, 1760, 4 vols. in-12.

Hurn, A. S., Voltaire et Bolingbroke. Paris, 1915.

Kaye, F. B., The Fable of the Bees (critical edition). Oxford, 1924, 2 vols. in-8.

Ladvocat, Dictionnaire historique-portatif. Paris, 1760, 2 vols.

La Mothe le Vayer, Cinq dialogues faits à l'imitation des anciens. Mans, 1671, in-12.

—— Critical discourse on the life and writings of Flavius Josephus, Works. London, 1733.

—— Œuvres. Paris, 1753–1754, 10 vols. in-12.

Lanson, G., "L'origine et le développement de l'esprit philosophique, etc."
Revue des cours et conférences, 1907–1909.

———— "Le Rôle de l'expérience dans la formation de la philosophie du
XVIIIe siècle en France." Revue du mois, 1908.

———— Voltaire. Paris, 1922.

———— "Questions diverses sur l'histoire de l'esprit philosophique en France
avant 1750," R. H. L. (1912), XIX, 1–29, 293–317.

———— (ed.) Lettres philosophiques, Paris, 1917, 2 vols. in-8.

Lantoine, A., John Toland, suivi de la traduction française du Pantheisticon.
Paris, 1927.

Lechler, G. V., Geschichte des Englischen Deismus. Stuttgart und Tübin-
gen, 1841.

Le Clerc, Jean, An Abstract and Judgment of Dr. Clarke's controversies
(Collins). London, 1713.

———— Bibliothèque choisie; vol. XXI, defense of Tindal; Eng. trans.: The
Right of the Christian Church adjusted. London, 1711.

———— Sentiments de quelques théologiens de Hollande sur l'histoire du
vieux Testament, composée par R. Simon, 1685.

Leibnitz, G. W. von, Annotatiunculae Subitaneae ad Librum de Christian-
ismo Mysteriis carente (1701). (Vol. II of Toland's Collection of Pieces,
1726.)

Leland, John, D.D., A View of the deistical Writers. London, 1764, 2 vols.

Locke, John, Essay on Human Understanding. London, 1690, in-fol.;
trans. by P. Coste (1700), Amsterdam, 1758, 4 vols. in-12.

———— Letters on Toleration. 1689.

———— Œuvres diverses. Amsterdam, 1732, 2 vols. in-12.

———— Reasonableness of Christianity, 1694; trans. by P. Coste (1694),
Amsterdam, 1731, 2 vols. in-8; 1740, 2 vols. in-12.

———— Some familiar Letters between Mr. Locke and several of his
friends. London, 1708.

Longchamp et Wagnière, Mémoires sur Voltaire et ses ouvrages. Paris,
1826, 2 vols.

Marsham, J., Canon chronicus aegyptiacus, haebraicus, graecus, et dis-
quisitiones. Londini, 1672, in-fol.

Mill, J., Variae lectiones in Novum Testamentum. 1707, in-fol.

Morgan, Thomas, A Collection of Tracts. London, 1726.

———— A Defense of the Moral Philosopher. London, 1737.

———— Moral Philosopher. London, 1737–1740.

———— Physico-Theology. London, 1741.

Morize, A., Candide, éd. crit. Paris, 1913.

———— "Le Candide de Voltaire." Rev. du XVIIIe siècle, 1913.

———— L'Apologie du Luxe au XVIIIe siècle. Paris, 1909.

———— Problems and Methods of literary History (Ginn and Co.), 1922.

Newton, Isaac, Arithmetica universalis. Lugduni Batavorum, 1732, in-4 (ed. 's Gravesande).

—— La Chronologie des anciens royaumes corrigée (trad. par Granet). Paris, 1728.

—— Observations upon the Prophecies of Daniel and the Apocalypse of St. John. London, 1733, in-4.

Niceron, J. P., Mémoires pour servir à l'histoire des hommes illustres. Paris, 1729–1745, 43 vols. in-12.

Nourrisson, J. F., Philosophie de la nature. Paris, 1887.

Pellissier, G., Voltaire philosophe. Paris, 1908.

Pelloutier, Histoire des Celtes. La Haye, 1750, 2 vols. in-12.

Petitfils, Un socialiste révolutionnaire au commencement du XVIIIe siècle, Jean Meslier. Paris, 1905.

Pierron, A., Voltaire et ses maîtres. Paris, 1866.

Pope, Essay on Man. London, 1734. (Trans. by E. de Silhouette, Lausanne et Genève, 1745.)

—— The Dunciad. London, 1728.

Prideaux, H., Histoire des Juifs et des peuples voisins. Amsterdam, 1728, 1 vol. in-12.

Reland, Adrian, Antiquitas sacrae veterum Hebraeorum. Trajecti Batavorum, 1708.

—— De Religione Mohammedica. Ultrajecti, 1705 (Fr. trans., La Haye, 1721, in-12).

Robertson, J. M., A Short History of Freethought. London, 1915, 2 vols. (Bibliog.)

Rousseau, J.-J., Lettres écrites de la montagne. Amsterdam, 1764, in-12.

Ruinart, T., Acta primorum Martyrum (against Dodwell). Amstelaedami, 1713, in-fol. (2d ed.)

—— Les véritables actes des martyres, trad. par Maupertuy. Paris, 1708, 2 vols.

Sayous, Edouard, Les déistes anglais. Paris, 1882.

Selden, De Synedris Hebraeorum. Amsterdam, 1679, in-4.

Shaftesbury, Characteristicks. London, 1711, 3 vols. (Trans. by Diderot: Principes de la philosophie morale. Amsterdam, 1745, in-12.)

—— Essai sur l'usage de la raillerie, etc. (trans. by Van Effen). La Haye, 1710, in-12.

—— Lettre sur l'enthusiasme (trans. by Samson). La Haye, 1708, in-18, and by Lacombe, Londres, 1762.

Sherlock, Thomas, The Use and Intent of Prophecy. London, 1725.

—— Trial of the Witnesses of the Resurrection of Jesus (answer to Woolston), 1729.

Sichel, Walter, Bolingbroke and his Times. London, 1902, 2 vols. in-8.

Simon, Richard, Histoire critique du vieux Testament (1678), in-4.

—— Histoire critique du texte du nouveau Testament. Rotterdam, 1689.

Skelton, P., Deism Revealed. London, 1749, 2 vols. in-8.

Sonet, E., Voltaire et l'influence anglaise. Rennes, 1926.

Spinoza, B. de, Miracles no Violations of the Laws of Nature. 1683, in-4.

—— Tractatus de Deo et Homine. Amsterdam, 1869.

—— Tractatus Theologico-Politicus. 1670, in-4. (Fr. trans. by Saint-Glain, 1678, in-12.) (*See* Boulainvilliers.)

Stackhouse, Tho., A Fair State of the Controversy between Mr. Woolston and his adversaries (Miracles). London, 1730.

—— Defense of Christian Religion. London, 1731.

—— The Life of the Reverend Mr. Thomas Woolston. London, 1733.

Stephen, Leslie, Dictionary of National Biography. (Articles on the deistic authors.)

—— English Thought in the Eighteenth Century, 2d ed. London, 1881, 2 vols. in-8. (Bibliog.)

Swift, Jonathan, A Tale of a Tub. London, 1704. (Trad. par Macé: Recueil de pièces sérieuses, 1721; par van Effen, La Haye, 2 vols. in-12.)

—— The Sentiments of a Church of England man, with respect to religion and government. (In the "Churchman armed," etc., vol. II, 1814.)

Tabaraud, M. M., Biographie universelle. Paris, 1828, vol. LI. (Article on Woolston.)

—— Histoire critique du philosophisme anglais, depuis son origine jusqu'à son introduction en France. Paris, 1806, 2 vols. in-8.

Tachard, Gui, Voyage au Siam. Paris, 1686, in-4.

Tallentyre, S. G., "English friends of Voltaire," Cornhill, 221 (1904).

—— Life of Voltaire. London, 1905.

—— The Friends of Voltaire. London, 1907.

Thorschmid, Urban Gottlob, Critische Lebensgeschichte Anton Collins. Dresden und Leipzig, 1755.

—— Versuch einer vollständigen Engelländischen Freydenker-Bibliothek, Magdeburg, Cassel, 1765–1766, 4 vols.

Tillemont, L. S. le Nain de, Mémoires pour servir à l'histoire ecclésiastique des six premiers siècles. Paris, 1701–1712, 16 vols. in-4.

Tillotson, John, A Discourse against Transubstantiation. London, 1684, in-4. (Trans. 1685, in-12.)

—— Works. London, 1701, in-fol.

Tindal, Matthew, A true Copy of the Last Will . . . of that famous Freethinker, M. T., LL.D. (Calculation of his Nativity; and a particular account of his Death.) London, 1733.

Toland, John, Critical History of the Celtic Religion and Learning, with an Abstract of the Life of the Author. London (1740?).

—— Toland's Life and Writings. London, 1720.

Torrey, N. L., "Bolingbroke and Voltaire: a Fictitious Influence," PMLA (September, 1927), pp. 788–797.

——— "Voltaire's English Notebook," Mod. Phil., XXVI (February, 1929), pp. 307–325. (See G. R. Havens.)

Van Dale, A., De Oraculis Ethnicorum. Amsterdam, 1683, in-8.

——— Dissertatio super Aristea de LXX Interpretibus. Amsterdam, 1705. (Dissertatio super Sanchoniatone.)

Villemain, A. F., Tableau de la littérature au XVIIIe siècle. Paris, 1882, 4 vols.

Warburton, William, Divine Legation of Moses. London, 1738–1741, 2 vols. in-8.

Waterland, Daniel, Scripture Vindicated. London, 1731–1732.

Whiston, William, Essay toward restoring the True Text, etc. London, 1722.

——— Literal Accomplishment of Scripture Prophecies. London, 1724.

Wollaston, William, Ebauche de la religion naturelle. . . . Traduite de l'anglais (Garrigue). La Haye, 1726, in-4.

Woodward, John, An Essay toward a natural history of the Earth. London, 1695. (Trad. par Nicéron, Paris, 1735.)

INDEX